THE CATHOLIC QUESTION IN AMERICA

A Da Capo Press Reprint Series

CIVIL LIBERTIES IN AMERICAN HISTORY

GENERAL EDITOR: LEONARD W. LEVY
Claremont Graduate School

THE CATHOLIC QUESTION IN AMERICA

by
William Sampson

DA CAPO PRESS • NEW YORK • 1974

Library of Congress Cataloging in Publication Data

Sampson, William, 1764-1836.
The Catholic question in America.

(Civil liberties in American history)
Reprint of the 1813 ed. printed by E. Gillespy, New York.
1. Confidential communications—Clergy—United States.
I. Title. II. Series.
KF8959.C6S24 1974 347'.73'6 73-22105
ISBN 0-306-70600-8

This Da Capo Press edition of *The Catholic Question in America* is an unabridged republication of the first edition published in New York in 1813.

Published by Da Capo Press, Inc.
A Subsidiary of Plenum Publishing Corporation
227 West 17th Street, New York, N.Y. 10011

Manufactured in the United States of America

THE

CATHOLIC QUESTION

IN

AMERICA.

Quos contra statuit æquos placitosque dimisit.—CICERO.

Whether a Roman Catholic Clergyman be in any case compellable to disclose the secrets of Auricular Confession.

Decided at the Court of General Sessions, in the City of New-York.

PRESENT,

The Honorable De Witt Clinton, *Mayor.*
The Honorable Josiah Ogden Hoffman, *Recorder.*
Richard Cunningham, } *Esqrs. Sitting Aldermen.*
Isaac S. Douglass, }

With the Arguments of Counsel, and the unanimous opinion of the Court, delivered by the Mayor, with his reasons in support of that opinion.

REPORTED BY
WILLIAM SAMPSON, Esq.
One of the Counsel in the case.

NEW-YORK:
Printed by Edward Gillespy, No. 24 William-street.

1813.

PREFACE.

The general satisfaction given to every religious denomination, by the decision of this interesting question, is well calculated to dissipate antiquated prejudices, and religious jealousies, and the Reporter feels no common satisfaction in making it public. When this adjudication shall be compared with the baneful statutes and judgments in Europe, upon similar subjects, the superior equity and wisdom of American jurisprudence and civil probity will be felt, and it cannot fail to be well received by the enlightened and virtuous of every community, and will constitute a document of history, precious and instructive to the present and future generations.

Report.

This case, like many others of importance, had its origin in a trivial occasion: One Philips, together with his wife, was indicted for a misdemeanor in receiving stolen goods, the property of James Keating. The vigilant justices of the police discovered that after lodging his information before them he had received restitution, and thereupon had him brought up and interrogated him with a view to further discovery. He shewed so much unwillingness to answer, that suspicions fell upon him and he was threatened with a commitment to bridewell. He was admonished that it was his duty on his oath to reveal the whole truth, and the duty of magistrates to enquire into it, and to enforce obedience to the law. He then mentioned that he had received the restitution of his effects from the hands of his pastor, the Reverend Mr. Kohlmann, Rector of Saint Peter's. Thereupon, a summons was issued to that gentleman to appear at the police office, with which he instantly complied. But upon being questioned touching the persons from whom he received the restitution, he excused himself from making such disclosure, upon the grounds that will be fully stated in the sequel. He was then asked some questions of a less direct tendency, as to the sex or colour of the person who delivered the goods into his hands, and answered in like manner. Upon the case being sent to the Grand Jury he was subpœnaed to attend before them, and appeared in obedience to the process, but, in respectful terms, declined answering. Bills of indictment were found, upon other testimony, against Charles Bradley and Benjamin Brinkerhoff, both coloured men, as principals, and against Philips and wife as receivers. These indictments were filed on the 3d of March, 1813, and on Friday, March 5, the parties having respectively pleaded not guilty, were put upon their trial. One jury was charged with both indictments.

The Court was composed of

The Honorable Piere C. Vanwyck, who sat in the absence of the Mayor, then attending the duties of his office as Lieutenant Governor, at Albany, together with Aldermen Morse and Vanderbilt.

The Jurors balloted and sworn were

Charles Gillard,	Augustus Colvin,
Wm. Sandford,	Philip Earle,
Wm. Englehart,	Elijah Fountain,
James M'Kay,	Samuel Keehards,
Wm. W. Todd,	Patrick M'Closky,
Caleb Street,	Laurence Powers.

Mr. Riker prosecuted as District Attorney, on behalf of the people.

Mr. George Wilson appeared as Counsel for the several Defendants.

Among the witnesses returned on the back of the indictment was the Reverend Anthony Kohlmann, who being called and sworn, was asked some questions touching the restitution of the goods. He in a very becoming manner entreated that he might be excused, and offered his reasons to the Court, which are here omitted to avoid repetition, but will be found at length in the sequel.

Mr. George Wilson objected also on behalf of his clients. The case was novel and without precedent, and Mr. Sampson, as amicus curiæ, interposed, and observed that in no country where he had been, whether Protestant or Catholic, not even in Ireland, where the Roman Catholic religion was under the ban of proscription, had he ever heard of an instance where the clergyman was called upon to reveal the solemn and inviolable secrecy of sacramental confession, and with the ready assent of Mr. Riker, obtained an adjournment of the trial until Counsel could be heard in deliberate argument. A juror was thereupon withdrawn and the following Monday was assigned for hearing the argument.

From various intervening circumstances the cause was deferred till the June session. In the interval, by a change of office Mr. Hoffman succeeded to Mr. Vanwyck as Recorder, and Mr. Gardinier to Mr. Riker as District Attorney.

On Tuesday, June 8, the traversers were put to the bar, and the following jury sworn :

Frederick Everts,	William Rhinelander,
John P. Schermerhorn,	David Mumford,
Samuel Ferguson,	Elijah Secor,
William Walker,	Jacob Scheffelin,
Robert Provost,	Joseph Blackwell,
Benjamin Styles,	William Painter.

The Court was now composed of

The Honorable De Witt Clinton, *Mayor.*

The Honorable Josiah Ogden Hoffman, *Recorder,*
(Who, on account of the importance of the case, took his seat upon the Bench.)

Isaac S. Douglass, }
Richard Cunningham, } *Esqrs. Sitting Aldermen.*

Mr. Kohlman was then called and sworn, and examined by Mr. Gardinier.

He begged leave of the Court to state his reasons for declining to answer, which he did in the following terms:

"I must beg to be indulged in repeating to the Court the reasons which prevent me from giving any answer to the questions just proposed; trusting they are such as to prevail upon the Court to dispense with my appearing as an evidence in the present case.

"Were I summoned to give evidence as a private individual (in which capacity I declare most solemnly, I know nothing relatively to the case before the court) and to testify from those ordinary sources of information from which the witnesses present have derived theirs, I should not for a moment hesitate, and should even deem it a duty of conscience to declare whatever knowledge I might have; as, it cannot but be in the recollection of this same honorable Court, I did, not long since, on a different occasion, because my holy religion teaches and commands me to be subject to the higher powers in civil matters, and to respect and obey them.* But if called

---

* See St. Mat. c. 22—v. 21. "Render, therefore, to Cæsar the things that are Cæsar's, and to God the things that are God's." St. Paul to the Romans, c. 13—v. 1, 2. "Let every soul be sub-

upon to testify in quality of a minister of a sacrament, in which my God himself has enjoined on me a perpetual and inviolable secrecy, I must declare to this honorable Court, that I cannot, I must not answer any question that has a bearing upon the restitution in question; and that it would be my duty to prefer instantaneous death or any temporal misfortune, rather than disclose the name of the penitent in question. For, were I to act otherwise, I should become a traitor to my church, to my sacred ministry and to my God. In fine, I should render myself guilty of eternal damnation.

"Lest this open and free declaration of my religious principles should be construed into the slightest disrespect to this honorable Court, I must beg leave again to be indulged in stating as briefly as possible, the principles on which this line of conduct is founded. I shall do this with the greater confidence, as I am speaking before wise and enlightened judges, who, I am satisfied, are not less acquainted with the leading doctrines of the Catholic Church, than with the spirit of our mild and liberal Constitution.

"The question now before the Court is this: Whether a Roman Catholic Priest can in any case be justifiable in revealing the secrets of sacramental confession? I say, he cannot: the reason whereof must be obvious to every one acquainted with the tenets of the Catholic

---

ject to higher powers: for there is no power but from God: and those that are, are ordained of God: and they that resist, purchase to themselves damnation." 1 Peter, c. 2—v. 13, 14. "Be ye subject, therefore, to every human creature, for God's sake; whether it be to the King, as excelling; or to Governors, as sent by him for the punishment of evil doers, and for the praise of the good."

Church respecting the sacraments. For it is, and ever was a tenet of the Catholic Church, that Jesus Christ, the divine Founder of Christianity, has instituted seven sacraments, neither more nor less.* It is likewise an article of our faith, that the sacrament of penance, of which sacramental confession is a component part, is one of the said seven sacraments.† It is, in fine, the doctrine of the Catholic Church that the same divine Author of the sacraments has laid the obligation of a perpetual and inviolable secrecy on the minister of the said sacrament.‡

"This obligation of inviolable secrecy enjoined on the minister of the sacrament of penance is of divine institution as well as confession itself: it naturally flows from the very nature of this sacrament, and is so essentially connected with it, that it cannot subsist without it. For, when the blessed Saviour of mankind instituted the sacrament of penance, as the necessary means for the reconciliation of the sinner, fallen from the grace of baptism by mortal sin, he unquestionably did it with the intention, that it should be frequented and resorted to by the repenting sinner. Now, it is self evident, that if Christ our Lord had not bound down his minister in the sacrament of penance to a strict and perpetual silence, it would be wholly neglected and abandoned; for, we want neither great learning nor deep sense to conceive, that, in that supposition, the last of the tempta-

---

* Concil. Florent. in Decreto Eugenii ad Armenos. Concil. Trid. Sess. 6. Can. 1.

† Concil. Trid. Sess. 14. Can. 1 et 6.

‡ Concil Cabilon. Cap. 33. Concil. Lateran. 4 in Canone: *Omnis utriusque sexus*, &c. &c.

tions of a sinner would be to reveal all his weaknesses and most hidden thoughts to a sinful man like himself, and one perhaps in many respects inferior to himself, and whom he knows to be at full liberty to divulge and disclose whatever may be intrusted to him. In short, the thing speaks for itself: Christ the incarnate Wisdom of God would have manifestly demolished with one hand, what he was erecting with the other; unless we believe that he has affixed by a divine and most sacred law the seal of inviolable secrecy, to all and every part and circumstance of what is communicated to his minister through the channel of confession.*

"If, therefore, I or any other Roman Catholic Priest (which God forbid, and of which Church History during the long lapse of eighteen centuries scarce ever furnished an example) if, I say, I should so far forget my sacred ministry, and become so abandoned as to reveal either directly or indirectly, any part of what has been entrusted to me in the sacred tribunal of penance, the penalties to which I should thereby subject myself, would be these: 1st. I should forever degrade myself in the eye of the Catholic Church, and I hesitate not to say, in the eye of every man of sound principle: the world would justly esteem me as a base and unworthy wretch, guilty of the most henious prevarication a priest can possibly perpetrate, in breaking through the most sacred laws of his God, of nature, and of his Church.

"2dly. According to the canons of the Catholic Church, I should be divested of my sacerdotal charac-

---

* Vide Concil. Cabilon. cap. eod. Vide Tournelly tract. de Sacram. Pœnit.

ter, replaced in the condition of a Layman, and forever disabled from exercising any of the Ecclesiastical functions.*

"3dly. Conformably to the same canons, I should deserve to be lodged in close confinement, shut up between four walls to do penance during the remainder of my life.†

"4thly. Agreeably to the dictates of my conscience, I should render myself guilty, by such a disclosure, of everlasting punishment in the life to come.

"Having thus briefly stated to this honorable Court, my reasons for not answering the questions of the Attorney General, in the present instance, I trust they will not be found trivial and unsatisfactory."

Mr. Gardinier, then put some leading questions to the witness, amongst others, whether he ever had the goods in his possession. Both the Mayor and Recorder stopped the examination, saying that the law either allowed him the exemption he claimed or it did not, but the Court would not permit that privilege to be frittered away, nor a discovery to be extorted by indirect means, which could not be directly enforced.

Mr. Sampson then said, that Mr. Riker and he stood ready as the Counsel for the witness, to argue the point, and the Court, with consent of parties, adjourned the jury till the following Monday, June 14, that the Court might have time not only to hear the argument, but to give an advised judgment.

---

* Vid. St. Greg. Cap. Sacerdos de Pœnit d. 6. Concil. Lateran. 4. in Canone mox citato.

† Ibid.

N.B. Mr. Riker, from the examination he had given to the cause, had become convinced that the exemption was legal, and now offered his services to maintain that opinion. Mr. Wilson was prevented from appearing by a domestic misfortune, the loss of a child, and Mr. Emmet, who would have taken a part in the argument, was prevented by indispensable engagements in another Court.

The day being already far spent, the cause was adjourned till the following day, Tuesday, June the 8th, when Mr. Riker opened the argument as follows:—

May it please the Court,

If in the discussion of the present question, I should discover more than ordinary solicitude, a sufficient apology, I trust, will be found in the novelty and in the magnitude of the cause. On the one hand, the exemption claimed by the Reverend Pastor, is now, for the first time, in this country, brought judicially under examination; and on the other, every enlightened and pious Catholic considers, the free toleration of his religion, involved in the decision that shall be made in this case.

Under these considerations, we respectfully ask of the Court, a patient and a dispassionate hearing: and, we confidently expect to satisfy your Honors, that the law and the constitution are on our side.

To render the argument definite and perspicuous, we shall advance, and endeavour to maintain, two propositions, either of which sustains the witness in the privilege which he claims.

Proposition 1st. That, under the explanation made by Dr. Kohlmann, the 38th Article of the Constitution of our state, fully protects him in the exemption which he claims, *independent of every other consideration.*

Proposition 2d. That the exemption is supported *by the known principles of the common law,* which will not compel any man, to answer a question, that subjects him to a *penalty* or *forfeiture,* impairs his *civil* rights, or may *degrade—disgrace*—or *disparage* him.

Before, however, I proceed to a vindication of those two propositions, it is proper, and may conduce to a more perfect understanding of the subject, to state some general and leading principles which must be conceded on both sides, and notice some British decisions, which may be supposed to have a bearing upon the case now under examination.

It will not be denied on our part, that the *general* rule is, that every person is bound, when called upon in a court of justice, to testify whatever he may know touching the matter in issue; nor will it be disputed by the Attorney General, that there are exceptions to this general rule, some of which are coeval with the rule itself.—As for example—That no man is bound to accuse himself. That a husband and wife cannot be witnesses against each other, except for personal injuries. That a Counsel or Attorney can never testify against his client. And in this country, the exception has been recognized, as applicable to the Secretary of the United States in certain cases.*

It is obvious, that these exceptions, are founded either upon the positive rights of the party claiming them, upon the maxims of policy, or the general fitness of things.

---

* Marbury, v. Madison. I. Cranch. 144.

They have been extended, or rather called forth, as the occasion has required, and a wise tribunal will always engraft them upon the rule, whenever it shall be demanded by the suggestions of reason and good sense.

But, it is contended that no professional character, other than a Counsel or Attorney, is exempted from testifying in a court of justice; and that therefore a Physician, a Surgeon, or a Priest, is bound to disclose all that has been entrusted to him, no matter under what circumstances it may have been confided.

It is, a little remarkable, that the modern elementary writers on the law of evidence* seem to take it for granted that a physician or a surgeon, is in all cases whatsoever bound to testify. They lay down the rule in the most unqualified terms, as if no doubt could exist on the subject, yet, when they refer the reader to authority for what they thus state, they rely solely upon the case of the Dutchess of Kingston.

It is proper to mention the facts in that cause, that we may duly appreciate its weight. The Dutchess of Kingston was tried in April 1776, in the house of Lords, for bigamy. She was indicted for marrying Evelyn Pierrepont, Duke of Kingston, in the life time of Augustus John Hervey, her former husband.

Mr. Cæsar Hawkins (a surgeon) was asked, "do you know from the parties of any marriage between them?" (referring to the first marriage):—To which he observed "I do not know how far any thing that has come before me in a confidential trust in my profession should be disclosed, consistent with my professional honor."†

* Peake 180.—M'Mally 247.—Swift 95.

† 11 State Trials 243. Fol. 6.

Upon the Lord High Stewart (the Earl of Bathurst then Lord Chancellor) stating the question proposed, Lord Mansfield observed, "I suppose Mr. Hawkins "means to demur to the question upon the ground, that it "came to his knowledge some way from his being em- "ployed as a surgeon for one or both of the parties; I "take it for granted if Mr. Hawkins understands that it "is your Lordships opinion that he has no privilege on "that account to excuse himself from giving the answer, "that then, under the authority of your Lordships judg- "ment, he will submit to answer it: therefore, to save "your Lordships the trouble of an adjournment, if no "Lord differs in opinion, but thinks that a surgeon has "no privilege to avoid giving evidence in a court of "justice; but is bound by the laws of the land to "do it; (if any of your lordships think he has such a "privilege, it will be matter to be debated elsewhere, "but) if all your Lordships acquiesce, Mr. Hawkins "will understand, that it is your judgment and opinion, "that a surgeon has no privilege, where it is a material "question in a civil or a criminal cause, to know wheth- "er the parties were married, or whether a child was "born, to say, that his introduction to the parties was "in the course of his profession, and in that way he "came to the knowledge of it. I take it for granted, "that if Mr. Hawkins understands that, it is a satisfac- "tion to him and a clear justification to all the world. "If a surgeon was voluntarily to reveal these secrets, "to be sure he would be guilty of a breach of honor, "and of great indiscretion; but, to give that information "in a court of justice, which by the law of the land he "is bound to do, will never be imputed to him as any "indiscretion whatever." The question was then put and answered.*

Upon this single decision, made on the spur of the occasion—without discussion, has the whole body of legal authority, on that point, been erected.

If however, the principle in the case referred to, be true, it by no means follows that a clergyman is bound to reveal what a penitent hath confessed to him in the exercise of a religious rite. The one is under no restraint but that which is imposed by the sentiments of honor—the other may be controlled by the pious convictions of duty, or by the imperious mandates of his religious faith.

Yet, it must be admitted, that the same elementary writers to which I have referred the Court, seem to consider the law as equally applicable to a Priest† as to a Physician or Surgeon, and that a clergyman is bound to disclose a confession, though made to relieve an agonized conscience, or for the holy and all important purpose of seeking pardon of the Almighty!

And now may it please the court, to bear with me while I examine the decisions upon which this rule is attempted to be supported. At the outset I boldly affirm, without fear of contradiction, that the Attorney General can produce but *two* cases, in which the question has ever been raised in relation to a clergyman; neither of which can be of authority in the United States, both having been decided since our revolution.—I go farther—I say the cases would not be binding in Great Britain.

---

* 11 State Trials 243. Fol. 6.

† Peake 180. M'Nally 253. Swift 95.

The first instance to be found in the books, in which a minister of the gospel, has been called upon, to testify what had been communicated to him by a penitent, was in the case of one Sparkes, who was tried before Mr. Justice Buller. It is not reported, but is cited in a subsequent case, where an interpreter between a client and counsel was not permitted to testify, and which was decided by Lord Kenyon, July 17, 1791. It is stated as follows by Mr. Garrow: "a case much stronger than this, " he said, had been *lately* determined by Mr. Justice " Buller on the northern circuit. That was a case in " which the life of the prisoner was at stake.. The " name of it was the King, v. Sparkes. There the pri- " soner being a Papist had made a confession before a " Protestant clergyman of the crime for which he was " indicted, and the confession was permitted to be given " in evidence on the trial, and he was convicted and ex- " ecuted. The reason (urged Mr. Garrow) against ad- " mitting that evidence was much stronger than in the " present case; there the prisoner came to the Priest for " ghostly comfort and to ease his conscience oppressed " with guilt."*

On this decision of Mr. Justice Buller, Lord Kenyon makes the following observation " I should have paus- " ed before I admitted the evidence there admitted."†

Thus we have the chief justice of England, expressing strongly his dissent, to the adjudication as stated to have been made by judge Buller. This alone, is sufficient to shake its authority.

---

* The Case of Du Barre. Peakes Cases. 78.

† Ibid. 79.

It must be recollected too, that it is the decision of a single judge, at the Circuit, which is never considered as binding.

There are other considerations which go far to destroy its influence, if those that have already been urged were not sufficient. The confession was made by a *Papist* to a *Protestant* Priest. It does not appear that the clergyman had any scruples to reveal what had been confessed to him, or that he made any objection thereto. On the contrary, it is expressly stated, that the evidence was *permitted* to be given; and Lord Kenyon remarks, that *he* should have hesitated before *he* should have admitted it to be given.

I may here appeal to every candid mind, and ask whether, the fact, of a clergyman never having before been called upon to testify in a court of justice, what had been thus communicated to him, for spiritual purposes, is not irresistible evidence that the law is otherwise? If the law had not been opposed to such examinations, would not the religious feuds which have agitated and afflicted Great Britain, have led long before to such inquiries? But allow me to call the attention of the Court to the only remaining case. It was decided in Ireland, in 1802, before Sir Michael Smith, bart. the master of the rolls.

In that case "a bill was filed praying to be decreed "the estates of the late Lord Dunboyne; the plaintiff "claimed the same as heir at law, and alledging the "will under which the defendant claimed as a nullity, "Lord Dunboyne having been a popish priest, and having conformed and relapsed to popery, which deprived him of power to make a will."

" Issue was joined ; and the plaintiff produced the
" Reverend Mr. Gahan, a clergyman of the church of
" Rome, to be examined, and interrogatories to the fol-
" lowing effect were amongst others exhibited to him :
" What religion did the late Lord Dunboyne profess
" from the year 1783 to the year 1792 ? What religion
" did he profess at the time of his death and a short
" time before his death ? The witness answered to the
" first part, viz.—That Lord Dunboyne professed the
" Protestant religion during the time &c. but demurred
" to the latter part in this way, that his knowledge of
" the matter enquired of (if any he had) arose from a
" confidential communication made to him in the exercise
" of his clerical functions, and which the principles of
" his religion forbid him to disclose : nor was he bound
" by the law of the land to answer."

"*Master* of the *Rolls* (Sir *Michael Smith* bart.)
" thought there was no difficulty in the case, though it
" had run into a great length of discussion, which he in-
" dulged as being most likely to give satisfaction upon a
" question which seemed to involve something of a pub-
" lic feeling. But he was bound to overrule the de-
" murrer. It was the undoubted legal constitutional
" right of every subject of the realm, who has a cause
" depending, to call upon a fellow subject, to testify
" what he may know of the matters in issue ; and every
" man is bound to make the discovery unless specially
" exempted and protected by law. It was candidly ad-
" mitted that no special exemption could be shewn in
" the present instance, and analogous cases and princi-
" ples alone were relied upon : and, there was no
" doubt, that analogous cases and principles were suf-

"ficient for judicial determination. But the principle
"must be clear as light, and the analogy irresistibly
"strong. That clearness of principle and strength of
"analogy did not appear in this case and demurrers of
"this nature being held strictly he was obliged to over-
"rule it."* He cited a case which is evidently inapplicable to the one before him.†

Upon this adjudication of the *Master* of the *Rolls,* I need only to observe, that it is unsupported by the authority to which he refers. It is a decision of a single magistrate. It is made in a country more remarkable for nothing, than the religious intolerance and biggotry of its laws. Precedents in such a country, and in such cases ought to be admitted, by us, with the most scrupulous caution; and finally, the fact enquired into of Mr. Gahan, had not been communicated to him in the administration of a sacrament of his Church, which in its nature is to be kept inviolably secret. I can see no reason to conceal, nor in our country would any Catholic Clergyman conceal, the fact that an American citizen had died in the Catholic faith. Mr. Gahan may have supposed, that it was his duty, as a pious man, to refuse to disclose, where the disclosure would defeat a person's Will, and work a flagrant injustice, as it obviously would have done in that case.

It may now be demanded, whether the two decisions to which I have referred—the latter before the *Master of the Rolls*—the former impeached by the *Lord Chief Justice* of England, would be binding, even in Great

---

* 1 M'Nally 254, 255.
† Vaillant, v. Dodemead 2 Atk. 524.

Britain. They clearly would not be binding. They have not the force of authority. Whoever has read their books of reports, knows, that the English judges do not feel themselves concluded by decisions much more solemn and imposing than those.

It may not be unapt, or time mispent, to recur to a few cases to shew the Court, the liberties which English judges have taken with each other, and how easily they overturn the law, which they themselves, after grave advisement have established! They cannot expect that we should shew them more deference or courtesy, than they shew to themselves.

In a cause before Lord Mansfield* a rule of law was urged. His Lordship said, "The law was certainly "understood to be so, and there are *an hundred cases so determined,*" but they struck him as "absurd and wrong," and he overturned them. Lord Kenyon was pleased to say, "I think that decision did him great honor."†

And we shortly afterwards find Lord Kenyon practising the example which had been set him, and actually overturning a decision of Lord Mansfield.‡ The opinion of that great man, formed after full argument, and sanctioned by the concurrence of all the other judges of the Court of King's Bench, yielded to the influence of Lord Kenyon. In this country, we have, in that instance, persevered in maintaining the law as settled by Lord Mansfield.

---

* Harrison, v. Beecles, cited 3 Term Rep. 688.

† Ibid. 3 Term. 689.

‡ Jourdaine, v. Lashbrook. 7 Term Rep. 601. In which the case of Walton, v. Shelly, 1 Term Rep. 296, is overruled.

Lord Loughborough pronounces a decision of Lord Chancellor Parker, *to have been long exploded.** Mr. Justice Ashurst says, "if there be several cases "which are not reconcilable with reason on one side, "and one sensible case to the contrary, we ought to de- "cide according to the latter."† Lord Mansfield and other distinguished judges of that country, have not hesitated to *make* the case.

But we all recollect what our own Courts have done—and done wisely.

It is only necessary to notice two prominent cases, in which our courts have unshackled themselves of former decisions, and put the law upon the footing of justice and sound sense.

The sentences of foreign Courts of Admiralty were long held as *conclusive* evidence of the facts decided by them, and are in Great Britain to this day, though now grievously complained of by some of its ablest judges. We had adopted the English rule in its full vigour.‡

In 1802, however, this principle was brought under review in the highest court in this state. It was upon that occasion, that one of the judges, whom I have now the honor of addressing,§ pursuing in his senatorial character the dictates of his own mind, overthrew, by the force of argument, the *conclusiveness* of foreign

---

* Sumner, v. Brady. 1 Hen. Blac. 655—referying to the case of Lewis, v. Chase. 1 Pierre Williams 620.

† 2 Term 574.

‡ Ludlow & Ludlow, v. Dale, 1799, 1 Johns. Cas. 16. Gorix, v. Low, 1800. Ibid, 341. Vandenheuval. v. United Insurance Company, 2 Joh. Cas. 452.

§ De Witt Clinton.

sentences. He has the satisfaction to find, within the short space of a few years, his opinion every where gaining ground, and a high judicial personage, even in Great Britain, adding thereto the weight of his authority, coupled with that of Lord Thurlow!! "I shall die "(said Lord Ellenborough) like Lord Thurlow, in the "belief that they ought never to have been admitted."*

The other case in which we maintained our judicial independence, is stronger and more emphatic in its character than that which I have just noticed. The rule of law was undisputed by all *legal* writers:—It was to be found in every book upon criminal law:—It was in the mouth of every student. I mean the doctrine *That truth is no justification on an indictment for a libel.*†

Yet, when this rule, came to be drawn into discussion in this state—when the vast talents of a man, now no more! ‡ who was indeed the pride of our bar, were arrayed against it—and when the authorities were maturely weighed, the rule was pronounced to be a legal heresy.—It was exploded. The Legislature by the concurrence of every member of both Houses, vindicated the law. They declared truth to be a justification, "Provided that the matter charged as libellous, was "published with good motives and for justifiable ends." The principle contained in Mr. Fox's libel bill was also recognized and adopted, that the jury should de-

---

* Donaldson, v. Thompson. 1 Camp. N. P. Cas. 432. 1808.

† 2 Hawk. P. C. 128. B 1. Ch. 73. S. 6. 4 Blac. Com. 150. 3 Term Rep. 428.

‡ Mr. Hamilton.

cide upon the whole matter, and determine the law and the fact. This *declaratory* act, which, pronounced what the law *was*, received the unanimous assent of the Council of Revision, composed, as is known, of the Chancellor and all the Judges of the Supreme Court.*

Having thus stripped the cause of embarrassment, and shewn, I trust, to the satisfaction of your Honours, that this Court is at perfect liberty, in the judgment that it shall finally pronounce in this cause, to follow the guidance of liberality and wisdom, unfettered by authority; I shall proceed to examine the first proposition which I undertook to maintain, that is, that the 38th Article of the Constitution, protects the Reverend Pastor in the exemption which he claims, *independent of every other consideration.*

The whole article is in the words following:

" And whereas we are required by the benevolent
" principles of rational liberty, not only to expel civil
" tyranny, but also to guard against that spiritual op-
" pression and intollerance, wherewith the bigotry and
" ambition of weak and wicked priests and princes have
" scourged mankind : This convention doth further, in
" the name and by the authority of the good people of
" this state, ORDAIN, DETERMINE AND DECLARE, that
" the free exercise and enjoyment of religious profession
" and worship, without discrimination or preference,
" shall forever hereafter be allowed within this state to
" all mankind. *Provided,* that the liberty of conscience
" hereby granted, shall not be so construed, as to ex-

* Act passed 5th April 1805. And see the case which gave rise to it:—The People, v. Croswell. 3 Johns. Cas. 337—413.

" cuse acts of licentiousness, or justify practices incon-
" sistent with the peace or safety of this State."*

Now we cannot easily conceive of more broad and comprehensive terms, than the convention have used. Religious liberty was the great object which they had in view. They felt, that it was the right of every human being, to worship God according to the dictates of his own conscience. They intended to secure, forever, to all mankind, without distinction or preference, the free exercise and enjoyment of religious profession and worship. They employed language commensurate with that object. It is what they have said.

Again, the Catholic religion is an ancient religion. It has existed for eighteen centuries. The sacrament of penance has existed with it. We cannot in legal decorum, suppose the convention to have been ignorant of that fact : nor were they so in truth. The convention was composed of some of the ablest men in this or in any other nation. Their names are known to the court. A few still live, and we revere the memories of those who are no more. They all knew the Catholic faith, and that auricular confession was a part of it. If they had intended any exception would they not have made it? If they had intended that the Catholics should freely enjoy their religion, excepting always, auricular confession, would they not have said so? By every fair rule of construction we are bound to conclude that they would have said so :—And as the convention did not make the exception neither ought we to make it.

---

* Constitution of the State of New-York. Art. 38. 1 Vol. Rev. Laws, 16 17.

Again there is no doubt that the convention intended to secure the liberty of conscience.—Now, where is the liberty of conscience to the Catholic, if the priest and the penitent, be thus exposed ? Has the priest, the liberty of conscience, if he be thus coerced ? Has the penitent the liberty of conscience, if he is to be dragged into a court of justice, to answer for what has passed in confession ? Have either the privilege of auricular confession ? Do they freely enjoy the sacrament of penance ? If this be the religious liberty, which the constitution intended to secure—it is as perplexing as the liberty which, in former times, a man had of being tried by the water ordeal, where, if he floated he was guilty —if he sunk he was innocent.*

Your Honors,

I can find but one case which bears any analogy to the present. It is an English case. It is that of *Sir Thomas Harrison* against *Allen Evans.* Mr Evans was a *Protestant Dissenter,* and a freeman of the city of London. He had been elected one of the sheriffs of that city, but by law could not take upon himself the office, because, he had not within one year before, received the sacrament of the Lords supper, *according to the rites of the Church of England.*† By a by-law of the corporation a penalty of 600*l* was imposed on all such as should refuse to serve. A prosecution was commenced by the Chamberlain of London against Mr. Evans for the penalty. He relied upon the toleration act.‡ He pleaded that he was a dissenter within the toleration act;

---

* 4 Black. Com. 343.
† Act of Parliament 6 May 1661
‡ Passed 1 Feb. 1 year of Wm. and Mary.

that he had not taken the sacrament in the church of England within one year preceding the time of his supposed election, nor ever in his whole life; and that he could not in conscience take it. It was conceded on all hands, that if he took upon himself the office, without having previously received the sacrament according to law, he was punishable.

Though it was obvious to every ingenuous mind that Mr. Evans was, by necessary implication, within the spirit and protected by the true meaning of the toleration act, yet, judgment for the penalty was rendered against him in the sheriffs court: and afterwards affirmed by the Court of Hustings in the city of London. To the honor however, of the house of Lords this affirmance was reversed *nemine contradicente,* notwithstanding the opinion of *Mr. Baron Perrot.**

The observations of Lord Mansfield upon this case, before the British Peers, are too fine to be omitted by me. He exposed, in a masterly manner, that uncandid —Jesuitical—sophisticated attempt to defeat the toleration act. And here let me observe—that our constitution is our great toleration act, made by the people themselves, in their sovereign capacity; and as the end intended to be secured was *religious toleration,* every thing, essential to that end, not leading to licentiousness, nor to practices inconsistent with the peace or safety of the state, is by necessary implication guaranteed by the constitution.

---

* 3 Brown Parl. cas. 465. 31 vol. journ. House of Lords p. 458, 470, 475.

When, says Lord Mansfield in the case of Mr. Evans, the Jesuits in France meditated the oppression, and the distruction of the protestants "there was no oc-"casion to revoke the edict of Nantz; the Jesuits* need-"ed only to have advised a plan similar to what is con-"tended for in the present case. Make a law to ren-"der them incapable of office; make another to punish "them for not serving. If they accept, punish them; "if they refuse, punish them; if they say yes, punish "them; if they say no, punish them. My Lords this "is a most exquisite dilemma, from which there is no "escaping; it is a trap a man cannot get out of; it is "as bad persecution as that of Procrustes. If they are "too short, stretch them; if they are too long, lop them. "Small would have been their consolation to have been "gravely told—the edict of Nantz is kept inviolable; "you have the full benefit of that act of toleration, you "may take the sacrament in your own way with im-

---

* This religious order has been traduced both by ill informed Catholics and Protestants. The Jesuits have been proscribed throughout all Europe, except in Russia. It would be doing the highest injustice to the United States of America, to allow it to go abroad to the world that they have participated in the abuse which has been heaped upon that order. It cannot be doubted by any intelligent or well informed man, that policy and prejudice, have conspired more than any thing else, to pourtray that learned body in an odious light, and to hold them forth as faithless—designing and subtle. The fact is, that no class of men have manifested greater zeal for the Christian religion—none have taken more pains to diffuse its benefits to mankind—none have laboured more to carry it to the distant regions of the earth than the Jesuits. In learning they have been surpassed by none.—We beg leave to refer the reader to a note on this subject in the appendix.

" punity; you are not compelled to go to mass. Was " this case but told in the city of London as of a pro-" ceeding in France, how would they exclaim against " the Jesuitical distinction! and yet in truth it comes " from themselves; the Jesuits never thought of it;— " when they meant to persecute, their act of toleration, " the edict of Nantz, was repealed."*

Apply this to the case now before the Court. We tell the Catholics—yes, you shall have the full benefit of the constitution; you shall have the " free exercise " and enjoyment of religious profession and worship;" you shall have your seven sacraments; your Priest shall freely administer the sacrament of penance; you shall all enjoy the consolation of auricular confession; and as we know that your Priest cannot according to his religious faith, reveal to any person in the world, what passes in confession;—we will not compel him—we will only consign him to prison, and peradventure superadd a fine which he can never pay:—or, if your Priest should violate the seal of confession, and reveal what the penitent hath disclosed—far be it from us to violate the constitution; the penitent shall freely enjoy " his religious profession and worship."—He has the full benefit of it. We only shut him up in the State

---

* See Lord Mansfield's opinion 41 vol. Gentlemans Magazine 65.

N. B. The Edict of Nantz, was in fact repealed by Lewis the 14th, and not by the Jesuits.—It could not be repealed by that order. Whether the revocation of the Edict of Nantz proceeded from a spirit of persecution on the part of the French government, or from a necessity of securing the throne against the incessant attemps made by the Hugenots, to subvert it, is a point of historical fact that cannot be rightly decided but by perusing the historians of both parties of that time.

Prison, or otherwise punish him according to law. Is there, in the republic, a man who does not see in this the most scandalous sophistry? Is there, on earth, a man who would not abhor it?

The decision of the Peers in the case of the dissenter is important as a rule of construction. The toleration bill "left the dissenters to act as their consciences shall "direct them, *in matters of religious worship*."* It secured nothing more. Yet the Lords rightly held, that by necessary implication, it extended to the exemption claimed by Mr. Evans. Our constitution is much more broad and explicit. The object was to secure, "to all "mankind the free exercise and enjoyment of religious "profession and worship, without distinction or pre- "ference." Every thing essential to that object, is by necessary implication, secured by the constitution; unless it leads to acts of licentiousness, or to practices inconsistent with the peace or safety of the State.

We have no *statutory* regulation upon the subject now under consideration, and the principles of the *common law* are accurately and strongly laid down by Lord Mansfield. His words are these, "*My Lords, there "never was a single instance, from the Saxon times "down to our own, in which a man was ever punished "for erroneous opinions concerning rites or modes of "worship, but upon some* POSITIVE LAW."

Thus it is clear, in every possible view which we have taken of the question, that the exemption claimed by Dr. Kohlmann, is fully supported by the *enacting clause of the Constitution*. It only remains to be seen, whe-

* 4 Blac. Com. 54.

ther this right be impaired by the *proviso* in the Constitution.

The words are, "Provided, that the liberty of con-
"science hereby granted, shall not be so construed, as
"to excuse acts of licentiousness, or justify practices
"inconsistent with the peace or safety of this State."
Now, unless it can be shewn, that auricular confession tends to the excuse of licentiousness, or justifies practices inconsistent with the peace or safety of the State, we cannot be affected by the proviso.

But let us see how it stands. Does auricular confession excuse acts of licentiousness? If the Catholics held that the confessor could unconditionally forgive every, or any sin, which might be committed; or if they held that he could forgive *upon condition that they confessed such sin;* a sinner, on such terms, might go on and repeat his sins at pleasure; and then it might be said, that auricular confession is within the proviso of the constitution. But from a book* that contains the Catholic creed on this point, and which my Rev. client has put into my hands, I find the fact to be altogether otherwise. The Catholic holds that his priests can absolve no one, but the "*truly penitent sinner,*" that he must come to them "making a sincere and humble
"confession of his sins, with a true repentance, and
"firm purpose of amendment, and a hearty resolution
"of turning from his evil ways; and that whosoever
"comes without the due preparation; without a re-
"pentance from the bottom of his heart, and a real in-

* The Council of Trent, Sess. 14.

"tention of forsaking his sins, *receives no benefit by the* "*absolution; but adds sin to sin by a high contempt of* "*God's mercy, and abuse of his sacraments.*"

*According to our faith,** give me leave to ask, whether a sinner, under such convictions and resolutions, looking to, and confiding implicitly in the Saviour of the world, would not, through the merits of that Saviour, be absolved from his sins? I answer he would. It is the faith of all Protestants.

It requires no observations of mine, to shew that nothing in the Catholic creed, in this point, excuses or encourages licentiousness. In the instance before us it has led to a restoration of the property to the true owner, and it is known to be attended in a multitude of cases with great good. The life of HENRY the FOURTH, of France, was undoubtedly saved by it, though he afterwards fell a victim to the fanaticism of Ravillac.(1) If we could legally and constitutionally compel the clergyman to reveal the name of the penitent, who would afterwards go to confession? What would be gained to the State?

Is auricular confession dangerous to the *peace* or *safety* of the State? We know that it exists and is practiced in Russia—In Spain—in France—in Portugal—in Italy—in Germany, and in most of the countries of Europe. Is *their* peace, or *their* safety disturbed by auricular confession?

---

* The Protestant faith.

(1) See appendix.

If, however, it be necessary for me to add any thing further, to repel this objection to auricular confession; I will do it by reading the sentiments of an elegant writer and an able lawyer; and if it gives weight to the argument, it may be observed that he was not friendly (at least in his writings) to Catholics or Protestant Dissenters. I mean Sir William Blackstone.

After speaking of Protestant Dissenters, and remarking, that the experience of their "turbulent dispositions" in former times, occasioned several disabilities to be laid upon them, he proceeds to notice the Catholics. He says, "as to the papists, what has been said "of the protestant dissenters, would hold equally strong "*for a general toleration of them;* provided their "separation was founded only upon difference of *opi-* "*nion in religion*, and their principles did not also ex- "tend to a subversion of the *civil* government. If once "they could be brought to renounce the supremacy of "the Pope, *they might quietly enjoy their seven sacra-* "*ments, their purgatory, and* AURICULAR CONFESSION; "their worship of relics and images; nay, even their "transubstantiation. But while they acknowledge a "foreign power, superior to the sovereignty of the "kingdom, they cannot complain if the laws of that "kingdom will not treat them upon the footing of good "subjects."*

Here then, we have the explicit admission of Mr. Justice Blackstone, that auricular confession is innocent, that it, with all the other rites and ceremonies of the

---

* 4 Black. Com. 53, 54, 55.

Catholics, might be quietly enjoyed by them; and but for their maintaining the supremacy of the Pope, he sees no reason why they should not be *universally tolerated.* With regard to the supremacy of the Pope, we know that to be merely spiritual. They consider him the head of the church; but politically, or as connected with government, or civil society, they acknowledge no supremacy whatsoever in the pope. History shews us, that Catholic princes have oftentimes gone to war against the Pope in his character of a temporal prince.*

The great body of the American people are protestants. Yet our catholic brethren have never hesitated to take up the sword with us, and to stand by us in the hour of danger. The Father of his country—the illustrious conductor of the Revolution, did not hesitate in the face of the nation to do justice to their revolutionary services—to their good conduct as citizens—and to the aid which they rendered us in the establishment of our free government. His sentiments are such as were to have been expected from that exalted character. "As mankind (says he) become more liberal, they will "be more apt to allow, that all those who conduct them-"selves as worthy members of the community, are "*equally entitled* to the protection of civil government. "I HOPE TO SEE AMERICA AMONG THE FOREMOST NA-"TIONS IN EXAMPLES OF JUSTICE AND LIBERALITY." "He concludes with wishing them "every temporal and spiritual felicity."†

---

* See appendix.

† General Washington's answer to the Congratulatory Address to him by the Catholics, in 1789.

Having said thus much upon the question as arising out of the constitution, I shall resign it to the very learned Counsel who is associated with me; in full confidence that if a doubt still exists, it will be dissipated by the force of his talents.

I now proceed to a discussion of the second proposition, that is, that the exemption claimed by Dr. Kohlmann, is supported *by the known principles of the common law,* which will not compel, any man, to answer a question, that subjects him to a *penalty* or *forfeiture* :—impairs his *civil* rights :—or may *degrade, disgrace,* or *disparage* him.

This is a subject of technical law. I shall treat it as such. I think I can say, with confidence, that I have fully examined all the authorities in relation to it.

I need not refer to books, to shew that a man is not bound to accuse himself of a crime. That he is not—is a maxim as old as the law itself. It is equally clear, that he is not bound to answer a question in a Court of justice, which subjects him to a penalty or forfeiture.*

It may however be contended that the other branches of the proposition, which is now under consideration are not so clear. 1st. Is a witness bound in a court of common law to impair his *civil* rights? I know that a doubt has lately been raised upon the question. I am aware of the case of Lord Melville in England, and of the *declaratory* statute which was passed in consequence

---

* Raynes qui tam, v. Spicer. 7 Term Rep. 178. 2 Fonb. Equ. 492. 1 Atk. 539. Wallis, v. Duke of Portland. 3 Ves. Jun. 494. Mitford's treat. 157, 158, 224. Swift's Ev. 77.

of it. But the Court will be pleased to recollect that the judges were divided amongst themselves* and the opinion of the majority is contrary to the language of the books.† In the United States the decisions are all against it.‡ In a late case in Pennsylvania the principle adopted in Lord Melville is noticed and explicitely rejected. The judge saying. "I recollect the case of "Lord Melville; it never received my approbation, "and as it took place since the revolution, it is of no "authority over this court. It was a decision in violation of the rights of man, and in opposition to the laws "of nature. I have always overruled a question that "would affect a witness *civilly*, or subject him to a "criminal prosecution; I have gone farther and where "the answer to the question would cover the witness "with *infamy* or *shame*, I have refused to compel him "to answer it."§

In Great Britain it has been decided by Lord Kenyon‖ that a witness, under a subpœna *duces tecum*, cannot be compelled to produce a paper which constitutes part of his title, or would expose him to an action. The principle has been recognized by Lord Ellenborough in a

* 1 vol. American Law Journ. 223 232.

† Peakes Ev. 184. 2 Raym. 1008. Hawkins, v. Perkins. 1 Stra. 406. 8 Term, 590.

‡ Stores, v. Wetmore. Kirby 203. Starr, v. Tracy. 2 Root 528 Clairbourn, v. Parish. 2 Washington. 146. Connor, v. Brady. Anthon's N. P. Cas. 71. Smith's Ev. 77.

§ The case of T. W. Bell. Brown's Rep. 376.

‖ Miles, v. Dawson. 1 Esp. Cas. 405. And see also Peake 191. Swift 107. 2 Fonb. 487.

subsequent case, in which he observed that it was "a "proposition too clear to be doubted."*

[Here the Attorney General interrupted Mr. Riker, and stated that he did not mean to deny the law, to be as the counsel had contended it was in his argument.]

It being thus conceded by the public Prosecutor, and supported by reason and authority, that a man cannot in a Court of common law, be compelled to give testimony which shall impair his civil rights; I shall proceed to examine the remaining branch of the proposition. 2d. Can a witness, by the principles of our law be forced to *degrade—disgrace,* or *disparage* himself?

And here too, some confusion prevails in Great Britain on this point. I know that it has there in a few instances, been held that a person is bound to answer where his answer may reflect upon himself: As where a bail was asked "If he had ever stood in the pilory for perjury."† I know too that a respectable writer on the law of evidence‡ declares that a witness who has been convicted of an *infamous* crime, and has suffered the execution of the judgment, may be questioned as to the fact; and may be asked "whether he ever was tried for, or *charged* with a particular offence," and is bound to answer the question. I know however that another learned writer who has treated of the same subject,§ and in the same country, has severely questioned the propriety of such examinations, and says "the highest and most enlightened characters in the profession are much divided

* Amey, v. Long. 9 East 485.
† Rex, v. Edwards. 4 Term. Rep. 440.
‡ M'Nally 258.
§ Peake 129.

on the point." He considers the law as unsettled.*
Some of the judges he observes "have laid it down as
"a rule that a witness shall not be rendered infamous,
"or even *disgraced* by his own examination."†

Lord C. J. Treby is decisive against such a mode of examination.‡ So is Sir W. Blackstone§ and Lord Ellenborough has in a late case branded it with his disapprobation|| so too has Lord Alvanley.¶ It is also shaken in the Kings Bench as late as the 47. Geo. 3.** The weight of authorities in Great Britain are, in my opinion unequivocally against it; and in this country the course and current of the decisions are clearly in opposition to it. So too is an American writer, on the law of evidence.†† I shall close this subject by referring the Court to a book in which all the cases are collected.‡‡

Apply then those rules to the case before us. Dr. Kohlmann informs us under the solemnity of an oath, that besides violating his religious faith and committing the greatest impiety, he should if he revealed what passed in confession, be degraded in the Church—he would forfeit his office—he would be stripped of his sacerdotal character—he would lose his clerical rights—he would be disgraced in the eyes of all Catholics—in fine he would be rendered infamous, and according to his belief have to do penance for the residue of his life.

* Peake 130. † Ibid. ‡ Ibid 135.
§ 3 Blac. Com. 370.
|| Rex, v. Lewis. 4 Esp. cas. 225.
¶ M'Bride, v. M'Bride. 4 Esp. Cas. 242.
** Rex, v. Inhabitants of Castell Careinion. 8 East 77.
†† Swift's Evi. 52. 53.
‡‡ 2 Vol. Goulds Edit. Esp. part 2. p. 101—104.

Your Honors,

I confess I feel a deep interest in this cause. I am anxious that the decision of the Court should be marked with liberality and wisdom. I consider this a contest between toleration and persecution. A contest involving the rights of conscience. A great constitutional question, which as an American Lawyer, I might, with strict right and perfect propriety have discussed, independent of adjudged cases. To compel the Reverend Pastor to answer, or to be imprisoned, must either force his conscience or lead to persecution. I can conceive of nothing, more barbarous—more cruel—or more unjust than such an alternative. To compel him to answer, against his religious faith or to confine his person, would be the highest violation of right that I have ever witnessed. It would cast a shade upon the jurisprudence of our country. The virtuous and the wise, of all nations, would grieve that America should have so forgotten herself, as to add to the examples of religious despotism!

I cannot express my convictions on this important and delicate subject, better than in the language of that enlightened judge whose opinion I before quoted.*
"Conscience is not controllable by human laws, nor
"amenable to human tribunals. Persecution or at-
"tempts to force conscience, will never produce convic-
"tion, and are only calculated to make hypocrites, or—
"Martyrs."

"There is nothing, certainly, more unreasonable,
"more inconsistent with the rights of human nature,

* Lord Mansfield.

"more contrary to the spirit and precepts of the Chris-
"tian Religion, more iniquitous and unjust, more im-
"politic than PERSECUTION. It is against natural re-
"ligion, revealed religion, and sound policy."

Thus have I closed a subject of vast interest to the parties concerned. I could have wished that my argument had been more perfect, and more persuasive. The learned counsel however who is associated with me will more than supply its defects. It only remains for me to make my acknowledgments to the court for the very attentive hearing which it has been pleased to give me, and to express the entire confidence which my reverend client feels, in the wisdom and in the purity of those, to whose judgement he now cheerfully submits himself.

After Mr. Riker had finished, Mr. Blake, who had come into court with the clergymen and trustees of the church, rose and made a few grave and impressive observations. He said that he had come unprepared to speak, and with a determination rather to be silent. For though the question must be considered of high importance to every member of the Roman Catholic Church, and to him among the rest, yet he was more willing that it should be discussed by the gentlemen into whose hands it had fallen, and from whom it could not fail to receive every justice. He approved of the view which Mr. Riker had taken of the question, and affirmed that as well by the principles of the common law, as by the constitution; the privilege of the witness was secured. He animadverted upon the doctrines of the British, and still more on those of the Irish code, as respecting the Catholic religion, and said, as it was the first, so he hoped it would be the last time that he should ever hear of such a question, being brought forward in a court of justice.

Mr. Gardinier, the District Attorney, began by saying, that, he had with great reluctance, consented to bring up the present question for discussion ; because it was not of so much public importance that the offence charged against the accused (receiving stolen goods) should be punished, as that the repose of a respectable religious sect should remain undisturbed. And he had therefore, upon hearing of the question, given out, that he should enter a *nolle prosequi* in this case. And should have done so, if he had not received a very earnest request from the Roman Catholic Church, urging to bring the point now before the court to a decision. That having concluded to do so, he hoped that what he had to say, would give offence to none. It was a question delicate and tender in its nature, and he foresaw, that it would be scarcely possible to touch it, even argumentatively, without giving some degree of pain. But his duty now compelled him to proceed, and to examine whether the priests of the Roman Church were indeed entitled to a privilege to which no other persons asserted the least pretention: that of concealing their knowledge of matters which it concerned the public good and the public safety to have disclosed? He proposed to examine this question on the basis of the common law and of the constitution.

First. The common law. It is a principle of that law, that one of the primary duties of a citizen, is to disclose all his knowledge concerning matters connected with the public good. On this point there can be no dispute. There is however, an exception to this principle. An attorney may not disclose his clients secrets. But then the exception only proves the rule ; and unless the counsel for the defendant can shew that, the knowledge obtained by a priest in the course of confession, has also been established, as an exception, the general rule must prevail, and the priest of course must answer. He said the counsel for the defendant had produced no case in which the privilege of such a priest had been recognized ; but that in all the cases cited, a contrary doctrine had been held. The counsel had indeed *endeavored* to shew that these cases did not go the full length of expressly establishing the rule, that the priest should answer ; with what success the court would decide. He should not press those cases, because they were not necessary to his argument, for the right to examine this priest in this case, grew out of the general rule that every citizen must answer ; and unless it could be shewn by some adjudged case that he is privileged, it is of no use to object either to the authority or argument of the cases cited. He should not therefore (he said) follow the counsel through those cases ; it was enough for the purpose of this argument—*first ;* that under the general rule, the priest is obliged, in common with every other member of the community to answer—*secondly ;* that there is no case in which he was ever exempted ; and, *thirdly ;* that the decision in one, and strong bearing of every case that has been decided, or agitated in relation to this point, is in support of the general rule ; and in exclusion of the exception attempted to be set up against it. At common law, therefore, the priest has no privelege.

It remains to enquire therefore,

Secondly. Does the constitution of the state give this privilege in this case.

It would not be disputed he said, that the people of the state of New York, were at the time of making their constitution, a *Christian, Protestant People.* But aware of the injustice and evils of religious intolerance, they wisely and magnanimously resolved, that not only every section of the great protestant church should be equal with every other, but that persons of other religions should also be equal to them—but it was never intended that any one should ever be *superior* to any other. To tolerate religious profession and worship is one thing ; to allow any person whatever, to conceal matters upon the knowledge of which the public safety may depend, is another, for said he, it is palpable that the pretention here set up, is inconsistent with the safety, and he should say of course therefore, with the rights of society : If the priest remains silent, crime remains unpunished—and therefore the dilemma is this, shall the priest of a particular sect, or the society which is composed of all the sects, prevail ?

Mr. Attorney then proceeded to prove that the punishment of crimes is essential to the public safety. That punishment cannot take place, if witnesses are excused from testifying to their knowledge of crimes. And by consequence that a tenet, which makes it a religious duty to conceal this knowledge, thus necessary to the public safety, however it may be seriously believed in, by its professors, comes within the spirit of the constitutional proviso ; which is in these words, "*Provided* "that the liberty of conscience hereby *granted*, shall "not be so construed as to excuse acts of licentiousness, "or justify *practices*, inconsistent with the peace or *safe-* "*ty* of this state." The liberty of conscience is *granted* let it be remarked, and by a *protestant* people to all *others*—but these cannot be entitled to do things, inconsistent with the peace and safety of the grantors. Yet if the priests of the Roman church are excused from answering, they are permitted to hold the safety of their benefactors in their hands—nay they are bound to disregard it. A protestant must answer all questions, and by those answers protect all the society, and the Roman with the rest. But the latter, according to the pretension set up, is to be indulged in endangering all the rest. And this is called liberty of conscience ! This, the equality in religious freedom, to which they aspire ! If it were merely claimed that they might be silent, when they should honestly deem it expedient—we should never be induced to yield the claim, because society can never acknowledge the expediency of concealing crime. But the pretension far exceeds this. They actually claim the liberty of unqualified and inviolable subjection to silence ! The liberty of not being permitted to speak—the liberty of being compelled to be silent—and that in cases, when it may concern the safety of the whole state, that a disclosure should be made. Can society endanger its safety, by yielding to such a claim ? Can it be supposed that the representatives of a *protestant* people, intented to be so very tolerating, as to deny to *Roman Catholic priests*, even the right of saving the state ? It would have been a suicidal act. Suppose a religious sect should sincerely believe it a duty to sacrifice the first born of every family, belonging to that sect—would it be permitted? Soppose a Roman Catholic priest knows the actors in a treasonable conspiracy, to deliver our city to the enemy, and if the persons can be known the plot may be defeated: Shall he be permitted to say, my religion forbids me from preventing the horrible effusion of blood, which must follow, for my knowledge is gained in confession!

Upon what principle is it, that *quakers* refusing to bear arms, are compelled to pay a fine or commutation! Fine is *punishment*; for what? For an *offence*. What is the *quakers offence*? that he refuses to yield his personal services, for the protection of the Commonwealth. *Why* does he refuse? because the word of God, does in his judgement, forbid man to shed man's blood. *The excuse is not received!* his personal services, are indeed dispensed with—but he is made to pay. The liberty of conscience is, in express terms, secured by the constitution of almost all the states. Yet in every one, is the quaker made to *pay* for his liberty of conscience. And why? because political lawyers can never acknowledge a principal in society, which excuses any individual from the duty of giving his aid, for the protection and safety of the society. In this state, our constitution has indeed specially provided for them. But in the other states not. They are every where compelled to pay, for omitting to do military duty—and just so is every other citizen.—Where is the quakers liberty, of conscience then? Lost in the superior duty he owes society. Whether the quakers have been justly dealt with; whether their liberty of conscienee has not been trifled with, is not *now* to be discussed. The pratice of every state, has established the principle that, the safety of the state being the first duty, the quaker shall pay a fine as a punishment, for omitting to do what his religion forbids.

Why then, shall the Roman priest be excused from the same great duty? why shall society allow *him* to omit doing that which is essential to its safety?

But confession is a *sacrament*. How can secrecy be a *part* of that sacrament? The penitent has a rigbt to confess. Let him confess; he is not punished for *that*, but for his *crime*. If it be his *duty* to confess, then that duty exists whether the confession be secret or not. And if he be a true worshipper he will confess at every hazard. If he be not, it matters little, whether he confess or not. Let confession be a duty—a sacrament. Let the texts of scripture speaking of it be considered decisive in its support. It is not from scripture that the right of secrecy is claimed to be derived. It is a compact or engagement of the priest with his church; and if you will, with the penitent. Secrecy is not of the essence of the sacrament; it is a privilege claimed because of its being reasonable—and of course is to be decided on the ground of reason and law, and those alone. The privilege claimed by the catholic penitent, in this case, then, is not, that he may ease his conscience by confession—but that such confession shall never rise up against him; the privilege claimed by the priest, is not, that he shall be allowed to hear, but that he shall be forbidden to tell. What has the constitution secured? "The free exercise and enjoyment of religious *profes-* "*sion* and *worship*, without discrimination or *prefer-* "*ence*." Now the priest discloses the confession.

How is the "*profession or worship*" of the catholic less free than if it were secret? Or how can it be maintained, that silence on the part of the priest, is part of the religious "*profession or worship*" of the catholic layman.

But, by the constitution, there shall be neither "*dis-" crimination nor preference.*" Now, what a protestant layman should confess to a protestant minister, that minister would be compelled to disclose. The catholic not. Is not here, then, a "*discrimination*," a "*prefer-" ence*," not only forbidden by the constitution, but dangerous to all the sects that compose the society.

Not only where life and limb, but where property is in controversy, the attorney is privileged from disclosing the secrets of his clients. This is not upon the mere ground that an attorney is necessary to the party—but because the law itself, has instituted this office, and made this privilege one of its inherent properties; and therefore is this privilege as immemorial as the law itself. If the principle were not as laid down, then would a physician, employed in the cure of a disreputable disease, be excused from answering, on the ground that the disease works a speedy dissolution, and the physician is *necessary* to prevent death. Yet in our own state the physician has been made to testify in such cases.

It has been insisted by the opposite counsel, that, as the Roman catholic church, might, and probably would take away this priest's office and salary, should he testify in this case, he ought therefore to be excused. But this reasoning is utterly fallacious. If the principle advanced be a sound one, then they might have made his office depend upon refusing to testify in any case, and under any circumstances, against any person in society. If I do testify, says the priest, in such a case, I lose my salary. In one way or other every one might be excused from testifying. Suppose a witness declines to testify, because he belongs to a society, which is bound, under oath, to take the life of any member who shall in any case testify against a fellow member, and he verily believes his life will be taken if he does; would he be excused? Nay, would the law permit the priest to lose his salary, because he had displeased them by obeying the law? Or his office? Would not a mandamus restore him? But he would have no hearers—he would be "*infamous.*" How infamous? In whose estimation? His infamy would consist in obeying the laws, and in the estimation of those who deem such obedience a crime. To be hated, to be despised is not infamy. To do wrong, is infamy. To disobey the public law, is infamy. Obedience to authority is the first of virtues, and among the highest of the christian duties.

The right of exemption, on the score of infamy or interest, rests on this principle, giving it the broadest basis. That a witness shall be excused, where the *facts* he discloses, convict him of moral turpitude, or prove him unintitled to life, liberty, or property. But, to say that a society to which he belongs will deprive him of support, if he becomes a witness *at all*, and to appeal to the *law* to say, that this society may be indulged in preventing him from being a witness, by such means, would be, to make the law establish a power superior to itself. It is very evident, that a society of mere laymen, adopting such an article in their constitution, so far from finding protection under it, would, and justly too, be considered as guilty of an original conspiracy against society. Is the case altered because a religious society has done this same thing? The true principle, it is apprehended, in our happy state of religious equality is this: every man shall be allowed to reconcile himself to his maker in the way he may think most effectual; and seeing that none can pretend to greater certainty than his neighbour, so, to no one of the various sects shall be given the privilege of dictating to others their course of religious worship. Thus, all stand equal; no one pretending to the right of dictating to the others. But whenever any one shall claim to do what may justly offend the others, he claims an unequal, and so an unconstitutional "*preference*." Thus, the jew may keep his own sabbath, but he shall not violate that of the christian. Under a religious tenet, no sect would be permitted to indulge in what society deems cruelty, dishonesty, or public indecency, for it would offend the rest, though the worshippers might deem themselves engaged in a holy rite. Nor ought any be allowed to conceal, when called upon in courts of justice, matters pertaining to the safety of the rest—for if they are so, allowed, they make for themselves a rule of evidence, contrary to a pre-existing principle of law, involving the safety of the whole community. If they say, our religion teaches us this, society replies all religions are equal—none shall be disturbed—each one may seek heaven as seems fit to its votaries, this is the toleration society has "*granted*" to all—but still society is superior to them all, and not, nor ever could be supposed to have granted to any, the right of silence, when its own interest and safety may be jeopardized by that silence.

The common safety, is the common right—and any pretension, whether of a religious or social institution, which claims the right to withhold from society the knowledge of matters, relating to its safety, soars above the level of the common equality, and demands such an unreasonable "preference," as society would be false to itself to allow.

Finally the constitution has granted, religious "*profession and worship*," to all denominations, "*without discrimination or preferance*:" but it has not granted exemption from previous legal duties. It has expelled the demon of persecution from our land: but it has not weakened the arm of public justice. Its equal and steady impartiality has soothed all the contending sects into the most harmonious equality, but to none of them has it yielded any of the rights of a well organized government.

When Mr. Gardenier closed it was near the usual hour of adjournment, and the Court assigned the following morning to hear the reply.

Wednesday, June, 9.

[PRESENT AS BEFORE.]

MR. SAMPSON IN REPLY.

May it Please the Court,

Before I enter on debate, let me be permitted on behalf of the Clergy and Trustees of the Roman Catholic Church, to discharge a debt due to the District Attorney for his liberal and manly conduct in this cause. That it may proceed and end, as it has began, in the spirit of peace and good will. When Mr. Gardenier proposed to enter a nolle prosequi, his motives were no doubt highly commendable. He knew that religious discussions, often, too often, ended in bitterness, and were pernicious in their result. He did not then so fully know, in how mild a spirit this question was pressed upon him. And it was not till he was strongly solicited, by those I have the honor now to represent, that he consented to bring it forward. His right to follow the course he first proposed was not disputed. His motive for that he has pursued will best appear when I shall have laid before the Court the written request addressed to him.

Mr. Sampson then read the following paper.

New- York, Court of General Sessions,

The People, *vs.* Daniel Phillips and wife.	*On an indictment for receiving stolen goods.*

Whereas it has been represented to the board of Trustees of St. Peter's Church in the city of New-York, that the Reverend Dr. Kohlmann, the pastor of said church has beeen called as a witness, to testify therein, and that thereupon he declared he knew nothing touching the matter enquired of him, but what had been communicated to him in the administration of the sacrament of penance or confession, in which he avowed himself to be bound both by the law of God and the canons of the Catholic Church to a perpetual and inviolable secrecy. That the knowledge thus obtained cannot, be revealed to any person in the world, without the greatest impiety, and a violation of the tenets of his religion. That it would be his duty, according to his religious principles, to suffer death, in preference to making the disclosure, and that this hath been the uniforn faith and doctrine of the Catholic Church. That he was advised by counsel, that the enlightened and liberal provisions of the constitution of this state protected him in the silence which his faith enjoins upon him, and therefore he respectfully requested the court to protect him in the exemption which he claimed.

And whereas, for the purpose of maturely considering the question, the District Attorney consented to delay the trial of the cause, until a future sitting of the court.

And whereas the Board of Trustees, sincerely consider the free toleration of the Catholic Religion, involved in maintaining the exemption claimed by the reverend pastor, and cannot but feel the deepest solicitude that a doubt should exist upon the subject, they therefore, respectfully request the District Attorney to bring the cause to trial at the next sitting of the court, to the end that a judicial determination may be had which shall ensure to all catholics, in common with the rest of mankind, and according to the words of the constitution, " the free exercise and enjoyment of their religious profession and worship."

The Trustees hope that the District Attorney, will be pleased to signify to them, at what time he will probably bring the question to a hearing.

By order of the Board of Trustees of St. Peter's Church.

DENNIS M'CARTHY, *Secretary.*

New-York, April 19th, 1813.

In complying with this request, the public prosecutor has done well. The gentlemen who presented it have done well. If the counsel for the witness shall have done justice to the cause, auguring from the liberal jugdgement of the Court upon the preliminary questions of evidence, I trust, the whole community will applaud the motives and rejoice in the event.

The decorous and prepossessing manner in which the reverend witness has expressed his reasons, is a good argument that this was not a challenge given in the spirit of bravado, and that if a victory is sought it is of that blessed kind, where every virtuous citizen is to share in the triumph, and none to suffer by the defeat.

Having much of necessity to say, upon a question so novel and important, I shall avoid repeating what my learned colleague has so ably urged. We have already agreed that each should take his part, as well to share the burthen of the argument, as to spare the Court the pain of a story twice told.

Mr. Riker has shewn by reason and authority, that no rigid rule of evidence can stand in the way of justice and convenience, so as to bear the exemption we lay claim to; that these rules are the handmaids, not the tyrants of a court of justice; and that when new cases occur within like reason as former ones, the same principles will govern them; and that the door of justice and propriety is never closed. The counsel did not, however rely entirely upon general reasoning, but shewed the current of authority to be so strong, that our ingenuous adversary was compelled to evade it, and driven to manœuvre with what dexterity he could, in the counter current and eddy of popular prejudices.

When this question first occurred, I humbly stated to the court, that in no country where I had been, whether Catholic or Protestant, I had ever heard of an instance of a similar kind. That in England, there was none to be produced; nor even in Ireland, where the people were catholic, and the law anti-catholic; where the few trample upon the many, and where no concessions were made to the feelings of the proscribed, or the dictates of humanity or piety. I spoke that with sincerity and truth, for the only case that ever has arisen, was decided since the epoch of my banishment, and not only since the independence of this country, but since the revolution that deprived Ireland of its independence and its parliament, and at a time when little good faith was observed by those whose opinions and sentiments are too apt to dictate, as conquerors do to the vanquished and subdued.

Two cases only have been cited, both adjudged since the period when they could be binding in this country as authority, and these only I shall notice. That of Dubarre is directly in point with us, as far as the opinion of the chief justice of England, can be in our favor. The case of the reverend Mr. Gahan, decided by the master of the rolls in Ireland, is not so much against us as I could wish it was. I am sorroy it is not equally in point, that by a decision directly in the teeth of it, the superiority of our constitution, our laws, and jurisprudence, might be more fully felt, understood, loved, and revered. I care not from what country precedents be drawn, if they be wise, and applicable to our exigencies, for reason and good sense is of every country; but if there be any country on the habitable globe, where we should not go to look for a pure and sound decision, upon the rights of Roman Catholics, it is surley that one from which this precedent is brought. Let us first enquire what they do and say on this, and the other side the Ganges; let us consult with canibals, but take no counsel from that Island, where for centuries past, a code has existed, and been in full and vigorous activity, which shames humanity. Let us first rake up the embers of every latent evil, and cut scions from the root of every desolating persecution, before we introduce the germs of that poisonous growth, so prolific in mischief, and malignity, that nothing like it can be found in the annals of the world. For every where else, though there may be madness, superstition, or idolatry, there may be some chance of impartiality; but in Ireland there can be none!

Abstract this Irish decision, from Irish politics, and Irish history, and mark upon what shallow reasons it was founded. What will the enlightened and unsophisticated judges, I have the honor to address, say to this argument, that because no case could be found, where a catholic clergyman had been exempted from an act of perfidy, and sacrilege, that therefore no such exemption could be lawful. Was that reasoning pure or solid ? Was it not more obvious, that since no case had happened of the kind, it was because so unwarrantable a stretch of power had never been attempted, even in the angriest times ? Was not the double argument of prescription and non-user in favor of the exemption ? For who is so ignorant of human history, as not to know, that in catholic countries, it would be blasphemy, and in protestant countries, until that very hour where was the instance of it ? And who that ever cast his eye upon the penal code of Ireland, but must see at the first glance, that if ever it had been lawful, it would not have been without some example, or instance that could be quoted. It would have been an easier snare for the destruction and extirpation of the catholic religion, and the catholic clergy, than those that were devised! It would have spared the tyrants of a misgoverned country, the pain, and their corrupt instruments, the shame of enacting and enforcing so many profligate and monstrous statutes. There would have been no need of such fearful penalties against the catholic clergy, as those laid on them for the offences of instructing youth, or celebrating mass, or matrimony, the latter of which, was punished with hanging, if one party proved to be protestant, the other catholic. There would have been no need of laws, giving fifty pounds for the mere discovery of an arch-bishop, twenty for a secular clergyman, and ten for the discovery of a school-master; nor inflicting pains, penalties, or premunires, for charitably harbouring them. These, and hundreds of other wretched extravagancies, may be found by any one who will look into the statute books ; and yet in the angriest times amidst all these frightful violations of nature, faith and honesty, this torture for the conscience and the heart was still unthought of, although it was well known that the sacrament of penance and confession, was an integral and vital part of the Roman catholic religion. It was known, as it has been proved in this cause, that the priest neither could, nor would reveal the secrets of that confession ; and nothing more would have been necessary than to summon the priest, in the case of every person accused of a crime, which he might be supposed to have confessed, and by putting the question to the priest, and using no other arguments than the counsel has used, commit him to prison till he answered, or in other words till he died.

By one of the ferocious statutes, made in the reign of Queen Ann, two justices of the peace, might summon any of the laity, to discover when he last heard mass, who celebrated it, and who was present, and also touching the abode of any popish clergyman, regular or secular, or any school-master, and fully to answer to all circumstances, touching such popish person, and if he had not money to ransom him, commit him to prison for twelve months,* yet in all this minute de-

* For these and other legislative enormities, see appendix.—Title, PENAL CODE ABRIGED.

tail of elaborate persecution, it was never attempted to force the confessor, to disclose what his penitent had revealed. Whether this arose from some lurking remorse, if remorse could find place in hearts so depraved; or whether it was from some politic source of the benfits that might result from confession even to the oppressors themselves, I cannot say; but I can say that it never was before attempted; and prove it by this alone, that no instance of it could be shewn.

When Lord Kenyon was told by Mr. Garrow (speaking from hearsay and for his client) that Mr. Justice Buller had obliged a protestant clergyman to disclose what a catholic penitent had confessed to him, what did he say? That his brother's opinion was entitled to respect. but that he should have paused before he made such a decision! What would he have said if it had been a catholic priest, called upon under pain of imprisonment, to violate his sacrament, abjure his faith, incur eternal infamy, and betray that holy trust, to which if he proved faithless, he cancelled every pious hope of heaven, and never could be true to any thing. Now it is not what any one of us may think upon this subject that should guide us, it is that christian charity that all should cherish. It is that precept that God has given, to pull the beam from our own eye, before we meddle with the mote that is in our neighbours. Strange then was the conclusion. that what in England was censured by so high authority, and what in Ireland never was attempted, though the rights, lives, liberties, and feelings of the catholics had been assailed through successive ages, in every wanton form that avarice, vengeance and malignity could devise, should yet be law, merely because no instance could be found where it had been attempted.

Indeed the history of that Irish case is its best comment. It is thus. Lord Dunboyne, who had been a catholic bishop, happened to succeed to one of those estates, which, together with the shadowy title of nobility, had been sufferered, after the perfidious breach of the treaty of Limerick, to descend to the rightful inheritor. And having conformed to the established church, from what motive I know not, devised it to the catholic college of Maynooth. This was a seminary lately established by government, grown wiser, if not better, by its long and many blunders. Before this institution, the young student, destined for the catholic ministry, was doomed to wander, like a poor exile, to some foreign land for education and instruction, and to receive in distant universities that charitable boon, which bigotry and fanaticism had denied him in his native soil. It was hailed as a happy relaxation of past oppression and intolerance. But still this was a poor step-child, and needed patronage and protection. If ever endowment was lawful it was this one. The devisor having no children, left to his sister and heir at law, already like himself, advanced in years, a very considerable estate. Why then was his will to be avoided? Not because it was vicious, but because he had, in the jargon of the penal code, "relapsed into popery." How does this sound in our ears? How should any one of us like the thought of having our acts avoided, when we were no more, because we had relapsed into presbyterianism, episcopalianism, or methodism? Our constitution does not forfeit the estate, or annul the acts, or avoid the wills even of convicted felons or outlaws. Nothing short of high treason can effect a forfeiture, nothing but fraud can avoid a grant or a devise. But in Lord Dunboyne's case, the question was not, whether there was guilt in the devisor, but simply, whether he took his leave of this and his flight to another life, pursuant to an Irish act of parliament, made in breach of a solemn treaty, and in the spirit of all uncharitableness. For who had he to cheat or to defraud? He had disposed of his worldly affairs. He had made his will. His last hour was approaching. The sleep of death sat heavy on his eyelids. He had no account but one to settle. It was that awful reckoning with his redeemer and his God. Forfeitures, premunires, prescriptions and pains lay on this side the grave; his way lay on the other. Still he perceives, as he looks back through the long misty dream of his past life, that he had upon that subject, which now concerned him most, been wavering and inconstant. He remembers that in the days of infancy and innocence he had been trained up in the religion for which his fathers suffered, and that when he grew up he had departed from it. He trembles to die in a faith which he had embraced from policy or from compulsion. He was a man, and the heart of man, like the hunted hare, still in its last extremities will double to its early layer. The world had no longer for him, bribe, terror, or persuasion. He offers to his almighty judge such prayers and sacrifices as he thinks most acceptable, and calls upon him as the God of mercy to pardon all his frailties. And who were those mortal inquisitors that sat to judge when God above should judge, and to condemn where he is merciful? What was that inquisition after death, that was to find the forfeiture, not because the party died *felo de se*, but because he did not? Not because he stood out in rebellion against his creator, but because he followed the best and only lights that his frail and exhausted nature afforded him, and in what concerned him more than all the universe, made choice of that road which his conscience and inward feelings pointed out as the path of his salvation. In an hour like that does any man commit fraud? If he prays to his God to direct him, and throws himself upon his mercy, and submits devoutly to his judgment, how virulent, how audacious is it in man to dare to judge and to condemn him.

Mr. Recorder, here asked the counsel, how that case of Lord Dunboyne was ultimately decided.

The Counsel. I will conceal nothing of it from the court. I wish the case to be understood, and fully weighed, for the reason and honesty of our case, will outweigh it, though twenty judges had decided it. From what appears in M'Nally's treatise, and what I gather from other sources, it ended at the rolls, with overruling the demurrer. But afterwards on an ejectment under the will brought by the heir at law, and tried before lord Kilwarden, in the month of August following, the same witness was called. Some subtle questions were put to him, to discover in what faith the testator died. He answered, like the reverend gentleman here, with modesty and discretion, that whatever knowledge he had, was imparted in religious confidence, and that he could not finish a life of seventy years by an act of sacerdotal impiety. He was committed upon this for a contempt of court, and sentenced to a weeks imprisonment in the common jail of Trim. The jury found specially upon other evidence, that Lord Dunboyne had died a catholic. The judge then observed, as the party had not suffered from the want of his testimony, and the law had been vindicated, he did not consider the clergyman an object for punishment, and immediately ordered his discharge. Let us charitably suppose that this judge felt the cruelty of the proceeding, and wished in some degree to wash his hands of it.

I have been told, and sometimes believed, that it was not without a heavy heart, that as Attorney General, he often moved for judgements upon men, whom he knew to be at least, as virtuous as himself, and as a privy counsellor, signed proclamations, at which humanity shudders. I was banished before his appointment to the bench, and long before his death. If he had those feelings of compunction, I could pity him, though he had persecuted me, and at no time could the world have bribed me to change places with him. He was not of the worst that governed in those times, and many regretted that the popular vengeance that lighted on his head, had not rather fallen on some others.

Mr. Sampson was again asked by the court, touching the event of the cause, and also whether the master of the rolls, was the same person who was once baron of the exchequer.

He was the same person, the title of baron being mere title of office, ceased with that office, he afterwards obtained the descendible title of baronet, and has since been known by that. As to the result of the cause, if I am not deceived, the will was finally established. But be that as it will, and let the personal merit of those judges be what it may, it affects not my argument. The system under which they acted; the barbarous code with which they were familiar, was enough to taint their judgement. No judge, no legislator, historian, poet or philosopher, but what has been tinctured, with the follies or superstitions of his age. Of this, one memorable instance may suffice. Sir Matthew Hale was virtuous, wise, and learned; the advocate of toleration, the enemy of cruelty. The revolutionary storms that shook the throne of monarchs, could not move him. Wealth could not corrupt, nor power intimidate him. When we find his great and philosophic mind, vilely enthralled in the grossest superstition of his time; treating of witch-craft, in the first and second degree, laying down quaint and specious rules, for the detection and conviction of those victims of barbarous folly, straining the plain rules of evidence, to meet these imaginary crimes, and because the practices of witches with the devil, and of conjurors with evil spirits, were *secret* and *dangerous*, holding that therefore, witches might be convicted without full proof. After this, may we not well suspect those Irish judges to have imbibed the poison of their cruel code, and to have eaten of the insane root that taketh the reason prisoner. And as a further lesson of circumspection, let us not forget, that after that ever memorable frenzy, which in a neighbouring state, hurled to destruction, so many innocent victims, when the actors in those bloody tragedies returned to their senses, overwhelmed with shame and with confusion, their apology was, that they had been deluded by the writings of Glanvill, Hale and Baxter. What I now relate is history, that strange as it may seem, cannot be disputed, so dangerous it is to give the reigns to cruel prejudices. At that time no eloquence could dissuade; no advocate had courage to oppose the torrent. The trembling wretch overawed by the frown of the magistrate, the fear of the law, and the dread of death, was no sooner denounced than he confessed; and many accusing themselves were received into favor as penitent witches or wizards, and used to convict others less guilty, but not so politic. At that epoch the peaceful society of Friends was thought little less dangerous, and thus did those who fled from persecution in England, become through ignorance most intolerant persecutors in America. Such is the nature of that fiendlike spirit, which it requires but a moment to raise and centuries to lay. Thank heaven it is laid in this land, and I trust forever. The best proof of which is, that we can discuss this question, in peace and charity without stirring one angry passion, or one malignant feeling. For there is no man on this side the Atlantic, that does not regard these errors of past times, as examples to be shunned, not imitated; nor should I revive their memory, but for that purpose. It seems indeed, as if providence had decreed this land, to be the grave of persecution, and the cradle of tolerance. The illustrious Penn, was imprisoned for his *dangerous* opinions in England; he came to America, and being invested with legislative authority, founded a code upon the principles of pure and unequivocating toleration. The storms of the revolution scattered back the precious seeds, and the British empire itself, after a long lapse of years, received practical lessons of that wisdom, it had banished from its shores. Even in Ireland the cheering ray pierced the gloomy night of oppression : the sympathetic charm awaked the sleeping genius of a reanimated people, and raised up those champions of civil and religious rights, within and without the walls of parliament, whose splendid eloquence, showed the native measure of many a thousand souls that bondage had degraded. How far that glorious spirit has since sunk into subjection; how far the unceasing workings of corruption and untoward events have again subdued the generous feelings of that season, I cannot, dare not say ; but with respect to catholic persecution, it received its death blow from the American revolution, and the constitution of the free states that compose this great commonwealth. It might be amusing and instructive too, to trace the progress of catholic emancipation, did our time admit of it. To see in the first trembling supplications of the abject petitioner for rights, that slaves would scorn to ask, the horrible relation of the oppressor and the oppressed. To be allowed to swear allegiance and fidelity, was granted with reluctance, as a too generous boon. To disclaim upon oath, charges of which no man was guilty, was an indulgence almost too great to ask for. That the son should no longer by the mere act of conforming to another church, be free to violate the order of nature and disinherit his own father, was a mighty concession. To hold a lease for years, or take by devise—he was a bold projector that dared to ask for that. To be a school-master, or a school-master's assistant, was too much to expect. To *" commit matri-*

mony" with impunity, was against all due subordination. At length a new and more auspicious era came, *et magnus ab integro sæclorum nascitur ordo.*

And now the patriot, soaring on the wings of enthusiasm, recommends a *gradual* emancipation, in the generous hope that the catholics would in the course o some indefinite period, or in some undetermined series of succeeding generations, inherit a capacity to take freedom. But still to have a gun to scare the crows, a steeple or a bell, or a vote at a vestry, was too dangerous a confidence. To be a juror or a constable, an attorney or a barrister, or to hold any station, civil or military, was not yet to be hoped or looked for. The thing had already gone too far. The alarm was rung. Protestant corporations, grand juries, committees and hired presses, poured forth their malignant ribaldry. The truth was this. The hour of danger was passed by, and with it the season of concession was gone. Then came the organized banditti. Then the no popery and peep of day men. Then the recall of faithless promises. And that government that refused to tolerate catholics, tolerated, instigated and indemnified a faction, whose deeds will never be forgotten. Then came hangings, half hangings, conflagrations, plunder and torture. Rape, murder and indemnity went hand in hand. And then it was, that a spectacle new and appalling, for the first time, presented itself; and presbyterian, churchman, and catholic were seen to ascend the same scaffold, and die in the cause of an indissoluble union. The great cause of human emancipation in spite of events, has still proceeded, and were the question that we are now debating, given against us, we might find to our astonisment, that on that very hour when an American tribunal had pronounced against the freedom of the catholic faith, the united parliament of Britain and Ireland had pronounced it free.

I am aware that the words I have spoken touching the penal laws of Ireland, must seem strange to many. It would be too cold and tedious to quote them from the statute book one by one, and perhaps too, foreign to the point. I have no principle to establish but this, that we should never look to Ireland for a precedent, where the rights of catholics were concerned. If what I have said be true, I think it is enough. And to shew that I have not exaggerated, I shall now refer to some of the expressions of the great Edmund Burke, upon the same subject. In the year 1782, when a bill for the *relief* of the Roman catholics was proposed by Mr. Gardner a member of the Irish house of commons, Mr. Burke in answer to a noble peer who had consulted him, used these words:

"To look at the bill in the abstract, it is neither more nor less, than a renewal act of universal, unmitigated, indispensable, exceptionless disqualification." Yet this of which he spoke, was a bill for the *relief* of the Roman catholics. If such was the character of the relief intended by their advocates, what must be the condition from which they sought relief?

Speaking of Mr. Hutchinson, then provost of the university, and a man distinguished in the Irish parliament and councils, who had proposed a few sizerships in Trinity College for the education of the catholic clergymen, Mr. Burke uses these emphatic terms: "Mr. Hutchinson certainly meant well; but coming from such a man as him, it shews the danger of suffering any description of men to fall into entire contempt, for the very charities intended for them are not perceived to be fresh insults. Where every thing useful is witheld, and only what is servile is permitted, it is easy to conceive upon what footing they must be in such a place. Mr. Hutchinson must well know the regard and honor I have for him; my dissenting from him in this particular, only shews that I think *he has lived in Ireland!* To have any respect for the character or person of a popish priest there, Oh! 'tis an uphill work indeed!" And alluding to the penalty of death for marrying a protestant with a papist, he continues, "Mr. Gardner's humanity was shocked at it, as one of the worst parts of that barbarous system, if one could settle the preference where almost all the parts were outrages upon the rights of humanity and the laws of nature." Mr. Burke then concludes his admirable letter thus: "Thinking over this matter maturely, I see no reason for altering my opinion in any part. The act as far as it goes, is good undoubtedly. It amounts very nearly to toleration in religious ceremonies; but it puts a new bolt on civil rights, and rivets the old ones in such a manner, that neither, I fear, will be easily loosened. I could have wished the civil advantages to take the lead, the others of religious toleration would follow as a matter of course. From what I have observed, it is pride, arrogance, and a spirit of domination, and not a bigotted spirit of religion that has caused and kept up these oppressive statutes. I am sure I have known those who oppressed papists in their civil rights, exceedingly indulgent to them in their religious ceremomies, and who really wished them to continue catholics in order to furnish pretences for oppression. These persons never saw a man, by converting, escape out of their power but with grudging and regret. I have known men, to whom I am not uncharitable in saying (though they are dead) that they would have become papists in order to oppress protestants, if being protestants it was not in their power to oppress papists. It is injustice, and not a mistaken conscience, that has been the principle of persecution, at least as far as has fallen under my observation."

The Court will excuse me for calling to my aid, the opinions of this eminent man, upon a subject where the truth is almost beyond credibility. Well might he say that injustice and not even a mistaken conscience had dictated these persecutions, for whoever reads the Irish history will see that these persecutions form two epochs. One before and one since the reformation. The one containing an era of about 400 years, the other about 300. Both equally fantastical and wicked. During the former, the natives of Ireland suffered for being Irish, or speaking Irish. They were pronounced aliens in their native land, and forced to sue out letters of denization. And in the reign of the third Edward they preferred a petition to be naturalized. It was refused. They rebelled—were defeated, and punished. It was no felony, and so enacted, to kill an Irishman in Ireland, and was forbidden under mônstrous penalties, to speak Irish, to use the fashions of Ireland, to wear the beard upon the upper lip, or wear wide sleeves. If any one was curious enough to read the ancient statutes and rolls of parliament, from the days of Edward the third, to those of Henry the eighth, he would find plainly enough, that mistaken conscience had nothing to do with the matter, nor religion nothing; but that the love of plunder, power, and confiscation was the sole and only motive. It was not until the axe was blunted by long use, till the mine was exhausted by the work of centuries, that religion served to whet the edge and rekindle the brand. Then streamed abroad the bloody banner of the church; then rose anew the yell of desolation; and then again the spoiler grew rich upon the soil, reeking and fattened with the natives blood. Thence the broad charters of desolated provinces, and *planting* of human beings, for so they termed it, amongst the bleaching bones of those destroyed by war and famine in the name of God!!! Were there rebellions? Were there massacres? Aye, to be sure, there were! They were the natural crop. For he that sows must reap! Away then with Irish cases and Irish authorities: for to adopt them here would be as mad as wicked. The Irish persecutors had their motives. It was their interest. They lived upon it. They had no living else than plots and forfeitures! They were not simple bigots, acting from mistaken conscience. They were pirates determined to hold what they had got, and rather than lose it scatter law and justice to the winds and waves. The cunning mariner will throw overboard the most precious of his effects, when his life and all is at stake. And so they did. But who except a maniac will do so in a season of tranquillity and calm? Indeed in later times the continuance of the catholic oppressions has taken the character of downright folly; and the wisest and keenest of British statesmen has so considered it.

and if so, every act and every decision that proceeds upon those antiquated errors, is at once a folly and a crime; shewing only how far "the evil that men do, lives after them." But to make a decision now which would be beyond all precedent, even in the worst of times, would be what I cannot give a name to.

What have our courts to do with these cases, or how do they apply to our condition? Unless it be to speculate upon such frightful histories, as the contemplative traveller ascends the vantage ground, and seating himself upon the border of some extinguished volcano, above the regions of mist or vapour, surveys above him the unclouded firmament, and below, the ravages of a convulsed world, the yawning crater, the sulphurous abyss, the scattered fragments of disjointed nature, the conjealed torrents of once streaming fire, under which lie buried and incrusted the treasures of civilization, wealth and arts; and moralizing on such awful objects, compares the benign laws of the creator with the efforts of the destroying spirit. To contrast these histories and barbarous codes with our happy constitution, and our enviable state, is to draw from them a moral, deep and wise. But though we use them, let us not be familiar with them. Let us apply all due precaution against their venomous contagion. I would hardly touch the volumes that contain them, till I had drawn on my gloves and said God bless me from all grammery. I would relegate them to some lonely desart, such as the barren Island. And there I would keep them fathoms under ground. Some wretch from the state prisons, who had ran the round of vice, and could not be inoculated with any new infection, should be their guardian. Once in the period of a lustre or olympiad, when the wind blew off our coast, they should be dug up; fasting, ablutions, and exorcisms, first performed; and if telegraphic signs, could be devised to communicate their terrible contents, it would be safest. But, bring such things into a court of justice? O! never, never.—Fie! fie! they are too rank. I think I could smell out that volume that treats of the dead Lord's will, and the inquisition held upon him, after death, for *"relapsing into popery."* Yes here it is! The whole system is already rotting above ground, let us hasten to inter its miserable remains. And now having done with Irish, let us turn to the English history. It is good to learn, even from an enemy. Mr. Pitt, who for years governed England by dint of ingenuity, was a good or a bad genius, I care not which. He was once a friend of parliamentry reform, but abandoned that; he was more than once desirous of reforming the penal code, and in that I believe he was more sincere, for he was sagacious enough to see the impolicy and gross absurdity of maintaining it any longer. In 1788, when a bill was proposed for the relief of the Roman catholics, a committee of the English catholics, waited upon him. He desired from them some authentic evidence of the catholic clergy, and universities abroad, that certain dangerous tenets imputed to them, were not avowed by the catholic church.

The three following queries were drawn up under his auspices.

1. Has the pope or cardinals, or any body of men, or any individual of the church of Rome, any civil au-

thority, power, jurisdiction or pre-eminence whatever within the realm of England ?

2. Can the pope or cardinals, or any body of men, or any individual of the church of Rome, absolve or dispense with his Majesty's subjects, from their oath of allegiance, on any pretence whatever ?

3. Is there any principle in the tenets of the catholic faith, by which catholics are justified in not keeping faith with heretics or other persons, differing with them in religious opinions, in any transaction either of a public or a private nature ?*

This was done no doubt, with a view to soften the King's conscience, which at that time was buckram against catholics. For his majesty had not then formed an alliance with the pope, nor sent his dragoons to guard his person, nor had England then spent as much blood and treasure, to put up the pope and the Bourbons as she had before expended to pull them down. These things fell out afterwards.

All great leaders of men have been addicted to oracles. In old times, they sent to Jupiter Amonon in Africa, or else to Diana at Ephesus, or else to the Delphic priestess, or to the old sybil. Mr. Pitt sent to none of these, nor did he consult the rioters of Moorfields, nor the priestly mob, nor the Orangemen. He did more wisely; he did very wisely. Let us do him justice. He sent his queries to six of the principal catholic universities of Europe. The Sorbonne at Paris, to Douay, to Louvain, to Alcala, to Salamanca, and to Valladolid.

---

* See the answers of the six universities at length in the appendix.

As politicians, mostly know the answer, before they ask the question, so I need not say that these universities all concurred in disclaiming, and firmly disavowing all these imputations, which no catholic ever thought of; unless it were in ancient times of war and contentions for kings and kingdoms, when the corruptions not of the church of Rome, but of some corrupt ministers of that church, had by forming leagues of "wicked priests and princes" dishonored that church. None but foolish ministers could have thought of visiting all those crimes of past ages upon the catholic church, because there had been weak or wicked priests, no more than of destroying all kings because there had been weak and wicked princes.

I should have venerated Mr. Pitt for this judicious step, if I could be quite sure that he was sincere. It would cover a multitude of his sins. And it is only to be lamented, that some minister, as sagacious, had not sent these queries to those six universities three centuries before. How much burning and ripping, would have been spared. I wish that Mr. Pitt had not, for his good name's sake, so soon after receiving this authentic testimony, tolerated that ferocious rabble of no popery, Orangemen, king's conscience men, and peep of day boys, whose atrocities are now as much history as his life and death. It is true, I will say it for him, he never loved them, he hated and despised them; but he knew them well, that they were always for evil, never for good, and having done all the mischief required, the sooner they were extinguished the safer and better it would be. But still he used them to carry his point, and overthrow the parliament of Ireland; which he had before corrupted to his ends. Having gained his point, he tried to put them down, but it is easier to excite wickedness than it is to subdue it. The hounds once uncoupled and set upon the tract of blood, ran riot on the hot scent, and the huntsman himself could not call them off. When he would have whipped them again into their kennel, they were savage and bayed him.

Having the authentic evidence of the six universities, that it was no tenet of catholics to break faith with heritics, he resigned his office, as he said, because he could not keep faith with the catholics. He resumed his place and did not keep faith with them. He was crossed in this by the peep of day boys, and by his other enemies, in his other projects, and he died, in what faith I know not, lamenting his incapacity to do justice, and exclaiming, Oh my poor country !

The Mayor. From what book do you take those queries of Mr. Pitt.

Counsel. I read them if it please the court, as general history, from Mr. Plowden's historical survey of the state of Ireland. They are I presume, upon the journals of the parliament.

Recorder. They are so, I have seen them.

Counsel. It is time now to take leave of foreign history. And as to those precedents of foreign law, the only weight they can have, is that of so much paper and calf's skin, for our own constitution is so explicit upon this important head of religious toleration, that nothing but the inveterate habit of running to foreign authorities, could have put it into the mind of any of us, to look elsewhere for instruction in so plain a case; unless we are to resemble that fabled race, that continued suckling till after their beards grew.

The constitution stands in need of no such illustrations. It is simple, and precise, and unequivocal. It may like other human institutions be perverted, but it cannot be easily mistaken. And judges who so well know its history will mistake it least of all. The people whose will it speaks, were not of any one church, as the learned attorney has said; but of many and various sects, all of whom had suffered more or less in Europe for their religious tenets, and many of whom had unrelentingly persecuted each other. All that came from England, and were not of the church established by act of parliament, of which the King of England was the head, all these were either catholics or protestant dissenters, and in one or the other character, liable to pretty heavy disabilities and penalties. The catholics it is true, bore the hardest burthen of all; but the others would be very sorry, I believe, to put aside our constitution and resume their ancient condition. And God forbid it should be so. For among the many losses that would light upon the community, we might be deprived of the respected magistrates that now sit to judge of our most precious rights. For if they dissented from the established church, then they could not hold any office in a corporation; and then they must come down from that bench which they fill so well, and pay a penalty moreover for having sat there, unless they could produce the certificate of a churchwarden, that they had taken a sacrament they did not acknowledge, in a church that was not their own; or unless they were through clemency, indemnified and pardoned as felons and outlaws are. I need not say more to the court, than refer to the test and toleration acts of England, and the indemnity bills passed for the relief of protestant dissenters. Mr. Attorney had forgot all this. I put him now in mind of it. Happy country, I again repeat it, where such things can be forgot. But I speak not only of what has been, but now is. At this day, a quaker, such is the term bestowed on the society of Friends, cannot be a witness in any criminal case, nor a juror in any case, nor can he vote at an election for members of parliament, nor can he hold any office in the government, unless he be sworn like other protestants. He cannot enforce the performance of an award, or the payment of costs, upon the credit of his affirmation. His religion forbids him to swear like other protestants, as that of the catholic clergyman forbids him to betray the secrets of confession, and therefore, in England, both are disqualified; but the constitution of New-York tolerates all religions, and neither is the Friend called upon by it to swear, nor the confessor to betray. The quakers are not committed to prison in this country by a justice for non-payment of tythes. Nor are they *fined* as in England for not serving in war. They enjoy in all these respects the full and equal measure of toleration, and a greater indulgence than others. All others must join the ranks of their country, and oppose its enemies. They are exempt. They are neither asked to go like their fellow citizens, nor yet to find a substitute, but for less than the hire of a mere labourer, they are defended. And this that the gentleman calls a fine, is a most signal benefit.—And from this fact I draw another conclusion, that the constitution has left nothing vague or undefined that was capable of being defined. And when it lays down the general rule, intending an exception, that exception is defined. And when it gave toleration to the religious professions and worship of all mankind, knowing that it was of the religion of the quaker not to fight, it pronounced the reasonable condition upon which that exemption was to be enjoyed. The catholic religion was surely as well known as that of the quaker. No christian could be ignorant of it: and for the same reason if the framers of the constitution intended any exception, they would have stated it. All catholics knew it because it was their religion. All protestants, because they must know that against which they protested or they know nothing. The catholic religion was as the genus, and the various species were composed of that and the essential difference. The subdivisions were but varieties. The catholic church contains at least two thirds of the christian population in the old world, and with respect to this article of auricular confession, it is still retained by the Greeks and oriental schismatics, after a seperation of 800 years. In this continent, looking to Canada on the north, and the vast and populous nations to the south, three fourths are surely catholic. If so, three fourths of the whole christian world are catholics. If the people who made this constitution were as the learned gentleman has said, a protestant people, they were then a christian people, and if they were a christian people, is it likely that they made a constitution tolerating the religion of all mankind, and subjoined, by way of parenthesis, a proviso putting under the ban of a new and unprecedented proscription, three fourths of the christians that inhabit the globe? Would not this be a moral monster, incongruous and amorphous, like some frightful sport of nature, with a foot bigger than the whole body, and trampling on its own head? Can we slander the fathers of our constitution by supposing they did this either in ignorance or through equivocation? No! For it needed little learning indeed to know all that I have stated. They needed not to be deep learned in the writings of the fathers, nor in the histories of general councils, canons, decretals, convocations, synods, or consistories; nor in legends, traditions, creeds, or catechisms, litanies nor liturgies, manuels nor missels, breviaries nor homilies. In that familiar volume of the commentaries cited yesterday, they would have found it all, set down under the head of offences against God and religion. They would have found as many models of proscription against jew and gentile, protestant and papist, as there are fashions or vagaries in a millener's shop. Some of which, I think, are great offences in themselves against God and religion.

It was with full knowledge of all this, and to close the door forever against religious contention, that the 38th article of our constitution was framed, by which all religions are put upon the very same footing, without preference or discrimination. From thence forward no frail man is to set himself up to judge his fellow, for his faith and usurp the power of the almighty judge, by whom all must be judged, nor are we to lay hands on one another, or punish either by death, by fine, or by prison, the free exercise of religious worship or profession. If there be any, who does not see the wisdom of this enactment, let him open the page of history, and read of the bloody religious wars of Europe, of which the wounds are still fresh and bleeding. Let him reflect who his own fathers were, and he will find the cogency and wisdom of the act. From the time of that constitution, the waters of strife were no more to be let loose; and as rights undefined, are wrongs concealed; as exceptions lead to contentions and equivocations; so the principle was established like a beacon on a rock, to be a light and guide to all the world.

Under this constitution, it is lawful for one to say, I hold of Christ, another, I hold of Paul, another, I of Cephas, another, I of Appollos. One only exception there is, and that is the proviso, that this liberty of conscience shall not be construed, to excuse acts of licentiousness, or justify practices inconsistent with the peace and safety of the state, and this brings me closer to the point.

The District Attorney has laid it down, as though it were conceded, that the general principle of law is with him, and that we who claim an exception, must shew ourselves entitled to it. I explicitly deny that proposition. The constitution here lays down the general rule, that all mankind shall be tolerated, without preference or discrimination, and we claim no exception from that rule. It is our adversary that would enforce the proviso, and take advantage of it against us; and it was for him to shew how we fell within it. It was for him to shew in what our acts were licentious, or our practices dangerous. The modest worth and unambitious courses of this pastor, often to be found by the bed of sickness, or in the abode of sorrow, but never in the repairs of revel or disorder, repels all idea of licentiousness. It remained then to fall back upon the subject of danger. And truly, Mr. Attorney with all his invention, was much put to it to imagine a case of danger. It was a dangerous pass for him and his argument. My colleague had pointed out from Blackstone's commentaries, that the danger which served as an apology for the proscriptions of the catholics in the British empire, was that of the pope and the pretender. The gentleman could not bring himself to say he was afraid of those persons. And yet Mr. Justice Blackstone had laid down that when the family of the one, and the temporal power of the other was reduced, or at an end, the catholics might safely enjoy their seven sacraments, auricular confession, and all. But if the gentleman had gone still further and maintained that the pope and pretender were on board Sir John Borlase Warren's fleet, it would have been little less surprising than the danger he did suppose, namely, that should there be a conspiracy of catholics to deliver up this city to the enemy, and that they should confess to the priest, and the priest conceal it, and so the city be lost. If the catholic is to hold his rights, and have the equal benefit of the constitution, upon the hard condition of satisfying the doubts of all doubters, and the cavils of all cavillers; if all possible things, however insupposeable, are to be supposed against him, this argument may do. But then the 38th article of the constitution is a dead letter to him; for under the pretence of dangers, figured merely in the imagination, all the old crimes, plots and massacres may be acted over again. But for my part I take all this as probably it is meant, in pleasantry; and in truth, I fear as little from this part of the learned gentleman's argument, as he probably does from the pope, the pretender, or the catholic plot he talks of. I shall therefore, knowing as we all do, who they are that compose the bulk of the Roman catholics in this city, content myself by *supposing* that they will not give the city to the English. No, not even if the troops of his holiness himself, should join in alliance with the British to invade it. And I maintain in the presence of my clients, and in their name, that doctrine boldly and firmly. That though the catholics must acknowledge the pope as supreme head of their church, yet they know, their duty as citizens would oblige them to resist him as a temporal prince, if in that character, he should make war upon that country, which is theirs, and theirs by choice, the strongest of all ties. Yes, and if the government was too slow in providing them with arms, they would with their pick-axe, or their spade, or their cart-rung, or paradventure, some old sanctified shillelah, the trophy of days that are past, drive the enemy from his cannon, as it has happened before. This is my supposition. And I suppose further, that there is one only way to make such persons dangerous; that is, to put their clergyman in prison for not betraying the most holy of all engagements towards God or man.

When my learned adversary advanced that this was a protestant country, and that a grant had been made by the protestants to the catholics, one would suppose that they stood in this relation, that the protestant was the liege lord, and the catholic the vassal. We came here to argue this question with good temper, and our good and reverend client, whose evidence is our text, has set us a good example of moderation and gentleness, which with due allowance for my humour, I will endeavour to follow. That the majority of the inhabitants and citizens of this state, were protestants when the constitution was formed, I do not dispute. But in establishing a constitutional code, different from that of England, they did nothing but unshackle themselves and the catholics together. I have read the case of a long and angry persecution of two Dutch calvinist clergymen in this very city, under the acts of conformity and uniformity, and for that I refer the gentleman to Smith's history of New-York, where it is fully detailed. But I will tell him further that if he should prevail so far as to do away the strong and wholesome provision of our constitution, he might himself that instant become a member not of a protestant, but of a catholic country. For when Lord Kenyon in Dubarre's case observed, the catholic religion is not *now* known to the laws of England, it was because the statute books had established another in its place. But all English statutes are abrogated in this state, and I should be glad to know what else prevents the catholic religion from being the common law of this land, as it was of England befoie those statutes? We know that it was the common law, and that the fathers of the law as well as the fathers of the church, were catholics! Alfred and Edward, Briton, Bracton, Glanvill, Heugham, the authors of the Mirror and Fleta, and many more such, were all catholics; and to crown the list, the revered Sir Thomas Moore, at once both witty, wise and great, the patron of judges, the elegant correspondent of Erasmus, lost his head upon the block, for adhering to his religion, and oppo-sing the lust of a King.

But let no man be alarmed. We claim no suprema-cy. We seek nothing but pure and perfect equality. From the bottom of our hearts we sincerely tolerate you all. We will lay hands on none of you, for your wor-ship or profession; and for ourselves, we claim neither more nor less. Hands off on all sides. And if any of you are aggrieved we will invoke the constitution in your favour, as we do in our own. We will join with all good citizens in loving, respecting, and defending it. For it is our own. If the protestant dissenters, as the English term goes, are not so foolish, so neither are we so simple, as not to know the difference between the toleration act of England and the toleration of the constitution of New-York. The one may ease the load, but the other takes it off. The former is from one set of subjects to another; the latter is a compact be-tween freemen. Let us have our rights to-day, that when it falls to our turn to judge, as it may to morrow, we may know of "no preference or discrimination." Every citizen here is in his own country. To the pro-testant it is a protestant country; to the catholic, a ca-tholic country; and the jew, if he pleases, may es-tablish in it his New Jerusalem. Not only so, but this very plank upon which I stand, as long as I continue to occupy it in arguing this cause, is my catholic plank; and if this gentleman be a calvinist, that, he stands upon, is his calvinist plank. These sayings are home-ly! No matter; they are plain. I wish to be plain; very plain—past all mistaking. As I am a friend to catholics, I would not have them vexed; were I their enemy, and thought them dangerous, I should not give them such advantage.

As to this idea of danger to the state, from the secrecy enjoined on the confessor by the catholic church, it is quite strange at this time of day, to call it in question, as dangerous to any state, seeing it has existed since christianity, under all the various forms and modulations of civilized society. Indeed, if this tenet could be assailed upon the pretence of danger, there is no part of the catholic religion that could stand; for it is that one of all their sacraments, that never has been attacked upon such score by the sharpest assailants; and those who have spared no other have been tender of this.—In a collection of German writings, by Martin Luther, p. 273, that author pronounces in its favour so strongly as this, "that he would rather fall back under the papal tyranny than have it abolished."

* The protestant ministers of Strasburg, also, after the reformation was fully established, regretted so much the abolition of auricular confession, that they petitioned the magistracy to have it restored, but were answered that it was then too late; for to restore that and not the rest would be like putting on a wooden leg. And in those queries of Mr. Pitt, it is not even glanced at as dangerous.

Having disposed of the argument of danger to the state, I must now proceed to shew the innocence and the excellence of this institution. For it would be hard that because I am not a Roman catholic I should not do justice to the sentiments of my much respected clients. They have put into the hands of their coun-

---

*Schaeffmacher, p. 282.

sel a little book, full of good matter, written by the Reverend John Gother. It has been cited by Mr. Riker. It is entitled, The papist misrepresented and represented. It contains a two-fold character of popery: giving on one hand a sum of the superstitions, idolatries, cruelties, treacheries, and wicked principles laid to their charge; and on the other it lays open that religion, which those termed papists own and profess; the chief articles of their faith, and the principal grounds and reasons which attach them to it. I shall read but one page of this little work, which I think will be satisfactory to the court. It is page 24, of the first American, from the nineteenth London edition.

"OF CONFESSION."

"The papist, *misrepresented*, believes it part of his religion to make gods of men; foolishly thinking that these have power to forgive sins. And therefore as often as he finds his conscience oppressed with the guilt of his offences, he calls for one of his priests; and having run over a catalogue of his sins, he asks of him pardon and forgiveness. And what is most absurd of all, he is so stupid as to believe, that if his Ghostly Father, after he has heard all his villainies in his ear, does but pronounce three or four Latin words over his head, his sins are forgiven him, although he had never had any thoughts of amendment, or intention to forsake his wickedness."

There spake bigotry!

"The papist *truly represented*, believes it damnable in any religion to make gods of men. However he firmly holds, that when Christ speaking to his apostles said, *John* xx. 22. *Receive ye the Holy Ghost; whose sins you shall forgive, they are forgiven; and whose sins you shall retain, they are retained;* he gave them, and their successors, the bishops and priests of the catholic church, authority to absolve any truly penitent sinner from his sins. And God having thus *given them the ministry of reconciliation,* and made *them Christ's legates,* 2 *Cor.* v. 18, 19, 20. *Christ's ministers and the dispensers of the mysteries of Christ.* 1 *Cor.* iv. And given *them power that whosoever they loosed on earth shall be loosed in heaven. Matt.* xviii. 18. He undoubtedly believes, that whosoever comes to them making a sincere and humble confession of his sins, with a true repentance and a firm purpose of amendment, and a hearty resolution of turning from his evil ways, may from them receive absolution, by the authority given them from heaven; and no doubt but God ratifies above the sentence pronounced in that tribunal; *loosing in heaven whatsoever is thus loosed by them on earth.* And that, whosoever comes without the due preparation, without a repentance from the bottom of his heart, and real intention of forsaking his sins, receives no benefit by the absolution; but adds sin to sin, by a high contempt of God's mercy, and abuse of his sacraments."

There spake charity!—Let us chuse between them.

No wonder then, this latter being the true character of confession, if the bitterest enemies of the catholic faith have still respected it; and that discerning minds have acknowledged the many benefits society might practically reap from it, abstracted from its religious character. It has, I dare say, been oftener attacked by sarcasm than by good sense. The gentleman who argued against us, has respected himself too much to employ that weapon, and I believe he has said all that good sense could urge against it, which we take in very good part.

But while this ordinance has been openly exposed to scoff and ridicule, its excellence has been concealed by the very secrecy it enjoins. If it led to licentiousness or danger, that licentiousness, or that danger, would have come to light, and there would be tongues enough to tell it. Whilst on the other hand, its utility can never be proved by instances, because it cannot be shewn how many have been saved by it; how many of the young of both sexes, have been in the most critical juncture of their lives, admonished from the commission of some fatal crime, that would have brought the parents hoary hairs with sorrow to the grave. These are secrets that can not be revealed.

Since however, the avenues that lead to vice are many and alluring; is it not well that some one should be open to the repenting sinner, where the fear of punishment and of the world's scorn, may not deter the yet wavering convert? If the road to destruction, is easy and smooth, *si facilis descensus averni*, may it not consist with wisdom and policy, that there be one silent, secret path, where the doubting penitent may be invited to turn aside and escape the throng that hurries him along? Some retreat, where, as in the bosom of a holy hermit, within the shade of innocence and peace, the pilgrim of this checquered life, may draw new inspirations of virtue and repose. If the thousand ways of error, are tricked with flowers, is it so wrong that somewhere there should be a sure and gentle friend, who has no interest to betray, no care, but that of ministering to the incipient cure? The syren songs and blandishments of pleasure, may lead the young and tender heart astray, and the repulsive frown of stern authority, forbid return. One step then gained or lost, is victory or death. Let me then ask you that are parents, which would you prefer, that the child of your hopes should pursue the course of ruin, and continue with the companions of debauch and crime, or turn to the confessional, where if compunction could once bring him, one gentle word, one well timed admonition, one friendly turn by the hand might save your child from ruin, and your heart from unavailing sorrow? And if the hardened sinner, the murderer, the robber, or conspirator, can once be brought to bow his stubborn spirit, and kneel before his frail fellow man, invite him to pronounce a penance suited to his crimes, and seek salvation through a full repentance, there is more gained, than by the bloodiest spectacle of terror, than though his mangled limbs were broken on the wheel, his body gibbetted or given to the fowls of the air. If these reflections have any weight at all; if this picture be but true in any part, better forbear and leave things as they are, than too rashly sacrifice to jealous doubts, or shallow ridicule, an ordinance sanctioned by antiquity, and founded on experience of man's nature. For if it were possible for even faith, that removes mountains, as they say, to alter this, and with it to abolish the whole fabrick, of which it is a vital part, what next would follow? Hundreds of millions of christians would be set adrift from all religious fastening! Would it be better to have so many atheists than so many christians? Or if not, what church is fitted to receive into its bosom, this great majority of all the christian world. Is it determined whether they shall become jews or philanthropists, Chinese or Mahommedans, lutherans or calvinists, baptists or brownists, materialists, universalists or destructionists, arians, trinitarians, presbyterians, baxterians, sabbatarians, or millenarians, moravians, antinomians or sandemanians, jumpers or dunkers, shakers or quakers, burgers, kirkers, independents, covenanters, puritans, Hutchinsonians, Johnsonians, or muggletonians. I doubt not, that in every sect that I have named, there are good men, and if there be, I trust they will all find mercy, but chiefly so as they are charitable each to his neighbour. And why should they be otherwise? The gospel enjoins it; the constitution ordains it. Intolerance in this country could proceed from nothing but a diseased affection of the *pia mater*, or the spleen.

The constitution is remediate of many mischiefs, and must be liberally construed. It is also declaratory, and pronounces toleration. What toleration? Not that exotic and sickly plant, that in other countries subsists by culture, bearing few blossoms and no fruit. No, but that indigenous tree, whose spreading branches stretch towards the heavens—in which the native eagle builds his nest. It is holy as the Druid's oak and sacrilege to wound it. If its authors are yet alive, or if looking down from a happier abode, they have now any care of mortal things, how must they rejoice to see it flourish, to see that all these churches, are but so many temples of one only living God, from whence his worshippers no longer sally forth with tusk and horn to gore each other, but meet like sheep, that are of one shepherd, but of another fold. If my neighbour cleaves to his own wife, shall I quarrel that he does not prefer mine, and love her better; and if he loves his own religion better, is that a ground of enmity ? I think it should not. The presbyterian may assert the independent tenets of his church, yet greet his catholic brother in gentleness and charity, fearing no evil, thinking no evil. Let the peaceful friend enjoy without molestation his silent devotion, his solemn meditation and his inward prayer, his simple communication, by yea and nay, by thee and thou. In like manner, let the methodist indulge the enthusiastic extacies of his devotion, without unkindness to his fellow citizen. Let the episcopalian, more like the catholic, add music, shew, and ceremony, to charm the senses and fix the wandering attention. I have been educated in that church. I am no bigot, I see in it no certain token of *axclusive grace*, and yet I claim the right to love it above all others, if so I am disposed; and I turn to it with the more affection, because those nearest and dearest to me, by every mortal tie, have been, and are its ministers, and have been good and virtuous men. I challenge for the catholic, the self same right, and I should despise him as I should myself, if force or violence should make him swerve from any tenet of a religion which he held as sacred. It is not however, nor never shall be, an offence to me, that the pious catholic glories in his faith, that he boasts of the long and uninterrupted succession of Christ's vicars, the sanctity of its apostles, the learning of its doctors, the holiness of its countless martyrs, its unity, integrity, catholicity, and apostolic origin; in the universality of its doctrines, dogmatical and moral; in the unanimity of its councils, in its miracles, victories, and sublime antiquity. What right have I to cavil at all this? It is enough for me, that amongst the friends I have had, none have been more true, more loyal, or more noble hearted, than catholics have proved. Without being a confessor, I have had occasions of knowing their inmost thoughts, in the hour of trial and sincerity, and I am convinced that a more intemperate or unreasonable construction could not be given to the proviso in question, than to apply the terms of either *dangerous* or *licentious* to any part of their religion or their practice!

We are not called upon to shew how the words of this proviso, may, or may not be satisfied. It lies upon the adversary to shew that they necessarily attach upon us. But I have no hesitation to meet the question, and I solve it thus: In as much as the constitution permits to all mankind, the free exercise of their religious worship, and the makers of it were aware that there were many heathen or pagan nations, whose devotional practices were repugnant to every acknowledged principle of law and morality; and yet that all these might in the course of time, become inhabitants and citizens of this country; it became necessary, therefore, to hold out some defence against the universal introduction of untried practices. To define them all, in like manner, as the exceptions in favour of the quaker was not possible; and however they might feel the necessity of clear and explicit definitions, the thing was here impossible.—They might have said, indeed, that Hindoo women should not burn themselves; that savage tribes should not make human sacrifices, or feed on human flesh, or drink blood by way of religious festival or triumph ; that bacchanalian orgies, or obscenities should not be tolerated under the name of liberty of conscience. They might have pointed out strange and freakish excentricities of self-professing christians, such as the denouncers of false judgments, and false pretenders to commissions from heaven, where they went so far as to break the peace by terrifying the innocent, and causing abortions and convulsions. They might have mentioned by name, the sect of the Adamites, that go naked in their devotion. But then, besides the difficulty of describing with certainty, things so remote and obscure, and little within their experience or observation, they had minds too extensive, and conceptions too congenial to the mighty subject entrusted to them, not to know that there might be people yet undiscovered by us, and to whom we are yet unheard of, who might, nevertheless, in the course of a few years, become our fellow citizens. Thence the necessity of this general proviso ; but to suppose that it meant, by a sidewind or indirect equivocation, to proscribe a vital part of the religion of three fourths of the christian world, and that of all others the most known, is a monstrous calumny upon those, whose memory should live in never-fading honor.

But I have been too long. The peculiar reasons I have had to dread and abhor every colour and shade of religious persecution, has communicated to my argument, perhaps, an over earnestness. Those who have not seen and felt as I have done, may think it common place. I think indeed, without so many words, the point was gained. In that case, I am more beholden to the patience of the court. So that our cause be gained

I go contented, I can do no more than those great doctors who pleaded half a day before the magnanimous giant, that he would replace their bells of notre dame, which he had taken down. He heard them graciously, and then informed them, that they had spoken right persuasively, so much so that all the bells were up before they came.

The sum of all is this: The constitution has spoken plain, the gospel plainer to our purpose. When Christ had put the Sadducees to silence, he was still tempted by a cunning lawyer of the Pharisees, asking, which was the great commandment. Mark his answer:

"Thou shalt love the Lord thy God with all thy heart, with all thy soul, and with all thy mind. This is the first and great commandment which I give unto thee, and the second is like unto the first, **THOU SHALT LOVE THY NEIGHBOUR AS THY SELF."**

On Monday, the 14th of June, the Jury were called, and all appeared; the Honorable **DE WITT CLINTON**, *Mayor*, then proceeded to deliver the **DECISION OF THE COURT**, premising, that the Bench were unanimous in their opinion, but had left him to pronounce the reasons of that opinion, and that responsibility he had taken upon himself.

In order to criminate the defendants, the reverend Anthony Kohlmann, a minister of the Roman catholic church of this city, has been called upon as a witness, to declare what he knows on the subject of this prosecution. To this question he has declined answering, and has stated in the most respectful manner the reasons which govern his conduct. That all his knowledge respecting this investigation, is derived from his functions as a minister of the Roman catholic church, in the administration of penance, one of their seven sacraments; and that he is bound by the canons of his church, and by the obligations of his clerical office, to the most inviolable secrecy—which he cannot infringe, without exposing himself to degradation from office—to the violation of his own conscience, and to the contempt of the catholic world.

In corroboration of this statement, a book entitled "The Catholic Christian instructed in the sacraments, sacrifices, ceremonies, and observances of the church, by the late right reverend R. Challoner, D. D." has been quoted, which declares, "That by the law of God and his church, whatever is declared in confession, can never be discovered, directly or indirectly, to any one, upon any account whatsoever, but remains an eternal secret between God and the penitent soul—of which the confessor cannot, even to save his own life, make any use at all to the penitent's discredit, disadvantage, or any other grievance whatsoever." Vide Decretum Innocentii XI. die 18 November, Anno. 1682 (page 120) and the same book also says, that penance is a sacrament, and consists, on the part of the penitent, of three things, to wit—contrition, confession, and satisfaction, and on the part of the minister in the absolution pronounced by the authority of Jesus Christ.

The question then is, whether a Roman catholic priest shall be compelled to disclose what he has received in confession—in violation of his conscience, of his clerical engagements, and of the canons of his church, and with a certainty of being stripped of his sacred functions, and cut off from religious communion and social intercourse with the denomination to which he belongs.

This is an important enquiry; It is important to the church upon which it has a particular bearing. It is important to all religious denominations, because it involves a principle which may in its practical operation affect them all; we have therefore, devoted the few moments which we could spare, to an exposition of the reasons that have governed our unanimous opinion: But before we enter upon this investigation, we think it but an act of justice to all concerned in it, to state, that it has been managed with fairness, candour, and a liberal spirit, and that the counsel on both sides have displayed great learning and ability; and it is due particularly to the public prosecutors, to say, that neither in the initiation nor conducting of this prosecution, has there been manifested the least disposition to trespass upon the rights of conscience—and it is equally due to the reverend Mr. Kohlmann to mention, that the articles stolen, were de-delivered by him to the police, for the benefit of the owners, in consequence of the efficacy of his admonitions to the offenders, when they would otherwise, in all probability, have been retained, and that his conduct has been marked by a laudable regard for the laws of the country, and the duties of his holy office.

It is a general rule, that every man when legally called upon to testify as a witness, must relate all he knows. This is essential to the administration of civil and criminal justice.

But to this rule there are several exceptions—a husband and wife cannot testify against each other, except for personal aggressions—nor can an attorney or counsellor, be forced to reveal the communications of his client—nor is a man obliged to answer any question, the answering of which may oblige him to accuse himself of a crime, or subject him to penalties or punishment.

In the case of Lord Melville, upon a witness declining to testify, lest he might render himself liable to a civil action, the question was referred to the twelve judges; and eight, together with the lord high chancellor, against four, were of opinion, that he was bound to answer. To remove the doubt which grew out of this collision, an act of parliament was passed, declaring "that a witness cannot by law, refuse to answer a question relevant to the matter in issue, the answering of which has no tendency to accuse himself, or to expose him to a penalty or forfeiture of any nature whatever, by reason only, or on the sole ground that the answering of such question, may establish or tend to establish that he owes a debt, or is otherwise subject to a civil suit, either at the instance of his majesty or of any other person or persons." This statute has settled the law in Great Britain. The point in this state, may be considered as res non adjudicata—but I have little doubt that when determined, the exemption from answering of a witness so circumstanced will be established.

Whether a witness is bound to answer a question, which may disgrace or degrade him, or stigmatize him by the acknowledgment of offences, which have been pardoned or punished, or by the confession of sins or vices, which may affect the purity of his character, and the respectability of his standing in society, without rendering him obnoxious to punishment, is a question involved in much obscurity, and about which there is a variety of doctrine, and a collision of adjudications.

After carefully examining this subject, we are of opinion that such a witness, ought not to be compelled to answer. The benevolent and just principles of the common law, guard with the most scrupulous circumspection, against temptations to perjury, and against a violation of moral feeling; and what greater inducement can there be for the perpetration of this offence, than placing a man between Scylla and Charybdis, and in such an awful dilemma that he must either violate his oath, or proclaim his infamy in the face of day, and in the presence of a scoffing multitude? And is there not something due to the feelings of human nature, which revolt with horror at an avowal that must exclude the witness from the pale of decent society, and subject him to that degradation which is as frequently the cause as the consequence of crimes?

One of the earliest cases we meet with on this subject, is that of Cooke (4 St. Tr. 748. Salkreld, 153——) who being indicted for treason, in order to found a challenge for cause, asked a juror whether he had not said he believed him guilty. The whole Court determined he was not obliged to answer the question—and Lord Chief Justice Treby said, "Men have been asked whether they have been convicted and pardoned for felony, or whether they have been whipped for petit larceny, and they have not been obliged to answer: for though their answer in the affirmative will not make them criminal nor subject to punishment, yet they are matters of infamy, and if it be an infamous thing, that's enough to preserve a man from being bound to answer. A pardoned man is not guilty; his crime is purged; but merely for the reproach of it, it shall not be put upon him to answer a question whereupon he will be forced to forswear or disgrace him."

In the case of Rex, vs. Lewis and others (4 Espinasses nisi prius cases, 225) the witness was asked if he had not been in the house of correction, in Sussex. Lord Ellenborough, relying upon the opinion just quoted, declared, that a witness was not bound to answer any question, the object of which was to degrade or render him infamous. In the case of Mac Bride, vs. Mac Bride (same book 243) Lord Alvanly, on a witness being asked whether she lived in a state of concubinage with the plaintiff, overruled the question, saying, that he thought questions as to general conduct, might be asked, but not such as went immediately to degrade the witness, and concluded by saying, "I think those questions only should not be asked, which have a direct and immediate effect to disgrace, or disparage the witness."

In the supreme court of New-Jersey (Pennington's Reports, the State, vs. Bailey, 415) the following question was proposed to a witness. Have you been convicted of petit larceny and punished? The Court after argument decided, that a witness could be asked no question, which in its answer might tend to disgrace or dishonor him, and therefore, in the particular case the witness was not bound to answer the question.

In the case of *Bell*, an insolvent debtor, which occurred in the Court of Common Pleas, for the first Judicial

District of Pennsylvania (Browne's Reports, 376) a question was asked the father of the insolvent, which went to impeach and invalidate a judgement he had against the insolvent, which question the Court overruled. *Rush*, the President, saying, "I have always overruled a question that would affect a witness *civilly*, or subject him to a *criminal prosecution* ; I have gone farther, and where the answer to a question would cover the witness with *infamy or shame*, I have refused to compel him to answer it."

In the case of Jackson ex dem Wyckoff, vs. Humphrey (1 Johnson's Reports 498) a deed was attempted to be invalidated at the circuit, by the testimony of the judge, taking the proof on the ground that the proof it was taken in Canada, and also, that the subscribing witness could not have known the facts respecting the identity of the grantor, as testified by him before the judge who took the proof, and also to impeach the general character of the witness. The testimony was overruled by the judge, and a verdict found for the plaintiff, and a motion for a new trial prevailed. The Court declaring, that "The judge, before whom the proof of the deed was made, was a competent witness to prove that it was done in Canada, and if that fact be established, the proof was illegal and void. Though the judge was a competent witness, *he would not have been bound to answer any questions impeaching the integrity of his conduct as a public officer*;" and we believe it to be the general if not established practice of our Courts to excuse a witness from answering questions which relate to sexual intercourse, in actions brought for a breach of promise of marriage, or by parents for seduction.

We have gone more particularly into this branch of the subject, because it has a very intimate connexion with the point in question. None of these propositions—*that a witness is not obliged to confess a crime, or subject himself to a penalty, or to impair or injure his civil rights by his testimony—or to proclaim his turpitude or immorality,* can be considered as including within its purview, the precise case before us. They all, however, touch upon it, in a greater or less degree. With the exception of the second position, there is this strong difference, they are retrospective and refer to past conduct, whereas in the case now pending, if we decide that the witness shall testify, we prescribe a course of conduct by which he will violate his spiritual duties, subject himself to temporal loss, and perpetrate a deed of infamy. If he commits an offence against religion; if he is deprived of his office and of his bread, and thrown forlorn and naked upon the wide world, an object for the hand of scorn, to point its slow and moving finger at, we must consider that this cannot be done without our participation and coercion.

There can be no doubt but that the witness does consider, that his answering on this occasion, would be such a high handed offence against religion, that it would expose him to punishment in a future state—and it must be conceded by all, that it would subject him to privations and disgrace in this world. It is true, that he would not be obnoxious to criminal punishment, but the reason why he is excused where he would be liable to such punishment, applies with greater force to this case, where his sufferings would be aggravated by the compunctious visitings of a wounded conscience, and the gloomy perspective of a dreadful *hereafter*; although he would not lose an estate, or compromit a civil right, yet he would be deprived of his only means of support and subsistence—and although he would not confess a crime, or acknowledge his infamy, yet he would act an offence against high heaven, and seal his disgrace in the presence of his assembled friends, and to the affliction of a bereaved church and a weeping congregation.

It cannot therefore, for a moment be believed, that the mild and just principles of the common Law would place the witness in such a dreadful predicament; in such a horrible dilemma, between perjury and false swearing: If he tells the truth he violates his ecclesiastical oath—If he prevaricates he violates his judicial oath—Whether he lies, or whether he testiffes the truth he is wicked, and it is impossible for him to act without acting against the laws of rectitude and the light of conscience.

The only course is, for the court to declare that he shall not testify or act at all. And a court prescribing a different course must be governed by feelings and views very different from those which enter into the composition of a just and enlightened tribunal, that looks with a propitious eye upon the religious feelings of mankind, and which dispenses with an equal hand the universal and immutable elements of justice.

There are no express adjudications in the British courts applied to similar or analogous cases, which contradict the inferences to be drawn from the general principles which have been discussed and established in the course of this investigation: Two only have been pointed out as in any respect analogous, which we shall now proceed to consider.

In the case of Du Barre &c. (Peake's cases at nisi prius 77) the following question was agitated, whether as the Defendant was a Frenchman who did not understand the English language and his attorney not understanding French was obliged to communicate with him by an interpreter, the interpreter ought to be permitted to give evidence, the Defendant's Counsel contending that this was a confidence which ought not to be broken, Lord Kenyon decided that the interpreter should only reveal such conversation as he had with the Defendant in the absence of the attorney. *Garrow* for the Plaintiff, said that a case much stronger than this had been lately determined by Mr. Justice Buller, on the Northern Circuit. That was a case in which the life of the prisoner was at stake. The name of it was, The King, vs. Sparkes. There the prisoner being a Papist had made a confession before a Protestant Clergyman of the crime, for which he was indicted and that confession was permitted to be given in evidence on the trial, and he was convicted and executed. Lord Kenyon upon this remarked, "I should have paused before I admitted the evidence here admitted."

The case referred to by Garrow, is liable to several criticisms and objections. In the first place it was stated by a Counsel in the cause, and is therefore liable to those errors and perversions which grow out of that situation. Secondly, it is the determination of a single Judge, in the hurry of a circuit, when a decision must be made promptly, without time for deliberation, or consultation, and without an opportunity for recurrence to books.

Thirdly, it is virtually overturned by Lord Kenyon, who certainly censures it with as much explicitness as one Judge can impeach the decision of his colleague, without departing from judicial decorum. Fourthly, the depositary of the secret was a Protestant Clergyman, who did not receive it under the seal of a sacrament, and under religious obligations of secrecy, and would not, therefore, be exposed to ecclesiastical degradation and universal obloquy by promulgating it.—And lastly, the decision of Mr. Justice Buller, was, to say the least, erroneous; for when a man under the agonies of an afflicted conscience and the disquietudes of a perturbed mind, applies to a minister of the Almighty, lays bare his bosom filled with guilt, and opens his heart black with crime, and solicits from him advice and consolation, in this hour of penitence and remorse, and when this confession and disclosure may be followed by the most salutary effects upon the religious principles and future conduct of the penitent, and may open to him prospects which may bless the remnant of his life, with the soul's calm sunshine and the heart-felt joy, without interfering with the interests of society, surely the establishment of a rule throwing all these pleasing prospects into shade, and prostrating the relation between the penitent and the comforter, between the votary and the minister of religion, must be pronounced a heresy in our legal code.

The other case was decided by Sir Michael Smith, Master of the Rolls of Ireland. On the 24th Febuary. 1802, (2 M'Nally, 153) a bill was filed praying to be decreed the estates of the late Lord Dunboyne, by the heir at law, who alleged that the will, under which the Defendant claimed, was a nullity, as Lord Dunboyne having been a Popish Priest, and having conformed and relapsed to Popery, had no power to make a will. Issue was joined, and the Plaintiff produced the Reverend Mr. Gahan, a Clergyman of the church of Rome, to be examined, and interrogatories to the following effect, were among others, exhibited to him: "What Religion did the late Lord Dunboyne profess from the year 1783 to the year 1792? What Religion did he profess at the time of his death, and a short time before his death?" The witness answered to the first part, viz. that "Lord Dunboyne professed the Protestant religion during the time, &c. but *demurred* to the latter part in this way, "That his knowledge of the matter enquired of (if any he had) arose from a confidential communication to him, in the exercise of his clerical functions, and which the principles of his religion forbid him to disclose, nor was he bound by the laws of the land to answer."

The Master of the Rolls determined against the demurrer; the reasons he assigns are loose and general, and very unsatisfactory, and the only authority cited by him in support of his decision, was that of Vaillant vs. Dodermead, reported in 2 Atkyns 524, which I shall now consider with a view of showing that there is no point of resemblance or analogy between that and the adjudication of the Master of the Rolls.

The Defendant in this case having examined Mr. Bristow, *his Clerk in the Court*, the Plaintiff exhibited interrogatories for cross-examining him, to which he demurred, for that he knew nothing of the several matters enquired of in the interrogatories, besides what came to his knowledge as clerk in court, *or agent for the Defendant* in relation to the matters in question in this cause. The

Lord High Chancellor overruled the demurrer, and compelled him to answer for the following irresistible reasons. Because the matters enquired of were antecedent transactions to the commencement of the suit, the knowledge whereof, could not come to Bristow as clerk in court, or solicitor: because this was a cross-examination, and whenever a party calls upon his own attorney to testify, the other side may examine him: and because he states that he knew nothing but as clerk or agent. Now the word *agent* includes non-privileged as well as privileged persons. The only privileged persons are Counsellors, Solicitors and Attorneys; *an agent* may be a Steward or Servant.

What analogy can be traced between the cases? Did the Catholic Priest cloak himself under any generality or indefiniteness, of expression? Did he obtain any information from Lord Dunboyne previous to his acting as his confessor, or in any other capacity than as confessor? Was he called upon by the Defendant to testify, and in consequence thereof exposed to the cross-examination of the Plaintiff? Surely not. The case then relied upon, does in no respect, in no similitude of principle or resemblance of fact quadrate with the case adjudicated, or in any degree, or to any extent support it.

With those who have turned their attention to the history of Ireland, the decisions of Irish courts, respecting Roman Catholics, can have little or no weight.

That unfortunate country has been divided into two great parties, the oppressors and oppressed. The Catholic has been disfranchised of his civil rights, deprived of his inheritance, and excluded from the common rights of man; statute has been passed upon statute, and adjud'cation has been piled upon adjudication in prejudice of his religious freedom. The benign spirit of toleration, and the maxims of an enlightened policy, have recently ameliorated his condition, and will undoubtedly, in process of time, place him on the same footing with his Protestant brethren; but until he stands upon the broad pedestal of equal rights, emancipated from the most unjust thraldom, we cannot but look with a jealous eye upon all decisions which fetter him or rivet his chains.

But there is a very marked distinction between that case, nd the case now under consideration. The Reverend Mr. Gahan did not pretend that he derived his information from Lord Dunboyne, in the way of a sacrament, but only as a confidential communication: he would not therefore be exposed by a promulgation, to degradation, breach of oaths, and a violation of his clerical duties. But the only imputation would be on his personal honor as a gentleman.

Penance implies contrition for a sin, confession of a sin, and satisfaction or reformation for a sin. Now can conversion to the church of Rome, in the eye of a Roman Catholic Layman, or a Roman Catholic Priest, require contrition, or confession, or reformation? And if it does not, a declaration of such conversion cannot be the sacrament of penance. In Gahan's case there was no sacrament, or religious obligation of secrecy. In the case of Mr. Kohlmann there is the strongest that religion can impose, involving every thing sacred in this world and precious in that to come.

But this is a great constitutional question, which must not be solely decided by the maxims of the common law, but by the principles of our government: We have considered it in a restricted shape, let us now look at it upon more elevated ground ; upon the ground of the constitution, of the social compact, and of civil and religious liberty.

Religion is an affair between God and man, and not between man and man. The laws which regulate it must emanate from the Supreme Being, not from human institutions. Established religons, deriving their authority from man, oppressing other denominations, prescribing creeds of orthodoxy, and punishing non-conformity, are repugnant to the first principles of civil and political liberty, and in direct collision with the divine spirit of christianity. Although no human legislator has a right to meddle with religion, yet the history of the world, is a history of oppression and tyranny over the consciences of men. And the sages who formed our constitution, with this instructive lesson before their eyes, perceived the indispensable necessity of applying a preventitive, that would forever exclude the introduction of calamities, that have deluged the world with tears and with blood, and the following section was accordingly engrafted in our state constitution :

" And whereas we are required by the benevolent principles of rational liberty, not only to expel civil tyranny, but also to guard against that spiritual oppression and intolerance, wherewith the bigotry and ambition of weak and wicked princes have scourged mankind, This convention doth further in the name, and by the authority of the good people of this state, ordain, determine, and declare, that the free exercise and enjoyment of religious profession and worship, without discrimination or preference, shall forever hereafter be allowed within this state, to all mankind. Provided, that the liberty of conscience, hereby granted, shall not be so construed as to excuse acts of licentiousness, or justify practices inconsistent with the peace or safety of this state."

Considering that we had just emerged from a colonial state, and were infected with the narrow views and bigotted feelings, which prevailed at that time so strongly against the Roman Catholics, that a priest was liable to the punishment of death if he came into the colony, this declaration of religious freedom, is a wonderful monument of the wisdom, liberality, and philanthropy of its authors. Next to William Penn, the framers of our constitution were the first legislators who had just views of the nature of religious liberty, and who established it upon the broad and imperishable basis of justice, truth, and charity: While we are compelled to remark that this excellent provision was adopted by a majority of one, it is but proper to say, that the colonial statute against Roman Catholic Priests, originated more from political than religious considerations. The influence which the French had over the six nations, the Iroquois, and which was exercised to the great detriment of the British colonies, was ascribed to the arts and management of the Jesuits, and it was therefore, in violation of all respect for the rights of conscience, deemed of essential importance to interpose the penalty of death against their migration into the colony.

A provision conceived in a spirit of the most profound wisdom, and the most exalted charity, ought to receive the most liberal construction. Although by the constitution of the United States, the powers of congress do not extend beyond certain enumerated objects; yet to prevent the danger of constructive assumptions, the following amendment was adopted: "Congress shall make no law respecting an establishment of religion, or prohibiting the free exercise thereof." In this country there is no alliance between church and state; no established religion; no tolerated religion—for toleration results from establishment—but religious freedom guaranteed by the constitution, and consecrated by the social compact.

It is essential to the free exercise of a religion, that its ordinances should be administered—that its ceremonies as well as its essentials should be protected. The sacraments of a religion are its most important elements. We have but two in the Protestant Church—Baptism and the Lord's Supper—and they are considered the seals of the covenant of grace. Suppose that a decision of this court, or a law of the state should prevent the administration of one or both of these sacraments, would not the constitution be violated, and the freedom of religion be infringed? Every man who hears me will answer in the affirmative. Will not the same result follow, if we deprive the Roman catholic of one of his ordinances? Secrecy is of the essence of penance. The sinner will not confess, nor will the priest receive his confession, if the veil of secrecy is removed: To decide that the minister shall promulgate what he receives in confession, is to declare that there shall be no penance; and this important branch of the Roman catholic religion would be thus annihilated.

It has been contended that the provision of the constitution which speaks of practices inconsistent with the peace or safety of the state, excludes this case from the protection of the constitution, and authorizes the interference of this tribunal to coerce the witness. In order to sustain this position, it must be clearly made out that the concealment observed in the sacrament of penance, is a practice inconsistent with the peace or safety of the state.

The Roman catholic religion has existed from an early period of christianity—at one time it embraced almost all Christendom, and it now covers the greater part. The objections which have been made to penance, have been theological, not political. The apprehensions which have been entertained of this religion, have reference to the supremacy, and dispensing power, attributed to the bishop of Rome, as head of the catholic church—but we are yet to learn, that the confession of sins has ever been considered as of pernicious tendency, in any other respect than its being a theological error—or its having been sometimes in the hands of bad men, perverted to the purposes of peculation, an abuse inseperable from all human agencies.

The doctirine contended for, by putting hypothetical cases, in which the concealment of a crime communicated in penance, might have a pernicious effect, is founded on false reasoning, if not on false assumptions : To attempt to establish a general rule, or to lay down a general proposition from accidential circumstances, which occur but rarely, or from extreme cases, which may sometimes happen in the infinite variety of human actions, is totally repugnant to the rules of logic and the maxims of law. The question is not, whether penance may sometimes communicate the existence of an offence to a priest, which he is bound by his religion to conceal, and the concealment of which, may be a public injury, but whether the natural tendency of it is to produce practices inconsistent with the public safety or tranquillity. There is in fact, no secret known to the priest, which would be communicated otherwise, than by confession—and no evil results from this communication—on the contrary, it may be made the instrument of great good. The sinner may be admonished and converted from the evil of his ways: Whereas if his offence was locked up in his own bosom, there would be no friendly voice to recal him from his sins, and no paternal hand to point out to him the road to virtue.

The language of the constitution is emphatic and striking, it speaks of *acts of licentiousness*, of *practices inconsistent* with the *tranquillity and safety of the state*; it has reference to something actually, not negatively injurious. To acts committed, not to acts omitted—offences of a deep dye, and of an extensively injurious nature: It would be stretching it on the rack so say, that it can possibly contemplate the forbearance of a Roman catholic priest, to testify what he has received in confession, or that it could ever consider the safety of the community involved in this question. To assert this as the genuine meaning of the constitution, would be to mock the understanding, and to render the liberty of conscience a mere illusion. It would be to destroy the enacting clause of the proviso—and to render the exception broader than the rule, to subvert all the principles of sound reasoning, and overthrow all the convictions of common sense.

If a religious sect should rise up and violate the decencies of life, by practicing their religious rites, in a state of nakedness; by following incest, and a community of wives. If the Hindoo should attempt to introduce the burning of widows on the funeral piles of their deceased husbands, or the Mahometan his plurality of wives, or the Pagan his bacchanalian orgies or human sacrifices. If a fanatical sect should spring up, as formerly in the city of Munster, and pull up the pillars of society, or if any attempt should be made to establish the inquisition, then the licentious acts and dangerous practices, contemplated by the constitution, would exist, and the hand of the magistrate would be rightfully raised to chastise the guilty agents.

But until men under pretence of religion, act counter to the fundamental principles of morality, and endanger the well being of the state, they are to be protected in the free exercise of their religion. If they are in error, or if they are wicked, they are to answer to the *Supreme Being*, not to the unhallowed intrusion of frail fallible mortals.

We speak of this question, not in a theological sense, but in its legal and constitutional bearings. Although we differ from the witness and his brethren, in our religious creed, yet we have no reason to question the purity of their motives, or to impeach their good conduct as citizens. They are protected by the laws and constitution of this country, in the full and free exercise of their religion, and this court can never countenance or authorize the application of insult to their faith, or of torture to their consciences.

There being no evidence against the Defendants, they were acquitted.

IRISH PENAL CODE ABRIDGED.

The law doth best discover the enormities.

THESE were the words of the English Attorney-General, to James I in his celebrated discourse, wherein, without any favour to the Irish, he lays open to his master the atrocious courses of their oppressors. To pursue a tragedy of seven centuries, is not the purpose of this publication; but it is due to the cause, to the court, and above all, to that magistrate who manfully assumed the responsibility of the reasons accompanying its unanimous decision, to shew how malignant the system was, upon which he passed a wise and deliberate animadversion. The massacres, robberies, and perfidies, practised by the English upon the Irish, are no longer buried in doubt, or darkness; they stand upon authorities past all contradiction; records rescued from oblivion, state papers, official reports, charters and title deeds. The historian who recites them, runs no risk; but if there be still surer ground it is that of transcribing from the statute book; for when the malice is so settled and confirmed as to become the characteristic genius of the law for an uninterrupted series of ages, then it may truly be said that "the law best discovers the enormities."

Whatever were the ancient glories of the Irish nation, they were faded and fallen when the invader found footing on their shores. The rancorous hostilities and petty warfares of numerous little Kings and tyrants, had merged all national pride; and Ireland was subdued by the vice of Irishmen. It happened to them as to every nation which exposes disunion to a crafty, jealous, and vigilant enemy.

The yoke once put on, is not easily shaken off, and ineffectual struggles, but draw the bonds the tighter. Seven centuries of miseries have not yet expiated the first fault of the Irish people; but their history is unlike that of Greeks, Romans, or other great people, subdued and fallen to brutal apathy. Too generous to acquiesce in slavery, and yet too disunited to join in any great effort for death or victory, they had wasted their strength in desultory struggles, and the same race who in all foreign countries have individually borne off the palm of constancy and courage, equal to every task, and faithful to every trust, have been and still are treated as aliens in their native land.

To give a succinct and intelligible view of the statutory code of Ireland, it may be well to divide it chronologically.

FIRST EPOCH.

From the English invasion to the reformation.

The Irish though far excelling their cotemporaries in refinement and education, were never known to invade the territory of other nations; but their country was still the seat of hospitality to strangers, who resorted there for learning or improvement. Let this short observation serve as a preface to the following English statutes, the earliest that are extant in print.

Stat. of Kilkenny, 40. Ed. 3. A. D. 1367, makes all alliance by marriage, nurture of infants, or gossipred with the Irish, high treason: and if any man of English race, shall use an Irish name, Irish language, or Irish apparel, or any other guise or fashion of the Irish, if he has lands or tenements, the same shall be seized till he has given security to the chancellor, to conform in all points to the English manner of living, and if he has no lands his body to be taken and imprisoned till he find sureties as aforesaid.

Stat. of Trim. 25. Hen. 6. A. D. 1447, enacts, that if any be found with their upper lips unshaven for the space of a fortnight, it shall be lawful for any man to take them and their goods, and ransom them and their goods as Irish enemies.

These statutes were levelled not more against the Irish, than the English settlers, who, won from their native ferocity by the social qualities of the Irish, or attracted by the charms of the sex, were treated as "*degenerate English,*" and punished by that title, as the Irish were by the more whimsical title of *aliens.*

28. Hen. 6. c. 3. A. D. 1450. Commits the punishment of every offender, to every private liege man of the King.

This is the frankest charter of murder ever granted.

Stat. Ed. 4. c. 2. A. D. 1465. enacts, "that it shall be lawful for all manner of men, that find any theives robbing by day or by night, going or coming, to rob or to steal, *in or out, going or coming,* having no *faithful* man of good name or fame in their company, *in English apparel,* upon any of the liege people of the king, to take and kill *those,* and to cut off their heads without any impeachment of our sovereign Lord the King, his officers, or ministers, or any others; and of any head so cut in the county of Meath, that the cutter of the said head, and his aiders there to him, do cause the said head so cut, to be brought to the Portreeve of the town of Trim, and the said Portreeve shall give him his writing under the seal of the said town, testifying the bringing the said head to him. And it shall be lawful for the bringer of the said head and his aiders to the same, to distrain and levy with their own hands, of every man having one plough land, one penny, and of every other cotter having house and smoke, one half-penny; and if the Portreeve shall refuse such certificate, he is to forfeit £10 recoverable by action."

The Irish Brehon law, to which the people were religiously attached was so humane that no capital punishment was allowed for any crime whatever. This statute, therefore, must have been peculiarly atrocious in the eyes of the Irish. What is meant by the distinction between robbing with a man of good fame in English apparel, and robbing without such a companion, requires a key, which is only to be found in the gross barbarity of the lawgivers. Perhaps the English were not only privileged to rob, but any one of them, might protect a whole gang. Such as it is, this statute was passed under the auspices and immediate government of Lionel duke of Clarence, son to the king.

LANGUAGE.

28 Hen. 8. c. 15. Every subject of the king inhabiting in this island, shall, to the uttermost of their power and knowledge, use and speak commonly the *English* language, and shall endeavour themselves to procure their children (if they have any) to speak the same, and according to their abilities, shall bring them up in such places where they shall have occasion to learn the same language, upon pain that every lord spiritual and temporal offending herein, shall forfeit for every offence 6*l.* 13*s.* 4*d.* every knight and esquire, 3*l.* 6*s.* 8*d.* every gentleman and merchant 40*s.* every free-holder and yeoman 20*s.* every husbandman, 10*s.* and every other of the king's subjects within this land, 3*s.* 4*d.* one half to the king, and the other to the party that will sue for the same by action of debt, &c. in any of the king's courts, wherein no essoin, shall be allowed.

If any spiritual promotion within this land (chargeable with the payment of first fruits to the king) at any time become void, such as have title to nominate, &c. shall nominate, &c. to the same, such a person as can speak *English*, and none other, unless there be no person that can speak *English* will accept it; and if the patron cannot upon inquiry (within three months after such avoidance) get any such person that can speak *English*, to accept the same, then he shall cause four proclamations to be openly made, at four several market days, in the next market town adjoining to the said spiritual promotion; that if any fit person that can speak *English*, will come and take the same, he shall have it: and if none come, within five weeks of the first proclamation, to take the same, then the patron may present any honest, able person, albeit he cannot speak *English*.

And if any patron do nominate, &c. one that cannot speak *English*, contrary to the form before recited, and being lawfully convicted thereof, upon inquiry or presentation, before any of the king's judges, then such nomination, &c. shall be void, and the king shall nominate, present, and give the same to any person that can speak *English*, and no other: and if the king be interrupted, he shall have a *Quare Impedit* against the disturber, and recover the presentation thereof for that time, in like form as he should have done for any other presentation of his own patronage; and if the king present any person that cannot speak *English*, then the same shall be void, and the patron's former gift to stand in force.—Such presentation of the king, shall not prejudice those who at that time had right to the same, but that they may (upon the next avoidance) nominate or give, &c. the same as though no such nomination, &c. had been had by the king.

And every archbishop, bishop, suffragan, and every other, having power to give order of priest-hood, deacon, or sub-deacon, shall at the time of giving such orders, give a corporal oath, to the person so taking any of the said orders as aforesaid, that he shall to the uttermost of his power, endeavour himself to learn the *English* tongue and language, and use the *English* order and fashions (if he may learn and attain the same by possibility) in the place where his cure or dwelling shall be, and shall move and teach all others being under his governance, to perform the same: and every such archbishop, &c. having power to admit, &c. any person to any spiritual promotion, shall, at the time thereof, give unto the person so addmitted, &c. a corporal oath, that he shall to his wit and cunning, endeavour himself to learn and teach the *English* tongue to all under his cure or governance, and shall *bid the beads*, and preach the word of God in *English*, (if he can preach;) and for his own part shall use the *English* order and habit, and move as many as he can to the same, and shall keep, or cause to be kept, within the place or parish where he shall be promoted, a school to learn *English*, if any children of his parish come to him to learn the same, taking for his salary (for keeping the same) as the custom of the country is.

Every archbishop, bishop, &c. having power to give orders or to admit, &c. offending herein contrary to the rules aforesaid, shall forfeit for every time 3*l.* 6*s.* 8*d.* one moiety to the king, and the other to that person that will sue for the same as aforesaid.—And every person promoted to any spiritual promotion, that does not observe the effect of the said oath, shall (upon conviction thereof as aforesaid) forfeit for the first time 6*s.* and 8*d.* for the second time 20*s.* and for the third, all such spiritual promotion; and the patron may present or give the same to any other sufficient and able person, in like manner and form as if the incumbent were dead.—This act shall not prejudice any beneficed within this land, that are bound to keep residence in any metropolitan cathedral or collegiate church, not being a student in any university, or in the king's service, or out of the land by the king's command; but that those who officiate under them, shall during their absence, teach the *English* tongue, and keep a school as the act directs, upon pain that every such parish-priest, for every year he omits the same, shall forfeit 20*s.*—*This act to take no effect until it be openly proclaimed in due form.*

SECOND EPOCH.

From the Reformation to the Revolution.

If the reformed religion had been presented to the Irish under any inviting or persuasive aspect; if the monarch who established it as law, had been a saint-like personage, of a holy and pious life, and faithful to all the relations of life; constant and steady in his own belief; tender of the rights and consciences of his subjects; patient, tolerant, and merciful, it would have been time enough to have accused the Irish for not instantly quitting the faith inculcated by the venerated Saint Patrick.

If the clergy sent over to teach the new religion had been able to instruct the Irish in its blessings and advantages, in a language that they could understand; men holy in their lives and reverend in their example, professing charity and doing good, it would have been less violent to treat them as wicked and obstinate. But if this reforming monarch was the greatest monster that history exhibits; who had established creeds and articles, and forced men under penalties to swear to them and believe them, and then for the purposes of lust and murder, violating every tender relation, and every feeling of human nature, established creeds and articles directly the reverse, under penalty of ruin, death, and infamy; and if the missionaries of the new gospel were the scum of the earth, low, vulgar, ignorant and rapacious; wantonly exposing their own religion to scorn, that fines might be levied for not conforming to it; with the sentiments of horse-jockeys and the hearts of wolves; then why should a people having no vicious motives, no wives to murder, no wish to bastardise their own issue, quit what they believed to be the word of God, to go to church and hear the word of Henry the Eighth, and the prayers and preachings of clergy who reviled what they held sacred, although they had themselves been so lately enjoined by statute to "bid the beads" to the Irish in the English tongue.

The statutes enforced against the Irish during this second epoch are of pure English manufacture, and may be found in any lawyer's library, in the English statutes at large, in all the abridgements of those statutes, and in the most familiar abridgements of the law, particularly that of Bacon,‡ and through all the reports and treatises, civil and criminal, under the heads of popery and papist, heresy, witchcraft, dissenters, recusants, offences against God and religion, conformity, uniformity, &c.In England they fell upon a smaller number, in Ireland they were visited upon a whole people. The operations of the ecclesiastical commissioners, the star chamber, (or castle chamber) and the spiritual courts, went hand in hand with the commissioners of defective titles, and between these and forfeitures by acts of attainder and forfeiture for treason and rebellion, there was scarcely an acre of land that was not seized and confiscated, and sometimes a second and a third time, even in the hands of the confiscators themselves.

The statute upon which most money was raised was 2 Eliz. c. 2. § 3. which commands all persons to resort to the parish church, or some usual place where such service of God, as in the book of common prayer, shall be used, and to abide there soberly and orderly during the time of prayer or preaching, upon pain of punishment by the censures of the church, and of 12 pence for every Sunday or holiday, to be levied by way of distress by the church wardens.

The ecclesiastical courts, says Bishop Burnet in his life of Bedel, p. 37, were managed by a chancellor who bought his place, and made of it all the profits he could, and their whole business seemed to be nothing but oppression and extortion. "The solemnest and sacredest of all church censures, excommunicatioon, went about in so sordid and base a manner that all regard to it as a spiritual censure was lost, and it became au intolerable tyranny. The officers of those courts thought they had a right to oppress the natives, and that all was well got that was wrung from them." Bulls went bare-faced, and the exchange they made of penance for money, was the worst of simony.

It is related by Carte, and also in the Analectica Sacra, that Sir Oliver St. John, on coming over from England as Lord Deputy, did put the statute 2 Elizabeth and all other penal statutes, in strict execution. He caused presentments to be made in the different parts of the kingdom. The effects of his rigor were dismal and extensive. The treasures of the rich were soon exhausted, and the poor, not being able to pay this tax upon their consciences, every where fled into dens and caverns, from the cruel collectors of it, where they were sometimes pursued by blood-hounds, set on and followed by a sheriff and a posse of disbanded soldiers, equally furious and unrelenting; and even the dead bodies of those who fell under those holy censurers, did not escape the cruelty, but were denied christian burial, and their corpses were thrown into holes dug in the high-ways, with every mark of ignominy that could be devised and inflicted by their wicked and bigotted judges. See also Doctor Curry. Mem. Civ. Wars, vol. 1. p. 102.

The Irish Commons once remonstrated to the king (Irish Com. Jour. v. 1. p. 258) that the judges of the ecclesiastical courts took money for holy water, for anointing, for mortuary muttons, mary gallons, St. Patrick's ridge, soul money, and the like: and that the protestant bishops exposed their religion to sale and to contempt in those ecclesiastical courts, and that the catholics were willing to redeem themselves from these exactions, by maintaining for the king Charles I. an army of five thousand foot and five hundred horse.— Against this there was a protest by primate Usher and twelve bishops, which was solemnly read by the bishop of Derry before the Deputy and Privy Council in Christ's Church. This prevailed; the offer was scornfully rejected, and the sufferers and their religion scurrilously abused.

Lord Strafford, the lord deputy, (State letters, v. 1. p. 76) informs the king that it was impossible to improve the revenue but by imposing 12d. a Sunday upon the recusants. This same deputy had before written [ib. p. 19.] that the duties from the Irish were indeed violent takings, rather ravishments of the poor, than the modest quiet levies of a pious and christian king. And yet he at another time proposed to his master to make him out a title to all Connaught; and writes (ib. p. 442.) that he had given orders to his managers in Connaught, that when he went there to hold *an inquisition* gentlemen of the best estates in the different counties should be returned on the juries which were to be on the first trials to be instituted on "*defective titles*," because the fear of a round fine in the Castle Chamber would produce a better effect than in persons who had little to lose.

In one case where a jury refused to find for the king against the proprietor (ib. v. 1.) he says, we bethought ourselves of a course to vindicate his majesty's honour upon this occasion, not only against the persons of the jurors, but also against the sheriff in a thousand pounds to his majesty; and we have fined the jurors four thousand pounds each. Their estates are seized, and themselves imprisoned till the fine be paid."

And in one of the above letters he says, I labour to make as many captains and other *offices*, burgesses of *this* parliament as I can, who having immediate dependance on the Crown, may sway the business as I please.

It is remarkable that this his own packed parliament voted against the grievances of his administration. The Irish Com. Jour. p. 94, refer to these very transactions, saying, "the jurors who give in their verdict according to their consciences, were censured in the star chamber, or castle chamber, in great fines; sometimes pillored with loss of ears, and bored through the tongue, sometimes marked in the forehead with an iron, and other infamous punishment." And Doctor Leland writes, vol. 3, p. 32. that the jurors of Gallway remained in prison till each paid his fine of £4,000, and acknowledged his fault upon his knees.

Thus were the Irish deprived of their estates by false inquisitions upon feigned titles, wherein neither traverse nor petition of right was admitted, and jurors who listened to the admonitions of conscience were devoted to ruin and disgrace. One hundred and fifty letters patent were declared void in one morning. See the remonstrance of Trim. sect. 2. Cartes Ormond, v. 3.

This corrupt deputy began his public career in conjunction with Pym and the others, but was gained over by the king and made a peer and governor of Ireland. He was afterwards impeached and convicted of high treason; the king signed his death-warrant and he was beheaded on Tower-Hill; a victim not so much of his real crimes as of party-spirit, and party-spirit on the other hand has held him up as a martyr.

THIRD EPOCH.

From the revolution to the present reign.

The persecutions of this period are purely *religious.* It is no longer for wearing the beard upon the upper lip, nor yet for being Irish that the people are robbed and murdered, but having been already plundered and impoverished for being Irish, for wearing their beards, and for not conforming to a church rendered odious to them, a new and curious system of torment is devised, under the title of "laws to prevent the further growth of popery."

In the former period we have seen how the English deputies bored the tongues of the jurors who could not find inquisitions for the king. We shall now see with what industry the tormentor sought out every tender part where the moral being could be afflicted, and cruelly conveyed the maddening poison through every organ of most exquisite sensibility; insulting religion, reversing the principles of law, violating parental affection, private friendship, filial duty, conjugal love, promoting family dissention, preventing education, proscribing industry, and having done all this, setting a bar against all future acquisitions of wealth, influence, or knowledge; in short, leaving nothing that hell could invent unattempted, in order to brutalise and enfeeble a race of beings whose courage and intellect was still formidable even in this abject state. To prove these assertions the statutes shall be distributed under appropriate titles.

EDUCATION.

7 W. 3. s. 1. c. 4. Sending a child abroad to be educated in the popish religion, either in a public seminary or a private family, or sending any thing for its maintenance, was punished with disability to

sue, or prosecute in law or equity for any wrong or any demand, or to be guardian or executor, to take any thing by legacy, deed, or gift, or to bear any office, with forfeiture of goods and chattles, land tenements, hereditaments, annuities, offices, and estates of freehold during life. And a single justice upon suspicion might summon and examine the persons suspected, to have evidence against themselves, and summon witnesses to answer upon oath; and if the offence seemed probable, bind the suspected party to the sessions, and there he was bound to answer *instantly*; and should the offence upon trial appear *probable*, then the offender is bound to prove where the child was, for what the money was sent, and the fact is to be presumed unlawful, till the suspected party prove *the negative*; and being entered on record shall be a conviction, not only of the supposed sender of the child, but of the absent child; and the infant convict shall incur the like disabilities: and of these forfeitures the booty is to be divided between the king and the pious informer.

There is indeed a proviso that the infant upon his return or twelve months after coming of age, may by prayer or motion in open court, obtain a trial; but upon that trial he must prove negatively that he was not sent contrary to the act, or it shall be taken for granted against him as if it had been fully proved. And if he should do so, still he shall lose his goods and chattles, and all the profits of his lands prior to his conviction, and the rest be restored only upon condition of swearing certain constrained oaths, and making forced metaphysical declarations of belief in open court.

N. B. To avoid future repetitions it may be here briefly stated, that the oaths, and declarations generally intended throughout, are those of allegiance, abhorrence, abjuration, and against transubstantiation.

2 Ann. s. 1. c. 6. Sending or suffering to be sent a child under 21, except sailors, ship boys, merchants apprentices, or factors, without special license of the queen or chief governor and four privy counsellors, like penalties.

A judge or two justices suspecting any child to be so sent may convene father, mother, relation or guardian, require them to produce the child within two months, and unless they prove it to be in England or Scotland, it is to be convicted as one educated in foreign parts, and suffer accordingly.

3 Ann c. 3. Protestants converted from popery must educate their children under fourteen, in the established religion or forfeit all offi-

ces of trust or profit, and be disabled from sitting in either house of parliament, or being barrister or attorney, and be for ever disqualified.

2 Ann. s. 1. c. 6. Where either father or mother is a protestant, the chancellor is to make an order for educating the child a protestant till eighteen, appointing where it shall be educated and how, and also by whom; the father to pay all the charges directed by the court: and the child may be taken away from the popish parent.

7 W. 3. s. 1. c. 4. Papists are forbid to instruct youth in any public school, and even in private houses, unless those of the family, under pain of fine and imprisonment.

8 Ann. c. 3. § 16. A papist teaching publicly or privately, or entertained as an usher to a protestant schoolmaster, to be esteemed *a popish regular clergyman convict*, and suffer all the pains inflicted upon such, that is, 1st. to be imprisoned in the common goal; 2d. to be transported; 3d if he return to his friends and native land, to suffer as a traitor: the following is his judgment.

1st. To be dragged along the ground to the place of execution; 2d. to be hanged by the neck; 3d. to have his entrails taken out and burned while he is yet alive; 4th. his head to be cut off; 5th. that his body be quartered or divided into four parts; 6th. that his head and quarters be at the *pleasure* of the *Queen*.

The legal consequences of this judgment are, attainder, *corruption of blood*, annihilation of all inheritable powers, from his ancestors and to his heirs.

Any person entertaining such teachers to forfeit 10*l.* to be distributed in equal shares between the king and the informer.

Any person *discovering* such teacher, to have £10, levied like money for robberies, all upon the papists.

All persons of sixteen years of age may be summoned and forced to become informers upon oath, touching the being and residence of such teachers, on pain of £20, or twelve months imprisonment.

A protestant permitting a child under fourteen to be educated a papist, to suffer as a papist.

MARRIAGE.

9. W. 3. c. 28. If a protestant maid being heir apparent, or having interest in lands, or a personal estate of £500, marry any man without a certificate from a minister, bishop, and justice, attested by two creditable witnesses that he is *a known protestant*, the estate shall go to the next of kin, and all popish intervening heirs deemed *dead* and *in-*

testate, and the protestant maid to be *dead in law:* and husband and wife to be for ever disabled from being guardian, executor, &c.; and the person who married them to be imprisoned a year and forfeit £10, half to the king, and half to the informer who will sue by bill or suit, and no essoign shall be allowed.

6. Ann. c. 16. If a woman persuade an heir apparent to marry her, by secret delusions, insinuations or menaces, she loses thirds dower, and all real and personal estate; and all accessaries before the fact, to suffer three years imprisonment.

Ib. §. 2. If any protestant shall marry any maiden or woman without such certificate, he is for ever disabled from being heir, executor, administrator, guardian, &c. or to sit in parliament, or bear any employment, civil or military, unless he procures her to be converted in one year, and a certificate thereof under hand and seal of the archbishop, bishop, or chancellor to be enrolled in chancery.

2 Ann. s. 1. c. 6. Any person having real or personal estate in the kingdom who marries a papist abroad—like disabilities and penalties as if he married within the kingdom.

9 W. 3. c. 28. Whoever marries a soldier to any uncertified wife, to be imprisoned till he pay £20, half of which is to reward the informer.

6 Ann. c. 16. § 1. 3. 6. If any person above the age of fourteen, by fraud, *flattery*, or fair promises, shall allure any maid or widow, having substance to mary him without consent of parents or guardian, and the person who celebrates the marriage be a popish priest; or if a popish priest celebrate any marriage knowing one party to be a protestant; he shall be deemed, and suffer all the pains, of a popish regular—be imprisoned, transported, and on returning be drawn, hanged, quartered, beheaded, embowelled, entrails burned alive, head and quarters given to the queen, and attainted and blood-corrupted.

8 Ann. c. 3. The knowledge of the fact is to be presumed against the priest, and he to be convicted, unless he produce a certificate from the protestant parish minister that neither were protestants.

12 Geo. 1. c. 3. § 1. A popish, or reputed popish priest, celebrating marriage between a protestant or reputed protestant and a papist, or between two protestants or reputed protestants—death, as a felon, without benefit of clergy.

N. B. 19 Geo. 2. c. 13. annuls such marriages without process, judgment, or sentence.

23 Geo. 2. c. 10, § 3, makes it felony in the priest, notwithstanding the marriage be annulled.

§ 1. And any two justices may summon all persons suspected to have been so married, or to have been present, and examine them on oath, where, by whom, with what form and ceremony such marriage was celebrated, and who were present; and upon neglect to appear or refusal to become informer against their friends, commit them to prison for three years without bail or mainprize, unless they will enter into recognizance to prosecute all the offenders.

7. G. 2. §. 6. A converted justice acting while his wife is a papist, or his children educated as such, to be imprisoned one year, pay £100 half to the king, half to the informer, and be for ever disabled to be executor or guardian.

7. G. 2. c. 5. §. 12. Barristers, six clerks, and attorneys, disabled unless they convert their wife in a year, and enrol a certificate thereof in chancery.

8. Ann. c. 3. A wife conforming in the life-time of her husband, may file a bill against him, and have all appointments or execution of powers, as he might make in her favour, if he were willing, decreed whether he will or not, and notwithstanding any disposition of his to the contrary, have one third of his chattles real and personal.

RELIGION—CLERGY.

7. 9. W. 3. S. 1. c. 26. §. 1. All Popish Archbishops, bishops, vicars general, deans, regular popish clergy, exercising any ecclesiastical jurisdiction, to leave the kingdom in three months, or be transported, wherever the chief governor shall think fit. And if he return, be dragged and hanged, quartered and beheaded, blood corrupted and attainted, entrails burned alive, and head and quarters at the king's disposal, to be piked or gibbeted, as was most for his royal pleasure and the honour of God, and forfeit all as in case of high treason.

§. 3. No such shall come into the kingdom, under pain of twelve months imprisonment, transportation, and in case of return, the same pains of high treason, hanging, dragging, emboweling, &c.

2. Ann. c. 3. §. 1. Extends these pains to every clergyman of the popish religion, secular as well as regular; and for their easier conviction, gives a trial in any county at the option of the queen.

7. & 9 W. 3. Above cited, enacts, that all such archbishops, &c.

shall repair to the city of Dublin Cork, Kingsale, Youghall, Waterford, Wexford, Gallway or Carrickfurgus, and there remain till there be conveniency for transporting them, and give in their names to the mayor or chief magistrate, who shall give their best assistance in transporting them.

Ib. §. 4. Concealing any person so ordered to leave the kingdom, or forbid to enter it, to forfeit for the first offence £20, for the second, £40, and for the third, lands, and goods, half of the goods to the king and half to the informer, provided, that the informer's share shall not exceed £100, however more the king's may be, the surplusage shall remain to the king; and shall be recoverable in any of his courts of record.

Ib. §. 3. The fines of £10 and £40, to be levied by a single justice, who has power to summon parties and witnesses, and to convict and commit to prison in default of payment.

Ib. § 8. 9, 10. Justices are commanded to issue their warrants *from time to time*, for apprehending and committing archbishops, bishops, &c. remaining in the kingdom, and give an accoant in writing of their proceedings on pain of £100 to the king and the informer.

8. Ann. c. 3. §. 33. Clergy, schoolmasters, and other Papists, ordered for transportation, are to be sent to the common goal of the next sea port, to remain there till transported, and if any merchant or ship-master refuse to receive their bodies, not exceeding five in one ship, the collector not to discharge the ship on pain of £30. The collector to allow *5l.* for transporting them to the West Indies, and *3l.* to any part of Europe. And by § 3. and 4. if any of them be found out of the custody of the master or merchant so receiving him, he is to suffer as in case of a popish regular, &c. drawing, hanging, quartering, embowelling, &c. &c. &c.

2 Ann. s. 1. c. 7. § 1. All popish priests to register their names, abode, age, parish, time and place of receiving orders, and from whom, and also to give security for their good behaviour, and not to remove to other parts of the kingdom, under like penalties of transportation, and the pains of high treason on return.

4 Ann. c. 2. § 2. Any other person officiating as a priest—the like. And in like case, of return from transportation, the like judgment and execution, bowelling, hanging, burning and drawing, and forfeiture of lands and goods, head and quarters to the Queen.

2. Ann. S. 1. c. 7. §. 4. & 8. Ann. c. 3, §. 19. Every Papist keeping a curate, deemed a Popish *regular*, and to suffer like pains.

All priests registered by virtue of these acts, to take the oath of abjuration, or else on celebrating mass or officiating as a priest—like pains.

8. Ann. c. 3. §. 21. Two justices may summon any Popish person of sixteen years or upwards, to give testimony on oath where he last heard mass, who celebrated it, what persons were present, and also touching the being and residence, of any popish clergyman or secular priest resident in the country, and upon neglect or refusal to become informer, commit him for twelve months unless he pay 20*l.*

8. Ann. c. 3. §. 16. & 20. Any person discovering against the clergy so as they may be prosecuted to conviction, to have for discovering an archbishop, or vicar general, 50*l.* for a regular or secular not registered 20*l.* and for a schoolmaster, 10*l.*. [*See Education*].

§. 24. Any person summoned by two justices to go before them, and swear *abjuration*, and neglecting or refusing, to pay 40*l.*; to be committed three months and disabled forever to *obtain any licence to carry any arms*. After three months, the same may be repeated and the party imprisoned six months and fined 10*l.* and be bound with two sureties to the sessions, or goal delivery, where, if he refuses to abjure, upon oath in open court; to suffer a prœmunire; that is, to be out of the king's protection, and forfeit land and tenements, goods and chattles to the king. And this offence was so odious, says Lord Coke, that whoever was attainted of it, might be slain by any other man, without danger of law, because the 25. Ed. 3. s. 6. c. 22. enacted, that any might do with him as the king's enemy. Still he can bring no action for any injury, however atrocious, and no man knowing him guilty can with safety give him aid or relief. 1. Hawk. p. c. 19.

1. Geo. 1. c. 9. Every justice may tender the oath of abjuration, to every suspected person.

8 Ann. c. 3. § 27. All magistrates required to demolish all crosses, pictures, and inscriptions, that are the occasion of popish superstition.

2 Ann. c. 7. § 2. Priests converted to have a maintenance till otherwise provided for, and to read the liturgy in the English or Irish language. This statute gives £20; by subsequent ones, it is increased to £40 yearly.

2 Ann. c. 6. §. 1. Persuading any person to be reconciled to the see of Rome, the reconciler and the party reconciled both subject to the pains of premunire.

N.B. The first English monarch that invaded Ireland, Hen. 2, did it by virtue of a bull from pope Adrian III. obtained on pretence of a sanctified regard for the promotion of the catholic faith.

BURIAL OF THE DEAD.

7 & 9 W. 3. st. 1. c. 26. None to bury any dead in a suppressed monastery, abbey, or convent, if it be not used for divine service according to the liturgy of the established church, upon pain of 10*l.* upon all that shall be present, one half to the informer, to be levied summarily by a single justice.

BATHING AND WATER DRINKING.

2 Ann. c. 6. § 26. Meetings and assemblies at certain wells or springs therein named, to be adjudged *riots*, and all magistrates required to be diligent in putting the law in force.

§ 27. And every person assembling there to forfeit on conviction before a single magistrate 10 shillings, or be publicly whipped within twenty-four hours. And every person selling ale or victuals there or any other commodities, upon like conviction to forfeit 20 shillings, or imprisonment.

HUSBAND AND WIFE.

[*See title* MARRIAGE.]

PARENTS AND CHILDREN.

2 Ann. s. 1. c. 6. §. 7. A child of a popish parent professing a desire to become a protestant, may institute a chancery suit against his parent, and be decreed a present maintenance, and a portion after the parent's decease.

8 Ann. c. 3. A child on conforming may also oblige his father to discover upon oath the full value of all his real or personal estate, and have a new bill, toties quoties.

N. B. Though the parent should abandon all his property, yet if he afterwards acquired any thing he might be vexed with a new bill as often as an undutiful child might think fit, to the end of his life.

2. Ann. Stat. 1. c. 6. 3. The eldest son by conforming, may, by filing a bill against his father, divest him of his fee, rendering him bare tenant for life, and take the reversion subject only, to maintenance and portions for younger children, not exceeding one third of the value.

Ib. § 5. No papist to have the guardianship of an orphan child, and if there be no protestant relation the child to be committed to a stranger, who shall be bound to use his utmost endeavours to make the child a protestant; and any papist who takes upon himself such guardianship to forfeit 500*l*. to the blue coat hospital.

6. Geo. 1. c. 6. Children of popish parents bred protestants from the age of twelve years, and receiving the sacrament of the established church, to be reputed protestants, and enjoy their rights, but if after eighteen they are present either at matins or vespers, to suffer the penalties of converted papists relapsing into popery.

For other rude violations of parental tenderness, and statutory temptations to filial and conjugal impiety, see the heads *Education*, and *Marriage*.

LAWYERS AND LAW OFFICERS.

3 W. & M. c. 2. § 4. A barrister, attorney, clerk, or officer in chancery, who without having taken the oaths and made the declaration against popery in open court, shall practise in any court, is disabled to hold any office of trust or profit, or to be executor or guardian, or to sue for any right in law or equity, or take by legacy, deed, or gift, and to forfeit 500*l*. half to the informer.

10 W. 3. c. 13. § 1. & 3. No papists to act as solicitor, except in their own cause, or as menial servants, on pain of 100*l*. to the informer, and like disabilities.

6 Ann. c. 6. § 1. 2. 9. No papist, or *reputed papist*, to act as above, on pain of 200*l*. and like disabilities, and any person seeing or knowing such person so to act, may openly in court cause the oaths and declaration [against transubstantiation, &c.] to be tendered to him, and on proof of his refusal he is to be recorded a *convict*.

Ib. § 4. NO LAWYER SHALL BE EXEMPT BY HIS PRIVILEGE FROM ANSWERING UPON OATH AS TO HIS KNOWLEDGE IN ANY MATTER THAT SHALL COME IN QUESTION UNDER THIS OR THE FORMER ACT.

It appears throughout this code that all principles of law are reversed, and go by contraries, and that what is law for protestants is not for catholics, and vice versa. It is not therefore wonderful that those familiarized to it by education and habit should judge in the same perverse sense, even where there was no statute, positively oversetting the principles of the law. When the lawyer's privilege is given up, the priest's must be little regarded.

§ 6. No officer to let any popish solicitor, &c. inspect or examine records, entries, rules, orders, &c. on pain of 50*l.* to the informer.

1 Geo. 2. c. 20. 1 Barristers, attorney's clerks, &c. applying for admission, must take the oaths, and repeat and subscribe the declaration appointed in 2 Ann, to *prevent the growth of popery.* And such as are converted or born of popish parents, must prove before the chancellor, judges, &c. that they have professed and continued to be protestants for two years before, and that their children then under fourteen, or born after the above period, have been educa tedprotestants.

21. & 22. Geo. 3. c. 32. s. 2. None but Protestant students are admissible to the king's Inn.

1. Geo 2. c. 20. §. 4. Sheriffs and their clerks, must have been five years Protestants, otherwise, to suffer like pains and disabillties as papists.

7. Geo. 2. c. 5. §. 3. Courts may *on suspicion* summons a solicitor, and on non appearance, punish him for contempt, with a fine of 50*l.* and imprisonment of six months.

§. 6. Drawing, dictating, or abreviating pleadings, or transcribing depositions—bring the party within the pains of these acts.

INTEREST IN THE SOIL.

To those not already pre-acquainted with this extraordinary code it is not easy to give an adequate impression of the statutes, in such a narrow compass, much less of their operation and effect.

2. Ann. s. 1. c. 6. Disables Papists from purchasing lands in their own name, or in trust, or even any rents, or profits issuing out of lands, or to take a lease for more than 31 years, and not that, unless two thirds of the yearly value be reserved—all other estates to be void.

Ib. §. 7. 8. & 9. No Papist who will not renounce his religion to take any estate, in fee simple, or in tail, by descent or purchase, but the next Protestant to take as if he were dead. The children of Papists to be taken as Papists, a Papist conforming, may be heir to a Papist disabled; wife, *if a Protestant*, to have dower.

8. Ann. c, 6. §. 10. The fee simple estate of a Papist, henceforth to descend to the sons share and share alike, and to their sons; and for

default of sons, to daughters, in like manner; and so for want of daughters to collaterals, any disposition by the ancestor to the contrary notwithstanding.

This singular rule of descent was obviously intended to break down all power or concentration of wealth, or influence in Catholic families, whilst primogeniture, being the rule in the descent of Protestants estates, jealouly preserved the opposite principle. It was *sui generis:* unlike the gavel kind of Kent, where the acquirer may devise his estate to whom he will; and more unlike the law of our state (New-york) where all is equitably distributed amongst sons and daughters. It was besides in barefaced violation of the treaty of Limerick, which was ratified by the king and queen, and Lords Justices, and guaranteed to all who were then in arms, their rights, titles, privileges and immunities, as by the laws theretofore in force. The whole of these laws to restrain the growth of popery; and which have made popery grow so much, were besides, their intrinsic enormity tainted with that odious stain of perfidy, and shew how safer it is to fight than to treat with implacable oppressors.

2. Ann. c. 6. §. 12. If the heir at law of a papist, be a protestant, he must enrol a certificate of that matter in chancery; if a papist he has a year, within which, if he renounce his religion, he may have his land.

English Stat. 1. Ann. S. 1. c. 32. §. 7. enacts, that the lands theretofore, forfeited and vested in trustees, should be sold to Protestants only, and if any title in the same shall accrue to any papist, he must renounce his religion, or as it was commonly expressed, the errors of the church of Rome, in order to enjoy the estate, and if any make or assign a lease to a papist, both grantor and grantee, to forfeit treble the yearly value; with the exception of a cottage or cabin, with two acres of land to a day labourer; and any Protestant, might file a bill of discovery against any person supposed privy to any trust, to which neither plea, nor demurrer was allowed, and on trial of any issue, none to be jurors but Protestants.

See further under the titles Education, Parents and Children, Marriage, &c. It is remarkable that these ferocious acts, as Mr. Burke has termed them, to prevent the further growth of popery, conduced more to the growth of it, than any other martyrdom in history.

RESIDENCE AND LOCOMMOTION.

2. Ann. c. 6. §. 23. No person or persons, that are or shall be papists or profess the Popish religion, shall come to inhabit in the city or suburbs of Limerick or Gallway, after the 24th of March 1703. And all then residing there to give sureties for their faithful bearing towards the crown: not to hinder seamen, fishermen, or day labourers, from dwelling within the suburds of those towns in houses worth *forty shillings* a year *or under*.

See further, title " *Religion and Clergy.*"

ELECTION FRANCHISE.

2. Ann. Stat. 1. c. 6. Papists who shall vote for members of parliament, without having *abjured* six months previously, to forfeit 100*l.* which the informer and the Queen are to divide, share and share alike.

1. 2. Geo. 1. c. 6. No papist to vote at a vestry for paving or lighting, except they be church-wardens, and then to have no vote for building or repairing churches.

JURIES.

6 Ann. c. 6 § 5. No papist to be on any jury in K. B. assizes, oyer and terminer, goal delivery, or sessions, unless where a sufficient number of protestants cannot be had, and in all trials under the popery laws, the prosecutor may challenge any papist juror.

It seems as if every sacred principle of law was selected for the purpose of being profaned by these inhuman and iniquitous legislators. Aliens are entitled to a jury half aliens; but Catholics were to be thrown on the mercy of their persecutors.

GUARDIANSHIP.

For this head, see the various other titles and disabilities there stated, and remark that Roman Catholic parents, were disqualified not only from being guardians to the children of others, but to their own; and liable to see their children taken from their arms, and committed to the bitterest of their enemies, who had it in charge by statute, to labour for their conversion, from the religion of their parents.

TRADE.

8. Ann. c. 3. §. 37. No papist *who is or shall be permitted* to follow any trade, craft or mystery (except hemp or flaxen manufactory) to have two apprentices, nor any for a less time than 7 years, on pain of 100*l.*

25 Geo. 3. c. 48. § 11 and 12. The 4000*l.* granted by this act, to be expended in apprentice fees, for apprentices taken from charter schools or hospitals, to *protestant tradesmen only*. See title Army, Arms, and Self-defence.

No person making locks or barrels for fire-arms, or swords, bayonets, skeins, knives, or other weapons, shall instruct an apprentice of the popish religion on pain of 20*l.* one moiety to the king, and one to the informer, and the indentures of apprenticeship shall be void, and such apprentice exercising, to suffer the like penalty, and refusing to take the oaths shall amount to a conviction.

ARMY, ARMS, AND SELF DEFENCE.

7 W. 3 St. 1. c. 5. § 1, 2, 3. All papists to deliver up their arms and ammunition, of what kind soever, in possession or held in trust for them, and all mayors, justices, &c. to issue warrants to search for and seize the same in any *suspected* house or place; and any person suspected of concealing arms, to be brought and examined upon oath; such as neglect to appear and submit to this examination, if a peer or *peeress*, to forfeit for the first offence 100*l.*, for the second a premuniere; if under the degree of peer or peeress 30*l.* and one year's imprisonment, and as much longer as the fine remains unpaid, and for the second offence a premunire.

The informer and the king to have equal parts in the penalties, which they may recover from the peer or peeress by an action of debt, in which no essoign, &c. shall be allowed.

Any nobleman or gentleman making proof to the Lord Lieutenant and council that on the 3d of October, 1691, he was an inhabitant of Limerick or other garrison in possession of the Irish, or officer or soldier of the late King James, or commissioned officers in the king's quarters, belonging to the Irish regiments then in being which were treated with, and hath not since refused to take the oaths, &c. when tendered to him; or if he be a gentleman of estate, then belonging to the town of Gallway, such persons may keep a *sword, a case of pistols, and a gun, for the defence of his house.*

12 Geo. 2. c. 6. § 1, 2, 3, 14, 15, 16, extends the above powers to every justice and chief magistrate of corporate towns, and imposes the fine of a peer or peeress for the *first* offence, encreasing it to 300*l.* and of every other person to 50*l.* and punishes the magistrate with a fine of 20*l.* for every neglect. And no papist, under any pretence whatever, to have any warlike stores, swordblade, barrel-lock, or stock of guns, or fire-arms, on pain of 40*l*, to the informer, and one year's imprisonment and afterwards, till the money be paid; and if a papist servant keep any such thing by consent of his master, the master to be deemed a papist and suffer the pains.

15 & 16 Geo. 3. c. 21 § 15. One or more justices and chief magistrates of towns and cities, or sheriffs, shall, as well by night as by day, search for and seize arms or ammunition, and enter dwelling-houses, out-houses, or offices, *or other place belonging to a papist*, or person suspected of concealing any such, and on *suspicion after search*, may summon and examine on oath the person suspected, and inflict for refusal to discover upon oath, fine, imprisonment, whipping, or pillory, at their discretion.

2 G. 1. c. 9 § 16. Every papist must send a fit *protestant* to serve in the militia, or forfeit double what a protestant would in case of non-attendance.

§ 18. And pay towards the militia double what a protestant pays.

6 G. 1. c. 11. § 4. 20*l.* to be levied by presentment upon the popish inhabitants for refreshments to the protestant militia on the days appointed for turning out.

1 G. 1. c. 47. Any papist enlisted in the army without a testimonial that he has renounced his religion, or declared to the officer or soldier enlisting him, that he was a papist, to suffer such corporal punishment, not extending to life or limb, as a court martial shall think proper to inflict.

10. W. 3. S. 2. c. 8. §. 4. No papist to be a fowler even for a Protestant, and any gun found with him though belonging to a Protestant, shall go to the informer.

HORSES.

2. Geo. 1. c. 9. §. 11. Horses of papists to be seized by proclamation when needful, all except breeding mares, stallions and horses, under four years old, and detained ten days, during which time any militia man, may tender to the *seizer 5l.* for the use of the owner, *deducting however the expence of seizing and keeping ;* and the property thereby to vest in the militia man. If no person chuses to tender this sum, the owner is only to pay for the seizing and detaining of his own horse, and have him again.

§. Papists who do not produce their horses on demand, or in three days, to be imprisoned till they pay 10*l.* half to the informer and half to the militia of the barony.

7 W. 3. S. 1. c. 5. § 10. Any chief magistrate or, two justices, may authorise any person professing the protestant religion, to break open the door of any papist, and bring the papist's horse before them, and if the protestant who broke the door and took the horse, will tender 5*l.* 5*s.* the property shall by these acts vest in him the same as if he had lawfully bought him in open market.

§ 11 Any concealing or aiding in the concealing a horse, if he be a papist, or suspected papist, or refuse the oaths against popery, to be committed to the common goal for three months, without bail or mainprize, and *forfeit to the king and his successors* three times the value of the horse, and continue in gaol till he pay the forfeit and be recorded—A PAPIST !

8 Ann. c. 3. § .34 and 35, Papists to have stud mares and stallions under five years old, but in case of any invasion likely to happen, or intestine war, the Lord Lieutenant may seize horse, mare and gelding. If he order them afterwards to be returned, the owner must pay the taker for every night he (the taker) detained his (the papist's) horse from him six pence.

WATCHMEN.

6 Geo. 1. c. 10. None but protestants to be watchmen, but *papists* must provide *approved* protestants, or be subject to distress.

OUTLAWRIES.

Under this head in the statute book may be seen the ungenerous severities against the too loyal soldiers of the wretched James.

CONCLUSION.

This summary may give an idea of the penal code, but none of its effects. It affords, however, a view of the Irish character as compared with the English during the same period. Whilst in the one nation, parliament and people, kneeled, fawned and addressed, and licked the bloody hand of their tyrant without other scruple than the fear of offending even by their adulation; fear that the crime they were extolling might already be denounced in favor of a new caprice, and that in the act of incensing their idol might devour them; whilst in Ireland no terror, no calamity could bring the stubborn soul to profess or swear to that at which conscience revolted, and death could not enforce prevarication!

SAD BUT HONORABLE MONUMENT.

APPENDIX.

THERE is perhaps no dogma of the Catholic church, which has been less correctly understood, and more grossly misrepresented by her adversaries, than that of the sacrament of penance. For these three centuries past, volumes have been written, and industriously circulated in every country, where the reformed churches have been established, or protected, in order to arrest, *this Popish imposition*, as they have been pleased to term it, and to purge Christianity of *this most licentious* practice, viz. Confession. No stone has been left unturned, no calumny has been thought too gross, which could warp the mind into a belief of its demoralizing effects. Hence we need not be surprised to see the minds of Protestants in general so prejudiced, and embittered against it, especially those of the United States, where the opportunity of reading such books is greater, and the means of correct information on the subject fewer, as well from the comparatively small circulation of Catholic books, as from the little regard that is paid to the reading of what is conceived, from a biassed education, to be false and dangerous. Few examine beyond report; and very few consequently are acquainted with the genuine and real doctrines of the Catholic church. Yet it is an undeniable fact, and which our adversaries seem to have but too well known, that the Catholic doctrine can never be attacked with any success, but by misrepresentation, and that it wants only to be known, to obtain the suffrages of upright men, and to silence the most inveterate of its enemies.

The public are presented in the subjoined Appendix, with a true exposition of the whole doctrine of the Catholic church, relating to confession, in order that the world may see how much she has been injured, and how very unlike she is to that many-headed monster which has been generally exhibited for her. The Catholic is far from being ashamed of his tenets when they are properly represented; and still less afraid to propose them to the public. He knows they are such as have stood the test of eighteen hundred years, and will remain unshaken to the end of the world; such as will strike conviction into every mind that will give them a fair perusal, and weigh the arguments by which they are supported; such in fine, as the divine founder of Christianity has himself established, and which have been handed down pure and uusullied through the channel of tradition, to the present day, and will continue through the same unpolluted stream to the consummation of ages.

Particular care will be taken through the whole of the Appendix to mark the authorities, and not to assert or hazard any thing from memory; in order that every point may be fairly and correctly stated.

NEW-YORK, JULY 14th, 1813.

A TRUE

EXPOSITION

OF

THE DOCTRINE

OF

THE CATHOLIC CHURCH,

TOUCHING THE SACRAMENT OF PENANCE, WITH THE GROUNDS ON WHICH THIS DOCTRINE IS FOUNDED.

It will not be amiss, in giving this exposition, to present the public previously, with a general notion of the sacramants, as they are understood and taught by the Catholic church; as it may serve to throw some light upon some of the matter contained in the preceding trial, and answer to some of the references.

SECTION I.

OF THE SACRAMENTS IN GENERAL.

The Catholic church has always uniformly taught, that, besides the graces which Jesus Christ diffuses immediately by himself without the ministry of the church, there are others which he has put as it were, into the hands of his first Pastors and their lawful successors, the Bishops and Priests of his church, by the institution of certain ceremonies which produce these graces, when they find in us the requisite dispositions. We call these ceremonies, *sacraments;* and reckon seven in number, viz. *Baptism*, *Confirmation*, *Holy Eucharist*, *Penance*, *Extreme Unction*, *Holy Orders*, *Matrimony*. This number is suited to all states and degrees, and serve to all the necessities of our souls, correspondent to those of our bodies: For as to our corporal necessities, we must first be born into the world; and to this *Baptism* answers, whereby we are regenerated, or born anew to God. 2. We must gain strength and growth, thereby to become perfect men: and to this answers *confirmation*, whereby we are made strong and perfect Christians. 3. We must have a daily competent sustenance for life; and to this the blessed *eucharist* corresponds, whereby our souls are fed and preserved to everlasting life. 4. When sick, we must have medicine and remedies to cure our wounds and diseases; and to this the sacrament of *penance* answers, whereby all the diseases and wounds made in our souls by sin, are healed. 5. We must have cordials and restoratives against the agonizing fits and pangs of death; and to this corresponds *extreme unction*, whereby our souls are strengthened in their agony, against despair, and the last assults of the devil. 6. We must be governed by laws and magistrates, to avoid injustice and confusion; and to this answers *holy orders*, whereby we are provided with pastors and spiritual superiors, to guide, govern and direct our souls. 7. We must increase and multiply, in a lawful and natural way, by marriage; and to this answers the sacrament of *matrimony*, whereby the married state is blessed and sanctified, not only to the having of children, but to the having and educating them to life everlasting.

The seven sacraments were instituted by Christ our Lord; because, he only who is the author of grace and nature, is able to give to natural things the virtue to produce supernatural effects of grace. They were ordained to sanctify our souls; that is, to render them holy and agreeable to God, while sin is blotted out, and sanctifying grace is given or increased in them.

St. John the Baptist administered a baptism of penance: but this baptism, as well as the other legal purifications, had no efficacy of itself; it was a mere symbolical ceremony to prepare to another baptism foretold by the holy Precursor. Jesus Christ after having received the baptism of John the Baptist, instituted a new baptism for *the remission of sins*, Acts 2. 38. He commanded his apostles *to teach and Baptize*, (Math. 28. 19.) declaring to them that he that believeth, and is baptized, shall be saved, Mark 16. 16.

Confirmation strengthens the faithful in the profession of the true faith, by a special communication of the Holy Ghost. We find an example of this in the acts of the Apostles. The new Christians of Samaria had not yet received the Holy Ghost, but had been baptized only in the name of Jesus Christ, when St. Peter and St. John *laid their hands upon them* and thereby caused the Holy Ghost to decend upon them. Acts 8. 17. This grace which was imparted to them at that time through the imposition of hands, was therefore different from the grace of baptism. We call it the grace of *Confirmation*, because it confirms or strengthens us in the faith. It was in consequence of their having principally received this grace, that so many martyrs triumphed over the most cruel torments.

Jesus Christ has declared that his *flesh is meat indeed*, and his *blood is drink indeed;* for adds he, *he that eateth my flesh and drinketh my blood, abideth in me, and I in him*, John 6. 56, 57. Now, we partake truly of his body and precious blood in holy communion. This sacrament is called the Eucharist, because the primitive church and the holy Fathers (vid. S. Just. S. Irenæus, Tertul. S. Cyprian. Concil Nicen. 1.) usually called it so; which word in the Greek signifies thanksgiving and is applied to this sacrament, because of the thanksgiving which our Lord offered in the first institution of it; St. Matt. 26. 27. St. Mark 14. 23. St. Luke 22. 19. 1 Cor. 11. 24. And because of the thanksgiving with which we are obliged to offer and receive this great sacrament and sacrifice, which contains the abridgment of all the wonders of God, the fountain of all grace, the standing memorial of our redemption, and the pledge of a happy eternity.

He has given to his Apostles the power of forgiving and retaining sins, with a promise that whatsoever they should bind on earth, should be bound in heaven; and whatsoever they should loose on earth, should be also loosed in heaven. John 20. 23. Matt. 16. 19. But his apostles and ministers cannot exercise this power with discernment, without knowing the state of the sinner; and they cannot know the state of the sinner, unless the sinner declare it. Hence, the obligation incumbent on him to make an avowal of the faults committed after Baptism, to obtain the remission of them in the sacrament of penance.

Is any man sick among you? Let him bring in the Priests of the church, and let them pray over him, anointing him with oil, in the name of the Lord: and the prayer of faith shall save the sick man: and the Lord shall raise him up: and if he be in sins they shall be forgiven him. James 5. 14, 15. Such is the effect of the sacrament of Extreme Unction, which at the same time that it confers grace, procures also the health of the body, when this health is conducive to the sanctifiation of the sick.

St. Paul makes mention of the grace which Timothy had received with the Apostolic mission through the imposition of the hands of the Priesthood, 1 Timothy 4. 14. c. 5. 28. 2. Tim. 1. 6. The Bishops, the heirs and successors of the Apostles, confer the same grace, and give the same mission by the sacrament of Holy Orders, with the right of exercising its functions, with the consent and by the authority of the first Pastors.

Jesus Christ by bringing Matrimony back to its primitive state, has declared that it was not in the power of man to dissolve it; Matt. 19. 4, 5, 6. and we believe that this indissoluble union representing the union of Christ and his church, Ephes. 5. 23. has been raised to the dignity of a sacrament, in order to give to the married couple grace to fulfil the obligations imposed on them.

Such is the doctrine of the Catholic church touching the sacraments, their number, and the special grace they confer upon the worthy receiver; and the Catholic in adhering to this doctrine has the infinite satisfaction to know that his faith, in this as well as in every other particular, is grounded on the authority of the unerring word of God infallibly delivered and interpreted by the Catholic church, which St. Paul declares to be *the pillar and ground of the truth ;* 1 Tim. 3. 15. which Jesus Christ has promised to be with, *all days even to the consummation of the world;* Matt. 28. 20. to which he promised to send another comforter to abide with her *for ever, even the spirit of truth;* John 14. 16. and finally against which the gates of hell were never to prevail; Matt. 16. 18. and that he believes no more than what the Fathers and Councils of the church, and all the saints of God have invariably always professed and believed in every age. From the proofs and arguments I shall adduce in support of the sacrament of Penance, which alone I intend to vindicate in this appendix, the candid reader may infer how firm and unshaken every other article of the Catholic creed stands, resting as it does, in all its parts, on the unerring authority both of the written and unwritten word of God, proposed and explained by the infallible Church.

SECTION II.

I shall now proceed to the examination of the great point in question, viz. the sacrament of penance, which I intend most fully, and I trust, equally satisfactorily, to prove and to vindicate. The aukward predicament in which Roman Catholics have been generally placed by their adversaries, as well learned as unlearned, who have been so very good as to draw up creeds for them, in order to combat and refute the same the more successfully, renders it necessary to place this subject first in its true and proper light, and previously to shew what the real doctrine of the Catholic church is touching the sacrament of penance. I shall therefore for the satisfaction of the public, transcribe the greater part of the fourteenth session of the Council of Trent, which presents a full exposition of said doctrine; and in order that every one may fairly understand, not what the Catholic willingly or unwillingly has been so illiberally made to believe, but what he believes *in reality.* This session was held under Pope Julius III. on the 25th of November. A. D. 1551.

AN EXPOSITION OF THE DOCTRINE OF THE COUNCIL OF TRENT,

ON THE SACRAMENT OF PENANCE.

SESSION XIV.

*THE holy Œcumenick and general council of Trent, in the Holy

---

* A council, is an assembly of Bishops, the lawful successors of the Apostles, in which those points are treated that relate to faith, discipline and morals. For councils are held either to support the truths of faith, when they are in danger of being shaken by the errors disseminated by heretics, or to examine and decide questions, which regard faith and morals, or to regulate what appertains to discipline.

The assembling of councils is as ancient as the church. We read in the Acts of the Apostles, of the Bishops having assembled at Jerusalem with the Priests, in order to examine what was to be done concerning the *legal observances,* and it was decided, that the Gentiles converted to the faith should not be compelled to observe them; and the church has always looked upon that council, as the model of all those that have been held afterwards.

There are different sorts of councils. 1st. The Œcumenick, or general councils, which represent the universal church: for all the Catholic Bishops are there assembled, and have a right to assist at them in quality of judges. The eight first general councils were

Ghost lawfully assembled, the same Legate, and the same Nuncios of the apostolic See presiding therein : Although in the decree respecting justification, much has been already said, in many places concerning the sacrament of Penance, the affinity of the subjects, having, as it

---

convoked by the emperors, but with the express consent and approbation of the Pope : The others were all convoked by the Popes, as may be seen by their bulls, which are placed at the head of these councils. This authority belongs to them by right, as being constituted over all the bishops in the world, being the Vicars of Jesus Christ. The bishops have a right to give their suffrage, and their right is a divine right. The Abbots and Generals of religious Orders, also give theirs, but by Ecclesiastical right only. The deputies of Cathedrals, Dioceses and Universities, assist at them in quality of witnesses, examiners, and counsellors. The Pope presides there either in person, or by his legates. The general councils, when lawfully assembled, and when the bishops give their opinions with perfect liberty, are infallible in their decisions because they represent the whole church, against which Christ has promised, Matth. 16. that the gates of hell shall not prevail. The bishops there propose the faith of their respective churches : now this testimony which each bishop renders of the belief and tradition of his particular church, enables them to know, whether all the churches agree in the same dogma and in one and the same practice.

National councils are composed of the bishops of many of the principal sees of a kingdom or nation ; and provincial councils are composed of the bishops of a metropolis, of the Diocesans, and of their clergy, that is to say, of the Abbots, Deans, Canons and Curates of a diocese. The decisions and judgments of particular councils are not infallible, and may be reformed by the general councils ; yet, when they are approved of and received by the whole church, their decision becomes entirely certain, and gives the same weight to their decrees as that of the general councils : for the unanimous consent of all the churches, in a point decided by a particular council, is an incontestable proof of the tradition, and carries as much weight with it as the decision of a general council.

The council of Trent, of which mention is made above, is the last of the general councils. It was held at Trent, a city on the frontiers of Germany. It was opened in the year 1545 and continued until 1563, so that it lasted nearly eighteen years, during the Pontificate of

were, necessarily required it, has judged, nevertheless, that it will be of no small utility to the public, in the great multiplicity and diversity of errors which appear at this time touching this matter, to give a more ample definition and explanation of it, in which, after having detected and destroyed all these errors, by the assistance of the Holy Ghost, the Catholic truth may appear in all its evidence and lustre, such as the holy council here exhibits it to all Christians, to be perpetually held and observed.

CHAP. I.

OF THE NECESSITY AND INSTITUTION OF THE SACRAMENT OF PENANCE.

If all who are regenerated by baptism were so to testify their gratitude to God, as to persevere constantly in the justice they received therein through *his grace* and bounty; it would not have been necessary to have instituted any other sacrament than Baptism, for the remission of sin. But because God who is *rich in mercy*, Eph. 2. knew the frailty of our weak nature, he has been pleased also to provide a remedy, whereby those, who after Baptism should be brought again under the bondage of sin and into the power of satan, may recover life, namely, the sacrament of Penance, through which, the merits of the death of Jesus Christ are applied to such, as have fallen after Baptism.

Penance has been, in all times, necessary to all men who had sullied their consciences by mortal sin, to obtain grace and justice, even to those who desired to be cleansed by the sacrament of Baptism, whereby renouncing and correcting their evil ways they detest the offence

---

five Popes, viz. Paul III. Julius III. Marcellus II. Paul IV. Pius V. and under the reigns of Charles V. and Ferdinand, Emperors of Germany, of Francis I. Henry II. and Charles IX. kings of France. There were present at it five cardinals, legates of the holy see, three patriarchs; thirty-three arch-bishops; two hundred and thirty-five bishops; seven abbots; seven generals of religious orders; and one hundred and sixty doctors of theology. It was assembled for the purpose of shewing what the true doctrine of the Catholic church was. This council contains twenty-five sessions, and has been received and approved by the whole church.

they had committed against God, joining thereto a hatred of sin and a grief of the heart. Whence the Prophet says: Ezek. chap. 18. *Be converted and do Penance for all your iniquities: and iniquity shall not be your ruin.* And our Lord says likewise: Luke 13. *Unless you do Penance you shall all likewise perish.* And St. Peter the prince of the Apostles, recommending Penance to the sinners who were to be baptized, said to them, Acts, c. 2. *Do Penance and be baptized every one of you.* But yet Penance was not a sacrament before the coming of Jesus Christ; neither is it after his coming, for any one who has not been baptized.

Now, our Lord Jesus Christ, principally instituted the sacrament of Penance, when after his resurrection he breathed upon his disciples, saying to them: *Receive ye the Holy Ghost: whose sins you shall forgive, they are forgiven them: and whose you shall retain, they are retained,* John 20. By which remarkable action and not less expressive words, the Holy Fathers, have always unanimously understood that the power of remitting and retaining sin, had been imparted to the Apostles and to their lawful successors for the reconciliation of the faithful, fallen after baptism. Hence the Catholic Church with very great reason formerly condemned and rejected as heretics, the *Novatians, who obstinately denied this power of remitting sin. Wherefore the holy council approving and receiving this sense of these words of our Lord as the true one, condemns the imaginary interpretations of those who, in opposition to the institution of this sacrament, wrest and falsely apply these words to the power of preaching the word of God and announcing the Gospel of Jesus Christ.

---

* The Novatians, were the disciples of Novatien, a Priest of the city of Rome, who lived in the third century, with whom Novatus, a Priest of Africa joined in opposition to St. Cornelius, Pope. This opposition occassioned a temporary schism in the church. They maintained, that the church had no power to remit sin committed after baptism. St. Cyprian, St. Pacien, Bishop of Barcelona, St. Ambrose, St. Basil, were the Principal Fathers who wrote against this heresy. It was condemned in several councils held both in Italy and Africa; and finally by the general council of Nice. It was in consequence of this schism that St. Cyprian wrote his admirable work, on the Unity of the Church.

CHAP. II.

OF THE DIFFERENCE BETWEEN THE SACRAMENT OF PENANCE AND THAT OF BAPTISM.

Moreover it is evident that this sacrament differs in many respects from baptism. For besides its being very dissimilar both in the matter and form, which constitute the essence of a sacrament; it is manifest also, that it does not appertain to the minister of baptism, to act in the capacity of a judge; the church exercising no jurisdiction over a person before his entry into her bosom through baptism. *For what have I to do*, says the Apostle, *to judge them that are without?* 1 Cor. 5. It is not so with the servants of faith whom our Lord Jesus Christ has once made members of his body, by the laver of baptism: for, with regard to these, he has been pleased, should they be afterwards contaminated with any crime, not that they should be purified a second time by a repetition of baptism, as this is in no manner allowed in the Catholic church; but that they should appear as criminals before this tribunal of Penance, in order that by the sentence of the Priests they may be delivered, not once only, but as often as repenting of their sins, they should have recourse to it.

Besides, very different are the effects of baptism from those of Penance, for having put on Jesus Christ in baptism, Gal. c. 3. we become entirely a new creature in him, obtaining a full and complete remission of all our sins; but by the sacrament of Penance, we cannot arrive at this total and entire renewal but by many sighs and great labours, which the justice of God exacts from us: insomuch that it is with great reason that Penance has been styled by the holy Fathers a painful and laborious baptism. Now, this sacrament of Penance is as necessary for salvation to those fallen after baptism, as baptism is to those who have not yet been regenerated.

CHAP. III.

OF THE PARTS AND EFFECTS OF THE SACRAMENT OF PENANCE.

The holy council of Trent moreover declares, that the form of this sacrament of Penance, in which its virtue and efficacy, principally consist, is contained in these words, which the minister pronounces. *Ego te absolvo, &c. I absolve thee, &c.* to which indeed, by a laudable custom of the holy church, are joined some other prayers; but they in no manner regard the essence of the form of the sacrament, and are not necessary to its administration.

The acts of the Penitent himself, namely: Contrition, Confession and Satisfaction are, as it were, the matter of this sacrament; and these same acts, which being of divine institution, are required in the Penitent for the integrity of the sacrament, and for a full and perfect remission of the sins, are also called in this sense, the parts of Penance. But as to the ground and effect of the sacrament, in what regards its virtue and efficacy, it consists in the reconciliation with God; which is often, in pious persons, who devoutly receive this sacrament, followed by a great peace and composure of conscience, and with great consolation of the spirit.

The holy council, explaining after this manner the parts and effect of this sacrament, condemns at the same time the sentiments of those, who maintain that faith and the terrors of an affrighted conscience are the parts of Penance.

CHAP. IV.

OF CONTRITION.

Contrition which holds the first rank among the acts of the penient, of which mention has been just made, is an interior grief, and a detestation of the sin committed, with a resolution of never sinning more. This notion of contrition has been at all times necessary for the remission of sin; and to a man fallen after baptism, it serves as a preparation for the remission of sin, when joined to a confidence in the mercy of God, and to a desire of doing whatever is requisite, for the worthy receiving of this sacrament.

The holy council declares therefore, that this contrition comprises not only a cessation from sin, and a resolution and a commencement of a new life, but also a hatred of the past, according to that of Ezekiel, chap. 18. *Cast away from you all your transgressions, by which you have transgressed; and make to yourselves a new heart, and a new spirit.* And certainly whoever will consider these transports of the saints: *To thee only have I sinned, and have done evil before thee:* Psal. 50. *I have laboured in my groanings, every night I will wash my bed,* Psal. 6. *I will recount to thee all my years in the bitterness of my soul,* Isaias 38. and others of this nature; he will easily perceive that they flowed from a vehement hatred of the past life, and a great detestation of sin.

The holy council declares moreover, that although it may sometimes happen that this contrition may be perfect from charity, and reconcile man with God, before he actually receives this sacrament, this reconciliation however must not be attributed to contrition alone, independently of the desire of receiving the sacrament of Penance, which is included in it.

And with regard to that imperfect Contrition, which is called Attrition, because it springs commonly either from a sense of the turpitude of sin, or from the fear of punishment and of hell, if with the hope of pardon, it exclude the desire of sinning, the holy council declares, that not only it does not render man a hypocrite, and a greater sinner, but it is even a gift of God; and an impulse of the Holy Ghost; who indeed is not yet abiding in the penitent man, but only excites and assists him in such a manner as to prepare him for justification. And although it cannot of itself without the sacrament of Penance lead a sinner to justification, yet it disposes him to receive the grace of God in the sacrament of Penance.

For it was with a similar fear, a fear filled with terror that the Ninnivites were so usefully struck by the preaching of Jonas, when they did penance, and obtained the mercy of God. Thus, it is falsely and without foundation, that some calumniate Catholic Authors, as if they had written, that the sacrament of Penance confers grace without any good motion from the part of those receiving it, which the church of God has never believed nor taught; and they advance also another falsity, when they teach that Contrition is a constrained and violent act, and not a free and voluntary one.

CHAP. V.

OF CONFESSION.

FROM the institution of the sacrament of Penance already explained, the Catholic church has always understood that an entire confession of sins was also instituted by our Lord, and that according to the divine law, this confession is necessary for all those who fall into mortal sin after Baptism: Because our Lord Jesus Christ, before his ascension into heaven, left the Priests as his Vice-gerents, and as presidents and judges, before whom all mortal crimes, into which the faithful might fall, were to be laid open, in order that they, by virtue of the power of the Keys which was given to them to remit or to retain sins, might pronounce sentence. For it is manifest, that Priests could not exercise this jurisdiction without cognizance of the cause, nor observe that equity in imposing the penalties, if the Penitent confessed his crimes in general only, and not in particular and in detail.

Whence it follows, that all mortal sins of which penitents find themselves guilty after a diligent examine of conscience, ought to be laid open in confession, however secret they may be; and although committed only against the two last commandments of the decalogue, as these sorts of sins not unfrequently wound the soul more dangerously than those which are done in the face of the world.

As to venial sins which do not deprive us of the grace of God, and into which we fall more frequently, although it be laudable, useful and in no manner presumptuous to confess them, as the custom of truly devout and pious persons sufficiently testify, yet they may be omitted without sin, and expiated by various other remedies.

But, as all mortal sins, even those of thought, render men children of wrath and enemies of God, it is therefore necessary to seek forgiveness of all from God, by a sincere and humble confession. When therefore, the faithful desire to confess all those sins which occur to their memory, they, no doubt, expose all to the divine mercy; but those who act otherwise and knowingly retain any, present nothing to the divine bounty which can be remitted by the Priest; for if the patient be ashamed to discover his wound to his physician, his art will not heal what he is ignorant of.

It follows also that those circumstances which change the nature of the sin, are to be also explained in confession: because without this, the sins themselves are not entirely exposed by the penitent, nor sufficiently known to his judge, (confessor) to enable him to estimate justly their grieviousness, and to impose an adequate penance upon the penitent. It is therefore, wholly inconsonant to reason to teach, that these circumstances have been invented by idle men, or that it is sufficient to confess one of them only, as for example to say, I have sinned against my brother. But it is moreover impious to assert that it is impossible to make one's confession in the manner thus pointed out, or that it is a rack and a torture to the conscience; for it is evident that in the church nothing more is required of penitents, than after each one has diligently examined himself, and explored to the bottom, all the hidden recesses of his conscience, to confess those sins by which he recollects to have offended mortally his Lord and his God.

But the other sins, which do not occur to the mind after a diligent examination, are understood to be included in general, in the same Confession: And it is with regard to these, that we confidently say with the prophet: *From my secret sins cleanse me O Lord*, Ps. 18. It is true that confession from the difficulty which it offers and the shame we undergo in laying open our sins, might appear indeed a heavy yoke, were it not rendered light, by so many consolations and advantages which are undoubtedly conferred by Absolution on those who worthily approach this sacrament.

Moreover as to the manner of confessing secretly to a Priest, although Christ our Saviour has forbidden no one to confess his sins publicly, by the way of punishment for his crimes and for his own humiliation, as well as for the edification of others and of the church which he has dishonoured; yet this is not commanded by divine precept, nor would it be adviseable, to require any human law that crimes, particularly such as are hidden, should be divulged by a public confession.

As therefore private sacramental confession which has been from the beginning and is now in use in the Catholic church, has always been commended by the general and unanimous voice of all the most ancient Fathers of the church; the empty calumny of those who are not ashamed to assert that it is of human invention foreign to the command of God, and took its rise from the Fathers assembled in the council of Lateran, is manifestly refuted. For the church in this council did not at all establish the precept of confession for the faithful, because they well knew that it was by the law of God already established and necessary, but they enjoined that this precept should be observed at least once a year, by all and each one of the faithful, as soon as they had arrived to years of discretion.

It is for this reason, that this salutary custom of confession is now observed in the Catholic church with so great fruit by faithful souls, and more particularly during the holy and favourable time of Lent: which custom this holy Synod adopts and highly approves of as being replete with piety and worthy of being retained in the church.

CHAP. VI.

OF THE MINISTER OF THIS SACRAMENT, AND OF ABSOLUTION.

With regard to the minister of this sacrament, the holy Synod declares all doctrines false and repugnant to the truth of the Gospel, which by a pernicious error extend the Ministry of the Keys to all men indiscriminately, Bishops and Priests alone excepted, explaining these words of our Saviour: *Whatsoever you shall bind upon earth, it shall be bound also in Heaven: And whatsoever you shall loose upon Earth, it shall be loosed also in Heaven, Matt.* 16. *and* 19. *And whose sins you shall forgive, they are forgiven them: And whose sins you shall retain, they are retained, John,* 20. As addressed to all Christians indifferently and promiscuously, contrary to the institution of this sacrament, so that each one has power to remit public sins, by reprehension, if the person reprehended submit himself to reproof, and private ones, by a voluntary confession to any person whatsoever.

It likewise teaches that even Priests who are in mortal sin, exercise the power of remitting sin as ministers of Christ, through the virtue of the Holy Ghost received in ordination; and that the opinion of those is erroneous, who contend that this power is forfeited by wicked Priests.

But although the Absolution of the Priest be a dispensation of the benefit of another, it is not however a simple ministry, or a simple commission to announce the Gospel, or to declare that the sins are remitted; but a species of judicial act, by which the Priest as judge pronounces sentence: And hence the penitent should not flatter himself, or confide so far in his own faith, as to think, that even without contrition on his part, or without any intention on the part of the Priest to act seriously and absolve really, he will nevertheless from his faith alone, be really absolved before God; for faith without penance can produce no remission whatsoever of sins: Nor can a person be otherwise than deemed extremely negligent of his salvation, who perceiving that a Priest absolves him in joke only, does not anxiously seek another, to discharge that duty seriously.

CHAP. VII.

[As this chapter treats wholly of reserved cases, it's insertion is deemed unnecessary.]

CHAP. VIII.

OF THE NECESSITY AND ADVANTAGES OF SATISFACTION.

FINALLY, with regard to satisfaction, which of all the parts of penance has been in all ages the most earnestly recommended to Christians by the holy Fathers: and which nevertheless under a specious pretext of piety is the most combatted in our days, by men who carry with them indeed the appearance of piety, but who have totally extinguished its virtue: This holy Synod declares, that it is every way false and repugnant to the word of God, to say that no fault has ever been remitted by our Lord without the whole penalty being likewise remitted; for independently of divine tradition, remarkable and illustrious examples may be found in the sacred writings, by which this error is manifestly refuted.

Moreover the course of divine justice seems also to require, that those who before Baptism have sinned through ignorance, should be received into favour differently from those, who having been once delivered from sin and the slavery of the devil, and received the gift of the Holy Ghost have not apprehended to profane deliberately *the temple of God*, 1. Cor. 3. *and to contristate the Holy Ghost*, Ephes. 4. And it is in every respect consistent with the divine clemency, not to forgive us our sins without some satisfaction, lest we might take occasion therefrom to consider them of less moment, and by an ungrateful and injurious conduct towards the holy spirit, fall into crimes more enormous, *treasuring to ourselves wrath against the day of wrath*,

Rom. 2. 5. For it is certain that these punishments imposed as a satisfaction for sin, render penitents more cautious and vigilant in future, withdraw them in a special manner from sin, and keep them within bounds, so as to destroy, by the practice of contrary virtues, those sinful habits contracted by a disorderly life.

It is moreover certain that there has never been considered in the church of God, a more salutary and effectual way of averting those chastisements with which God continually threatens the sinner, than that of having frequent recourse to these works of penance, with sincere and heartfelt sorrow. Add to this, that whilst by satisfaction we suffer for our sins, we become conformable to Jesus Christ, who has satisfied for our sins, having from thence a certain pledge, that if we partake in his sufferings we shall likewise partake in his glory.

But this satisfaction by which we atone for our sins, is not so much ours, as that it is not effected through Jesus Christ. For who of us can do any thing, of ourselves but with the assistance of him who strengthens us, we can do all things. Thus, man has nothing in which he can glory, but all our glory is in Christ, in whom we live, in whom we merit, in whom we satisfy, bringing forth worthy fruits of penance, which derive their force and efficacy from him, are offered to the Father by him, and through him are received and accepted by the Father.

The Priests of the Lord ought therefore, as far as the Holy Ghost and their own prudence shall suggest, to enjoin a salutary and proportionate satisfaction, suitable to the quality of the crime and the circumstances, state and condition of the penitent; lest it should happen that by conniving at the sins of, and acting too indulgently with penitents, by enjoining a slight satisfaction for the greatest crimes, they themselves become partakers of the sins of others. They should always reflect that the satisfaction which they impose, is not only a preservative in their new state of life, and a remedy for their infirmities, but likewise a retribution and a punishment for their past sins.

For the ancient Fathers of the church always believed and taught that the keys were given to Priests, for the purpose of binding as well as loosing, nor did they think that the sacrament of penance was a tribunal of wrath, or of torments, which no Catholic ever thought, or that by our satisfactions, the virtue and efficacy of the merit and satisfaction of our Saviour Jesus Christ, was in the least weakened or diminished. But whilst innovators did not wish to understand this, they taught, that a change of life was the best penance, that they might thus destroy the entire efficacy and practice of satisfaction.

CHAP. IX.

OF WORKS OF SATISFACTION.

THE holy council teaches moreover, that so great is the bounty and liberality of God, that we can satisfy God the Father through Jesus Christ not only by the punishments we voluntarily embrace, as a chastisement for our sins, or which are enjoined us by our confessor according to the measure of our fault; but also as the last pledge of his love, by suffering with patience the temporal afflictions, he is pleased to send us in this world.

SECTION III.

HAVING for the information of the public, fully shown what the real tenets of the Catholic church are, concerning the sacrament of penance, as they are explicitly laid down in the above mentioned session of the council of Trent, and held throughout the whole Catholic world, I shall now proceed, for a further elucidation of this interesting matter, to exhibit the principal grounds upon which the doctrine of sacramental confession is founded, and the testimonies by which it is supported. I shall *first* produce the passages of the Gospel proving it to be divinely instituted; *secondly*, shew how the holy Fathers, who certainly ought to be acknowledged the best interpretors of the sense of the scripture, have understood these passages; *thirdly*, how the councils, as well general, as particular, have always understood them; *fourthly*, what the universal practice of the church is, and has been in all ages, from the times of the Apostles down to our present time; and, finally, the opinions and belief of many of the Reformers themselves touching this all important matter.

CHAP I.

THE OBLIGATION OF CONFESSION PROVED FROM THE GOSPEL.

THE holy council of Trent in the fifth chapter of the 14th session, declares the confession of all mortal sins to the Priests of the church, the lawful successors of the Apostles, to be* necessary, by the divine law, to all who fall after Baptism.

To proceed with method, I shall condense the whole force of the divine testimonies in favour of the above doctrine into the following syllogistic form:

MAJOR. *All who have fallen into mortal sin, are bound by the divine law to do penance, and to seek a reconciliation with God:*

MINOR. *But the necessary means to a reconciliation with God after Baptism is the confession of all mortal sins to a Priest:*

CONCLUSION. *Therefore, all who have fallen into mortal sin after Baptism, are bound by the divine law, to confess all mortal sins to a Priest.*

Proof. The Major proposition viz: *All who have fallen into mortal sin are bound by the divine law to do penance, and to seek a reconciliation with God:* is proved from these and innumerable other texts of the divine Scripture: *Do penance*, Mat. 3. 2. *Unless you do penance, you shall all likewise perish*, Luke 13. 3. *Be converted and do penance for all your iniquities: and iniquity shall not be your ruin*, Ezek. 18. 30. As this proposition is denied by no one; I shall proceed immediately to the proof of the *Minor*, couched in these words: *But the necessary means to a reconciliation after Baptism, is the confession of all mortal sins to a Priest.* This is the great point in question; to prove which, I shall again reduce my argument into a syllogistic form, viz:

MAJOR. *Christ has instituted the Apostles and their lawful successors, the Priests of his church, to be judges upon earth, invested with a*

* The sense of the council is: that confession is necessary to all *generally;* for where confession is impossible, as for example, where a Priest cannot be had, contrition with a desire of confession, suffices to salvation, as the council expressly says in the fourth chap. of the same session.

power, that, without their sentence, no sinner fallen after Baptism can be reconciled:

Minor. *But the Priests of his church cannot form a right judgment, unless they know the sins:*

Conclusion. *Therefore all who have fallen after Baptism are bound by the divine law to reveal their sins to the Priests of his church:— And hence the confession of sins is a necessary means to effect the reconciliation of those who have fallen after Baptism.*

The Major proposition alone in the above syllogism is to be proved, viz: that *Christ has instituted the Apostles and their lawful successors the Priests of his church, to be judges upon earth, that, without their sentence no sinner fallen after Baptism can be reconciled;* for the *Minor* is so evident in itself, that no one, I believe, will ever pretend to deny it: for, without a cognizance of the cause, it is impossible for any judgment to be formed, even in thought. Let it be supposed for example, that a private individual should present himself before a civil court, requesting a decision of his case and desiring to be informed of the penalty, if any, attached to his transgression. What answer think you, would the judge naturally make him? He would tell him: "My good friend, I should be glad to know first what your case is; what law have you infringed? What has been your transgression? How often, &c. Otherwise how shall I be able to determine any thing about you?"—The whole difficulty therefore rests in the major proposition, which having proved from the Gospel, viz. that the Apostles and their lawful successors, the Priests of the church, have been constituted judges by Jesus Christ in the causes of Penitents, I shall at once have proved, that the confession of sins made according to their respective species to a Priest, is indispensably necessary by the divine law.

There are three principal passages in the gospel from which this judicial power is most clearly demonstrated.

I. First, where Christ thus addresses St. Peter, Math. 16. 18. *Thou art Peter, and upon this rock I will build my church.........and I will give to thee the Keys of the kingdom of heaven: and whatsoever thou shalt bind upon earth, it shall be bound also in heaven: and whatsoever thou shalt loose upon earth, it shall be loosed also in heaven.*

II. Secondly, where he makes the same promise and in the same terms afterwards to his other Apostles, Math. 18. 18. *Amen I say to you, whatsoever you shall bind upon earth, shall be bound also in heaven: and whatsoever you shall loose upon earth, shall be loosed also in heaven.*

III. Thirdly, where he finally accomplishes his promise and explains to them in the clearest manner, the sense of his former promise, and the nature of the power he had promised, John 20. 21.

As the Father hath sent me, I also send you. When he had said this, he breathed on them: and he said to them: Receive ye the Holy Ghost: Whose sins you shall forgive, they are forgiven them: and whose you shall retain, they are retained.

The first passage cited above contains a promise made to Peter alone: But neither Catholics nor Protestants doubt of St. Peter's having received the keys, not only to use them himself, but also to communicate the same to other Priests.

The second passage contains a promise made to all the Apostles or a certain prediction of that power which the Apostles and their lawful successors were afterwards to receive. And as the eternal truth cannot deceive, nor utter a falsehood, although we should not read any where this promise realized, we could never entertain the least doubt of their having received this power.

The third passage contains the final accomplishment of the promise, the very concession of the power itself, and the complete establishment of the whole sacrament.

But as the adversaries of the Catholic Church do not deny this power of loosing and of binding; or of forgiving and retaining sin, to have been indeed promised and given to the church in these passages; but attempt to interpret this power as applying only to the ministry of preaching and announcing to penitents the remission of their sins, and to impenitents the anger of God and eternal damnation, it is incumbent on us to shew that the true power of absolving and of retaining sin with authority, is derived most evidently from these texts, and that by virtue of this power, are in reality constituted judges in the causes of sinners, in the room of Christ.

I. This is first manifest from the very metaphor of the *keys*, of which mention is made in the above text: *I will give to thee the keys of the kingdom of heaven, &c.* For in the first place, it is not customary for keys to be given to signify merely, that, the door is shut or open; but to open and to shut it in reality.—Again, do we not see, even among men, keys given to magistrates as a mark of their power? and in the ordination of the porter or door-keeper, one of the minor orders of the clergy, the keys of the material church are given him, not that the door-keeper should declare whether the door of the church be shut or open, but to shut and to open it in reality. Lastly, when it is said in the Apocalypse, (chap. 3.) of Christ: *Who hath the key of David: he that openeth, and no man shutteth; shutteth and no man openeth;* all agree that the word *key* implies a true and real power, by which Christ can both absolve and bind with judicial authority, and not merely intimate and declare who is bound and who loosed.

Wherefore, when Christ gave the keys to his apostles and their lawful successors, he imparted to them a true power, to bind and to loose, with judicial authority. And as no one can enter a house when shut, unless he who is charged with the keys open the door, so also neither can any one enter heaven, shut against him by reason of his crimes, unless it be opened through the ministry of the priests, the lawful successors of the apostles, who alone have the keys. For if there should be any other way to it, the apostles would have received the keys, evidently, to no purpose. For what necessity would there be for keys, when, without keys, and even in spite of the door-keeper, access could be had? *Let no one say*, says St. Austin in his 49th Homily, *I do penance privately with God who knows my sins: for then in vain was it said: whose sins you shall forgive, they are forgiven them. Were then the keys given in vain to the church of God? We frustrate the gospel, we frustrate the words of Christ.*

Nor does it in the least weaken the force of the above argument to say, that in baptism even they who have not the keys can open to man a way into heaven, as in the case of infants baptized by laymen in a case of necessity, and who die shortly after. For the power of the keys is a judicial power, and therefore is properly exercised towards those only, who are already in the church by baptism. For what have I to do to judge them that are without, says St. Paul in his first epistle to the Corinthians, 5th chap. Therefore, by baptism men are admitted into the church, and are subject to the power and judgment of the priests: but, if afterwards they fall into mortal sin, they can in no manner be reconciled (the case of impossibility, as mentioned above in a note, being excepted) without the benefit of the keys.

II. It is proved in the second place from the metaphor of binding and of loosing: for *to bind* and *to loose*, certainly does not signify to announce or to declare, but actually to confine with bonds and to liberate from them, and especially in the above texts of St. Matthew, chap. 16 and 18, otherwise our divine Saviour would not have said: *whatsoever thou shalt loose, shall be loosed*, or, *whatsoever you shall loose, shall be loosed;* but rather, *whatsoever thou shalt loose, was loosed*, and *whatsoever you shall loose*, was *loosed.*

But some may say, this is true: priests have the power to bind and to loose, but it does not follow, that it is necessary to appear before their tribunal: for Jesus Christ does not say: and whatsoever you shall not loose, shall not be loosed. Wherefore, they have indeed the power to loose, should any one be inclined to make use of their ministry: but a sinner can be also reconciled in another manner independently of their ministry. As in the case where public judges are constituted with judicial authority; they are empowered, it is true, to judge all who shall recur to them; yet those who have cause are not compelled to appear before them, they may choose their own arbitrators, or may even settle their differences by themselves.

But this objection is easily answered. For although private individuals are able to adjust the differences they may have among themselves, without the decision and interference of public judges constituted for that purpose, it does not follow, however, that they are able to adjust those which they may have, for example, with a king or the first magistrate of a country as such, unless they present themselves before him whom the king or first magistrate shall have delegated as judge in his place. Now, all sins are causes which we have with God himself, and consequently as God has entrusted the judgment of sin to the priests of his church, those who are members of the church cannot, if they have such causes, obtain a reconciliation with God without the judgment of the priests. Wherefore, although this negation: Whatsoever you shall not loose, shall not be loosed, be not expressed in this passage of the gospel, yet it manifestly flows as well from the above affirmation, *Whatsoever you shall loose, shall be loosed*, by which priests are constituted the future judges in all causes against God, as also from that: *whatsoever you shall bind, shall be bound;* for, to bind is not only to add a new bond, as for instance, that of excommunication, but also, is to confirm and retain the bonds of sin, as is explained in another passage of the gospel, and in short to be unwilling to loose. Because, should the guilty be able to obtain the absolution of their sins, without the sentence of the priests, the promise of Christ, *whatsoever you shall bind shall be bound*, &c. would certainly not be true.

III. The third and principal passage upon which the belief of the Catholic church respecting the divine institution and absolute necessity of confession is grounded, is found in the 20th chapter of St.

John, where Christ after his resurrection thus addresses his disciples, v. 21, 22. *As the Father hath sent me, I also send you. When he had said this, he breathed on them, and he said to them: Receive ye the Holy Ghost: whose sins you shall forgive, they are forgiven them, and whose you shall retain, they are retained. By which remarkable action and not less expressive words*, says the Council of Trent, in the 1st chap. 14th session, *the holy fathers have always unanimously understood, that the power of remitting and of retaining sin was imparted to the apostles and their lawful successors for the reconciliation of the faithful, fallen after baptism.* And indeed, either the words of Christ just quoted mean nothing at all; (which, it would be impious even to think,) or, they manifestly mean, that Christ did grant thereby to his apostles and their lawful successors, the power not only to forgive, but also to retain sins. This being once supposed, which cannot be denied, the Catholic divine in support of the necessity and divine institution of confession, forms this unanswerable argument: Christ in the above passage has constituted the apostles and their lawful successors judges between God and the sinner, and accordingly has invested them with the power not only to forgive, but also to retain sins: but unless confession be of divine institution and of absolute necessity for the sinner's reconciliation, the use and exercise of this power would be altogether nugatory and useless, nay, even utterly impossible, which cannot be asserted without blasphemy: therefore, confession is of divine institution and of absolute necessity for the sinner's reconciliation. The major proposition being made up of the words of Christ wants neither explanation nor proof. The minor is equally certain; for it is not less clear than evident, that if confession be not of divine institution and of absolute necessity for the reconciliation of the sinner, that is, if there be other ordinary means to obtain the remission of sins committed after baptism, different from confession, the use and exercise of the power of forgiving and retaining sins would be rendered thereby wholly useless and nugatory. For who is there, if he knew of any easier mode of reconciliation than that of confession; that would not prefer it? Who is there that would be so fascinated by the charms of humiliation and self-denial, as to submit, in opposition to his most darling passions of pride and self-love, to the mortifying law of auricular confession? For the correctness of this reasoning, I appeal to the reader's own good sense. But supposing even that some sinners should be found pepetrated with so vehement a sorrow and contrition as to recur to the Priests for their greater humiliation, even yet, the use and exercise of the power granted them would be impossible without confession. For, as they have received the power not only to forgive but also to retain sins, a power which conformably to the intention of Christ, they are to exercise not at random, but prudently and with discretion, it must be a part of their office as judges, to discern what sins they are to bind, and what to loose, what sins to retain, and what to forgive. Now, how are they to form a just judgment, how can they make a just discernment, how can they distinguish amongst a crowd of supplicants the penitents to be absolved, from the penitents to be excluded, if they know not the sins which have been committed? And how are they to know the sins, if the penitents themselves do not declare them? How could a civil or criminal judge, ever be able to decide and determine, agreeably to the invariable rules of justice and equity, the degree of punishment proportionable to the number, quality and aggravating circumstances of the culprit's crimes, unless he be made acquainted with them? As little would it be possible for the apostles and their successors to enjoin a penance proportionate to the guilt of the sinner, without knowing the degree of this guilt. The absolute and indispensable necessity of confession, therefore, flows naturally from the above words of Christ. It is essentially connected with the power granted thereby not only to forgive, but also to retain sins, a power, the exercise of which, without sacramental confession, would manifestly be vain and useless, nay even impossible.

But it may be objected, that although Christ gave power to his Apostles to bind and to loose, to forgive and to retain sins, it does not follow that their successors have that power.

This objection is so futile in itself, that I should have deemed it unworthy of notice, had I not been assured of its being frequently urged to prop a bad argument.—The power of binding and loosing was certainly given to be exercised till the end of the world, no less than the commission of preaching, baptizing, &c. which, though addressed to the Apostles, was certainly designed to continue with their successors, the Pastors of the church, for ever according to that of Christ, Matt. 28. 20. *Behold I am with you all days, even to the consummation of the world.*

But it will be farther objected, that from the doctrine contended for above, this monstrous absurdity would follow viz. that man can forgive sins, which is a prerogative belonging *only* to God.

To this I answer, that the Jewish scribes and Pharisees were formerly under a similar impression, but they were severely reprehended for it, and put to confusion by our Saviour Christ; for when our Saviour (as we read in St. Matthew and St. Mark,) had told a man who was sick of the palsy, that his sins were forgiven him, some of the scribes and Pharisees who were there present, concluded immediately, in their hearts, that this was blasphemy, *this man*, say they, *blasphemeth*, for *who can forgive sins except God alone?* But our blessed Redeemer, who came on purpose into the world for the remission of our sins, was instantly sensible of this wrong notion of the Jews, and therefore before they could even express their thoughts, he said to them, *Why do you think evil in your hearts?* For, *that you may see that the son of man hath power on earth to forgive sins*, he turns to the sick man saying, *Arise, take up thy bed, and go into thy house.*

The Jews were here under two mistakes: In the first place, they thought our Saviour was not God; and in the second place, they thought that being man, he could not forgive sins; therefore, our Saviour Christ, for our instruction concerning the remission of sin, was pleased on this occasion to pass by (in some degree) the first mistake, and more expressly to confute the second; on which account it ought to be noticed, that he does not say, that you may see that I am God, or that you may see that in quality of *God*, I can forgive sins; but to let you see that in quality of *man* upon earth, I have power to forgive sins.

It might be said that our Saviour would have used (against the Scribes and Pharisees to prove himself God from their own principles) some such argument as this; you grant, that he who forgives sins is God; now by this miracle which I have wrought, I shew you that I can forgive sins; consequently, according to your own principles, it follows that I am God. But our blessed Redeemer did not openly make use of this argument; for although tacitly and in fact, especially in discovering to the Jews their own thoughts, he gave them sufficiently to understand that he was God, the searcher of hearts: yet in the curing of the man sick of the palsy, what he more expressly made appear was, that even in quality of *man*, he had power to forgive sins; this being the intention of the miraculous cure, *that you may know*, says he, that (not only the Son of God, but also) *the son of Man has power even upon earth to forgive sins, arise* sick man, *take up thy bed and go into thy house.* Upon this, as it is related in the chapters above cited, all the people were astonished and seized with fear, and all *glorified God*, not because God himself had such power which they knew before, but because *he had given such power even to men.*

Now as from the *divinity* of our Saviour down to his *humanity* is derived and descends an unlimited power of remitting sin, so from our Saviour, who is our head, down to the ministers of his church who are his members, is also derived and descends a power of remitting all sins, of what kind soever they be, not indeed in their name, or by their own authority, but in the name and by the authority of God. *As the Father hath sent me, so I send you.* John 20, 21. He hath sent me to save the world; you shall also become in some sort its Saviours. He has sent me to destroy sin, to sanctify sinners, to reconcile men with him. Go, complete this great work, and to this effect, *receive ye the Holy Ghost, whose sins you shall forgive, they are forgiven them, and whose sins you shall retain they are retained.* John 20.

There is no absurdity therefore in saying, that man can forgive sins when empowered by God so to do. It would indeed be not only absurd but blasphemous to say, that he can forgive sins by his own power, as no man by his own power can raise the dead to life; because both the one and the other equally belong to the power of God. But as God has sometimes made men his instruments in raising the dead to life; so the Catholic believes that he has been pleased to appoint, that his ministers should in virtue of his commission, as his instruments and by his power absolve repenting sinners; and as this is evident from the texts cited above, it cannot be but false zeal, under pretext of maintaining the honour of God, to contradict this commission which he has so evidently given to his apostles and their lawful successors.

The same doctrine is proved from the Fathers of the church, who unanimously expound the above cited passage of the scripture to signify, that the Priests are actually constituted judges by Christ and invested with the power truly to forgive sins, and not to declare them simply, to be forgiven. I shall forbear, (to avoid repitition) giving their testimony in this place as I intend to arrange it afterwards in different chapters according to the different centuries in which they lived.

The same is also proved by various reasons.—In the first place, if Priests be not indeed judges and have no power truly to remit sins, but simply to declare them to be remitted, it is certain, that no one would be lost from this cause alone, viz: that they could not procure a Priest to reconcile them. But St. Austin in his 180th epist. to Honoratus explicitly writes, that some desiring to be reconciled, and of course believing in Christ, were eternally lost, because (having neglected the opportunity when it presented itself) they died before they could be absolved by the Priest. *Do we never reflect, says he, when danger is extreme and when there is no possibility of escaping it, how great a concourse is usually in the church, of both sexes, and of every age; some demanding Baptism, some to be reconciled, some again the very action of penance itself, and all the consolation and completion of the sacraments and their distribution? When, should the ministers be absent, how great is the misfortune that attends those who depart this life, either without having been regenerated* (baptized) *or without having been loosed?* (without having their sins remitted them.) *How great also is the lamentation of the faithful, their relatives, who will never have them with them in the enjoyment of eternal life?* Thus far St. Austin. Nor does St. Leo write differently in his 91st epist. to Theodorus. From which places we may gather, that sacramental reconciliation, has the virtue to justify, and that it is not a simple declaration only of justification either already received, or about to be received.

In the second place, if Priests do not remit sins in any other manner than by declaring the divine promises; it would be certainly equally vain and ridiculous to absolve the deaf and those deprived by sickness of the use of their senses. *Where there is no hearing*, says the wise man in Ecclesiasticus, chap. 32. 6. *pour not out words.* But in the primitive church, not only the deaf, but also those who by violence of sickness were bereft of reason, were sometimes reconciled, as is manifest from St. Austin, lib. 1. de adulterinis conjugiis capit. ult, and from St. Leo, in his epist. cited above to Theodorus, and from the 4th council of Carthage, can. 76, and the Arausican council, can. 12.

In the third place, if absolution were merely a declaration of the remission of sins, either it would be rash, or it would be superfluous. For when the minister says, *thy sins are forgiven thee*, he pronounces this, either absolutely, or hypothetically, that is, provided he believe and repent as he ought. If absolutely; he pronounces it rashly, as he knows not whether he who solicits to be reconciled, be truly penitent and have faith, such as is requisite for justification, and besides although the minister may in some degree know this, yet the penitent knows it better and consequently does not stand in need of that declaration of the minister, which can add nothing to his certitude. But if the absolution be conditional, (as Calvin teaches) such an absolution can never render a penitent secure and certain, as it depends upon an uncertain condition, and yet our adversaries rarely admit any other end in the absolution, than to render the individual certain of his justification.

In the fourth place, if the absolution be not a judicial act, but a simple enunciation of the divine promise, which stands recorded in the gospel, any individual, a layman, nay even a woman, a child or an infidel, will be able to absolve no less than the Priest: and although our adversaries admit this, because it flows evidently from their principles, yet it is contrary to the consent of all the Fathers, contrary to the practice of every church, of every age, and even of sound reason.

Before I conclude this chapter, I must bring in confirmation of the above truth, one more proof drawn from the figures which have preceded sacramental confession; from which a two-fold argument may be formed. In the first place, if the confession which God exacted in the old law was a mere figure, as indeed it was; as *all these things happened to them in figure*, as St. Paul tells us in his first epist. to the Corinth, chap. 10, it is certainly necessary, that in the new law, there should be a confession of sins commanded by God, and a confession as much more perfect and exact as the thing figured is above the figure. And in the second place, if confession made before a minister of God was deemed necessary at that time, when no power was given to the Priests to remit sin; who is there that will not infer that it was far more necessary that confession should be enjoined in the new law, when we can confess with so much benefit as to obtain a certain and speedy absolution of our sins, by a worthy confession?

The first figure therefore is found in the 3d and 4th chap. of Genesis, where God first exacted from Adam and Eve, and afterwards from Cain the confession of his sin. In these places confession is exacted, not of the heart only, but also of the mouth, not in general only, but also in particular, not to God only, but also to his minister: for the interrogation was made by an angel appearing in human shape, as appears from *his walking in paradise at the afternoon air*, Genesis, 3. 8. From which there appears so great a similarity between that confession and the confession which is now made to a *Priest*, who is also *an angel of the Lord,* according to Malachy, chap. 2. 7. that the one may be said with reason to be the figure of the other. Wherefore, this figure is beautifully treated by Tertullian in his second book against Marcion, also by St. Ambrose, in lib. de paradiso, cap. 14. and lib. 2. de Cain and Abel, cap. 9. also by St. Greg. lib. 22. Moralium, cap. 13. and also by St. John Chrysostom, homil. 18. in Gen. who all expound these places as having a bearing upon confession and say, that God wished to extort a confession from them, that they might wipe away by confession what they had committed by transgressing.

The second figure may be found in the 13th and 14th chap. of Leviticus, where the judgment of the leprosy is committed solely to the Priests, and the lepers were obliged to shew and present themselves to the Priests, and according to their determination either to remain out of the camp, or after their cure, to return to the same: which law our Lord also approved in Matt. chap. 8. when he said to the leper who had been healed by him: *Go shew thyself to the Priest, &c.*—That this was a figure of sacramental confession, St. Chrysostom lib. 3. de Sacerdotio, and St. Jerom in cap. 16. Matthæi, equally testify. For from this St. Jerom infers, that the Priests ought to know the different species of the sins; and St. Chrysostom shews, that the office of Christian Priests is far more excellent, than was formerly that of the Jews, as they had the power not to heal the leprosy, but to declare it healed: whereas ours have power not to declare the sins healed (that is, remitted;) but to heal (to remit) them in effect.

The third figure is the confession which God instituted in the old law, and in addition to which he exacted as a satisfaction, the oblation of a sacrifice; of which we have a proof in Numb. chap. 5. and also in Levitic. chap. 5. For unquestionably, if figurative confession was instituted by God and necessary by the divine law, how much more ought the confession prefigured to be esteemed instituted by God, and necessary by the divine law? The words of the scripture in the book of Numbers, chap. 5. are these, *and the Lord spoke to Moses saying: say to the children of Israel: when a man or woman shall have committed any of all the sins, that men are wont to commit, and by negligence shall have transgressed the commandment of the Lord and offended, they shall confess their sin.* Here two things are to be observed: first, that the Hebrew word correspondent to the term *confess* is in the conjugation of *hitpael,* which augments its signification; so that it may correctly be interpreted: they shall expressly and distinctly confess. Secondly, these words: *they shall confess their sin,* are more clear and explicit in the Hebrew: for thus we there read; *they shall confess their sin which they have done.* From which we infer, that in this place, an open confession of every sin according to their different species was commanded; for if it was sufficient to confess them in general only, the scripture would not say, *they shall openly confess their sin which they have done,* but simply, they shall confess their sins.

In Leviticus, chap. 5, where our version has: *Let him do penance for his sin;* in the Hebrew we find the same expression as in the book of Numbers; for thus we there read: *And it shall be, when he shall sin in any one of these* things, *that he shall openly confess the sin which he hath sinned.*

Moreover, the testimonies of the Rabins, and the practice of the nation sufficiently shew, that this precept is to be understood of distinct confession, and according to the species of the sin, for the expiation of which, sacrifice was to be offered. Respecting the practice of the Hebrews, Thomas Walden in his second tome on the sacraments, chap. 137, writes, that he was informed in Austria of this their custom, by the Jews themselves: and St. Antoninus in the third part of his sum. Theologic, tit 14, chap, 6, § 1, says, that the more learned among the Jews were always careful, before their death, to confess all their sins to some Levite, if perchance one could be had. For the testimonies of the Rabins, see Peter Galatinus, lib. 10 chap. 3. who proves from many testimonies of the Rabins, that they conceived it to be necessary in confession to make a full declaration of their sins, according to their different species and circumstances.

Add to this, that it is more than probable, that the book of Ecclesiasticus in the 4th chap. exhorts to the observance of this legal precept, when it says: *Be not ashamed to confess thy sins:* for there is, generally speaking, very little shame attending a confession made to God alone, or which is made in general terms only to men; but the reverse is but too often the case in a confession made to men, according to the different species of the sin, as experience sufficiently proves.

The fourth figure is found in St. Matthew, chap. 3, and St. Mark, chap. 1, where we read, that many went out to John (the baptist,) and were baptized by him *confessing their sins:* for as the baptism of John was a figure of the baptism of Christ, so also was the confession which was made to John a figure of the confession, which was to be made to the ministers of Christ. Here it must be also remarked, that those who went out to John, did not declare themselves in general terms, to be sinners, for this would not, in any manner, be conformable to the words of the Evangelists; but they most evidently made an open and thorough confession of all their sins according to their different species; for both Evangelists expressly say, that they went out *confessing their sins, confitentes peccata sua*, or as the Greek has it, *ἐξομολογούμενοί τὰς αμαρτίας αυτῶν*. Now, it is certainly one thing to confess one's sins to a person, and another, to confess or acknowledge one's-self in general terms to be a sinner.

From which passages therefore, it is manifest, that confession was more than once enjoined even in the law of nature—that it was afterwards more clearly instituted and ordained by God in the old law—that it was always considered by the Jews themselves to be of divine institution, and consequently obligatory upon them, and finally, that it was every where practised among them. Which then being the case, how strongly may we infer, that confession in the ne law is equally of divine institution and no less obligatory, when it i. the thing figured, as the holy Fathers unanimously declare? I s all forbear producing other figures, confirmatory of the same, such as the resurrection of Lazarus, of which St. Ireneus (lib. 5. c. 13.) says; that *this was the symbol of a man who had been fettered by the chains of his sins, and therefore our Lord said,* (to his apostles, as St. Austin tract. 49. in Joan. and St. Gregory, homil. 26. in Evangel. testify) *loose him and let him go,* John 11, in order to proceed to shew the practice of confession in the days of the apostles, and how the texts, *Whatsoever you shall bind on earth shall be bound also in heaven, &c. and whose sins you shall forgive, &c.* were understood in the primitive church.

CHAP. II.

THE SAME TRUTH IS CONFIRMED BY OTHER PASSAGES OF THE NEW TESTAMENT.

In the preceding chapter we have shown that confession is of divine institution: we shall now prove from the most undeniable testimony, that the apostles and first disciples were impressed with this belief, and acted accordingly.

The first remarkable passage which presents itself, is found in the Acts of the Apostles chap. 19, where we read these words: *And many of those who believed, came confessing and declaring their deeds: and many of those who had followed curious things, brought their books together and burnt them before all.*

This text, in the first place, is to be understood of the confession of the faithful after baptism; for, they only are properly called believers, as is evident from the 2d. chap. of the Acts, v. 41. and 44; and also, 1st Epist. Thess. 1, and many other places: nor is this denied by our adversaries. In the second place, the scripture unquestionably speaks here of the confession of sins according to their different species, as appears from these words: *confessing and declaring their deeds:* And lastly, of a confession made not to God alone, but also to men: for they came to St. Paul, in order to confess their acts. And because there was at that time no law or constitution of the church commanding the confession of sins, it necessarily follows, that this confession must have been ordained and instituted by Christ.

Luther in his version declares, that the word *deeds* in the above passage signifies *miracles*, and is joined in this opinion by John Brentius in his commentary on this passage.

But this exposition is not only rejected by the unanimous consent of all catholics, and especially by venerable Bede, in chap. 1. of Mark; but by far the greater part of the Reformers themselves, as Melancthon, Calvin, Beza, Bullinger, Sarcer, upon the Acts of the Apostles, Illyricus Centur. 1. Book 2. c. 4. col. 347. and Kemnitius in the 2d part of his Exam. page 987. See also the Polyglott of Walton. Besides it is unheard of, that *miracles* should be termed *our deeds*, when they are certainly works purely divine; and still more absurb to pretend, that the words *confessing their deeds*, signify proclaiming, or boasting of the miracles which they had wrought. We may also add, that the occasion of this confession, as St. Luke testifies in the same chapter, was a great fear which had fallen upon them, in consequence of the signal punishment which God had inflicted upon those, who had abused of the name of Jesus. Now the terrors of divine justice do not generally incite persons to proclaim their own praises, but rather to acknowledge and to confess their sins. In short, the Syriac edition, instead of *deeds*, has the word *offences*, which certainly does not imply *miracles*.

Kemnitius in his book cited above, attempts to give two solutions to our argument; viz. 1st. That the scripture in this place speaks only of general confession, wherein the Ephesians acknowledged that their deeds were not according to the law of God. 2d. That they might have confessed some sins in particular, by way of example, but not all.—But this solution is most easily refuted. For, in the first place, the words *their deeds* evidently indicate, that the confession was here made of all sins, according to their different species: for no one can be properly said, to confess his *deeds*, who simply avows himself in general terms, to be a sinner. Besides, the word *declare*, or the Greek word ἐναγγέλλω, which St. Luke here makes use of, signifies, to relate something distinctly, and in the Syriac edition, we find a word, which signifies the same as the Hebrew, *Saphar;* and may be properly translated, *numbering their sins,* which certainly imports a detailed confession. In a word, how else did St. Paul know that they had followed curious things, so as to order their books to be burnt, unless they had previously confessed their sins in detail?

The other solution, which is the same as that given by Calvin, in his Comm. Act. and Magdeburgensium Centur. 1. lib. 2. chap. 4. col. 360, is manifestly repugnant to the whole scripture. For whenever the scripture speaks of sin in general, it is, and must be understood of all sins; and should it be understood of some only, and not of all, the most absurd and ridiculous sentences might be found in holy writ. Thus for example: Daniel iv. 24. *Redeem thou thy sins with alms.* Math. 1. *He shall save his people from their sins.* Math. 9. *Son, be of good heart; thy sins are forgiven thee.* Luke 11. *Forgive us our sins.* John 1. *Behold who taketh away the sins of the world.* Acts 24. *That they may receive forgiveness of sins,* &c. In these and innumerable other places, the scripture speaks of sins in general terms only, yet it is manifest, that it intends and includes all sins; and although each one in particular be not expressed, they are nevertheless evidently understood; and no one will ever doubt, but that *Redeem thy sins with alms; He shall save his people from their sins; Son be of good heart, thy sins are forgiven thee,* &c. &c. means one and the same thing with, *Redeem* all *thy sins with alms; He shall save his people from* all *their sins;* Son be of good heart; all *thy sins* without exception, *are forgiven thee,* and so of the rest. Wherefore, according to the manner of speaking of the scripture, *to confess and to declare their deeds,* or sins, can mean nothing else, than to discover and to reveal all their sins.

Besides this solution, which we have briefly refuted, Calvin has thought proper to propose a few antitheses in his commentary upon the Acts, between the confession of these Ephesians, and the confession, as it is now in use, of the catholics, in order to make it appear, that the above cited text, does not in the least favour us: *We read,* says he, *that these confessed but once; but the Papal law commands us to confess at least once every year. These went forward of their own accord: but the Pope imposes it as a duty upon all. Luke says, that many came, not all; but under the Papal law there is no exception. These humbled themselves before the assembly of the faithful: but the Pope has issued a very different command, viz. that by secret whisperings, the sinner shall auricularly reveal his sins to his Priest. See how dexterously they accommodate the scriptures to prove their fallacies.* Thus Calvin,

But such light and puerile calumnies scarcely deserve refutation. For, although we read but once of the Ephesians having confessed, it does not however follow, that they did not do it oftener: otherwise it might be concluded these same Ephesians, because we read no where of their having received either baptism or the Eucharist, according to Calvin's logic, had never received either baptism or the Eucharist.

As to their having gone, of their own accord, to make their confession, this ought not in the least to surprize us, as well because there was no law at that time compelling any one to confess within a given time, as because, even in our days, many go spontaneously to confession, not only at Easter, when alone they are obliged by the ecclesiastical law to go, but also repeatedly through the year. Wherefore, although there had been, even at that time, a law compelling all to confess yearly, the Ephesians could still have gone freely and spontaneously to confession.

But many came to confession, not all. What opposition has this to that law, which obliges all to confess their sins, at least once a year? Neither does this law absolutely include all, but those only, whose consciences are defiled by mortal sin; nor does it even oblige these at all times, but only once a year. Wherefore supposing this ecclesiastical law to be in force at the time of St. Paul, still some of the Ephesians could have made their confession, when all did not make it.

Finally, as to what regards their having humbled themselves in the assembly of the faithful, I do not know whence Calvin has taken this, unless from his own brain; for St. Luke makes no mention of it: *many* says he, *of those who believed came confessing and declaring their deeds.* But whether they came before the assembly of the faithful, or in a private manner, to St. Paul, or to any one else, St. Luke does not say. Besides, do not Catholics even in our days humble themselves before the assembly of the faithful, when in our confessionals ranged in the middle of our temples, the whole congregation looking on, they cast themselves at the feet of the Priest, and secretly make their confession to him? See how dexterously Calvin accommodates his Antitheses to to weave in his calumnies.

II. The second passage I shall adduce in confirmation of this truth, is taken from the second epistle of St. Paul to the Corinthians, chap. 5, which is expressed in these words: *He hath given to us the ministry of reconciliation.......and hath placed in us the word of reconciliation. We are therefore ambasssdors for Christ, &c.* Calvin himself, acknowledges in the fourth book of his Instit. c. 1. §. 22. that these words refer to the power of the keys, and frankly confesses, that this power is to be exercised, as well publicly, as privately, towards the faithful who have been baptised. Now certainly those who are sent as ambassadors, invested with a power to reconcile the enemies of a king, with the king himself, cannot properly discharge their ministry, unless they know from the guilty, what they have done, what the nature of the offence is, which they have committed, what satisfaction they are disposed to make, &c. &c. Wherefore this ministerial power necessarily carries with it, the power of hearing the causes of the guilty, and consequently of exacting and receiving their confessions: nor is it lawful for the ministers to reconcile at pleasure any, without having previously heard them.

III. The third passage, is taken from the Epist. of St. James chap. 5. wherein St. James, exhorts the faithful to confess their sins. His words are these: *Confess your sins one to another:* which exhortation manifestly shows confession to have been already instituted, and that it was to be made not only to God, but also to man. And this agrees manifestly with the above words, according to the explanation which the Fathers give them. For, a little above, the Apostle St. James, had admonished the sick *to bring in the priests of the church,* in order *to pray over them, anointing them with oil,* and likewise added: that the effect of that sacred unction and of the prayers would be, *to save the sick and raise them up, and if they should be in sins,* to remit and deliver them from them. But in order that the reader might not conclude from these words, that those deadly or mortal sins, of which a person might be guilty, would be remitted by the sacred unction, he subjoined: *Confess, therefore, your sins, one to another:* for the sacred unction does not remit those mortal sins of which a man may have a knowledge, since these are to be cleansed by the sacrament of Confession; but such as are venial, or even mortal, which we have no knowledge of, and which are commonly called the remnants of sin.

But our adversaries object, and particularly Melancthon in his apolog. confess. art de confess. and satisfac. and John Calvin lib. 3. Istitut cos. 4 § 12, the words *one to another*, for, say they, these words compel us to say, that St. James does not speak of sacramental confession, which is made to the Priest only, but of the confession of an injury done to an offended brother, in order to be reconciled wtih him, and to obtain his pardon or, of the confession of sins, which is made to a pious and holy man, in order that he, knowing our spiritual infirmity, may instruct us, and offer up prayers to God for us. Thus Melancthon and Calvin.

But this objection is easily removed. For Origen in his second homil. in Levit. St. Chrysostom, book 3d de sacerdot. St. Augustin homil. 12, ex lib. 50 hom. and St. Bernard in his book of meditations, chap. 9, all maintain that this place is simply to be understood of confession which is made to a priest; and as venerable Bede in his commentary upon this passage, and Hugue de S. Victor, book 2, on the sacraments, correctly expound, these words *one to another* are to be taken, as the agreement of the words of the scripture require; consequently *confess your sins one to another* implies the same, as, you being men, confess to men; you who stand in need of absolution, to those who have the power to absolve from these words: *whose sins you shall forgive, they are forgiven them.* As in the first epist. of Peter chap. 4, when the Apostle says: *Using hospitality towards one another without murmuring, as every man hath received grace, ministering the same one to another, as good stewards of the manifold grace of God. If any man speak, let him speak as the words of God: if any man minister, let it be as from the power which God administereth, &c.* he certainly does not wish to give to understand by the words *uniting hospitality towards one another*, that all without discrimination are to receive the rights of hospitality from all, or that all are to be taught, or all to be cured, &c. but that those who have no house, or are in need should be hospitably received by those who have, or who are in easy circumstances; that the ignorant, should be instructed by the learned; the sick should be cured by physicians; the poor supported by the rich; and not, that the rich should be supported by the poor, or the physicians should be cured by the sick, or the learned, instructed by the ignorant, or finally, those who abound in houses should receive the rights of hospitality from those who have none: So also, ought those therefore, who are bound by the chains of sin, to recur to those to whom it has been said: *Whatsoever you shall loose on earth, shall be loosed in heaven.*

The succeeding words also of the same Epist. viz. *Pray for one another, that you may be saved*, signify, that the Priests should pray for the sick and not the sick for the Priests: for St. James manifestly alludes to what he had said before; *Is any man sick among you?*

Let him bring in the Priests of the Church, and let them pray over him. This the Greek version clearly points out; for in the same passage where we have the words, *that you may be saved,* the Greek text has the word ἰαθῆτε which refers properly to the health of the body.

CHAP. III.

CONFESSION PROVED FROM THE TESTIMONIES OF THE COUNCILS.

I shall now add the testimonies of the ancient councils of the church, which have been held at different periods, and in different countries, from which the doctrine of the Universal Church may be gathered. These testimonies of the councils which I shall adduce, although they may not go directly to establish the truth, viz. that confession is of divine institution, contain nevertheless, the ancient custom, and frequently also indicate the necessity of confessing sins to the Priests. From which it will be easy to infer, that it must therefore have been commanded by God himself, as well because the origin of this practice is no where found in any council; as, because it is by no means probable, the faithful would have consented to a precept so difficult and repugnant to nature without reclaiming against it, especially, if by confessing to God alone, by a confession or made in general terms, they could have obtained the remission of their sins.

In the first place the practice of confession is proved from the council of Laodicea, held in the East as early as the year 364. In the second Canon we read these words: *To those who fall under the guilt of different sins, and who by prayer, confession, and penance shew a perfect conversion from their evil ways, a time of penance must be allotted according to the quality of the sin.*

In the Canons also of the sixth Synod, held by the Greeks about the year 500; we read in the 102d Canon, these words: *It is proper that those who have received from God the power of loosing and binding, should consider the quality of the sin, and exert a becoming zeal for the conversion of the sinner, and thus apply a proper remedy to the disease.*

In the Latin church, in the 31st Canon of the third council of Carthage, which was held in the year 350, we find these words: *The time of penance must be determined, according to to the judgment of the Bishop, agreeably to the difference of the sins.* And we find the same Canon repeated in the African council, can. 10. There certainly can be no doubt, that all sins must be revealed in confession, if the time of penance, or the period during which the sinner is to do penance, is to be determined according to the difference of the sins.

We read also in the 8th Canon of the first council of Chalons, held in the year 654, these words: *We judge it to be highly useful that a penance, be imposed by the Priest on the penitent, his confession having been made.*

Again in the 32d canon of the second council of Chalons held in the year 850, we read thus: *We have remarked this also as requiring correction, namely, that when persons confess their sins to the Priests, they do not fully develop them. Wherefore as man is formed of two substances, viz. the soul and the body, and sometimes he sins by an act of the mind, and at other times by the frailty of the flesh, they must, by a strict enquiry examine into these sins, that a full and entire confession may be made of both; viz. that those sins may be confessed which are committed by the body, and those also which are committed simply in thought.*

In the third council of Tours, which was held about the same time chap. 22. we read as follows: *Bishops and Priests ought cautiously to consider, how they determine the time of abstinence with respect to those who confess their sins to them.* We find a similar testimony in the council of Rheims, equally as ancient as the above, in can. 12. v. 6. and in the Parisian, chap. 32. and 46. All these councils are of the Gallican church.

If we examine the Church of Germany, we shall find testimonies equally strong. For in the council of Mentz, held under the archbishop Rabanus, in chapter 26 it is thus decreed: *Particular care must be taken by the Priests, that those sick who are in danger of death, make a clear and sincere confession; the quantity of penance must not however be imposed upon them.* See also chap. 27.

In the council of Worms held in the year 868, it is thus set down in the beginning of that council, chap. 25. *Priests are to regulate the penance of the penitents, according to the difference of their sins. Each Priest, therefore, in prescribing the penance, ought to consider the causes of each singly, also the origin and circumstances of the sins, and diligently to examine the disposition and repentance of the delinquents, to know them thoroughly, as well as to examine into the qualities of the times, persons, places and ages, in order that he should not be inattentive to what is laid down in the sacred canons respecting the places, ages, times, or quality of the crimes. and of the grief of each delinquent.* From these testimonies it appears how differently the ancient churches of the East and West, thought and taught, concerning Confession, from what the multitude of present sectaries and innovators think and teach.

To these testimonies we may add the general Councils: the Council of Lateran, under Innocent III. chap. 21. that of Constance, Sess. 8. of Florence in Instruct. Armenorum, the council of Trent, which I have inserted above at large, which, although rejected by our adversaries, by reason of their being of a more recent date than the others, are, however, rejected without reason. For they transmit to us a faith and doctrine perfectly conformable to all the most ancient Councils, and contain the sentiments of the whole Catholic church, during the space of four hundred years, so that they cannot be said to be in error, without admitting, at the same time, that the whole church of Christ has erred with them, (which is impossible,) and consequently, that the gates of hell have indeed prevailed against her, notwithstanding the promises of Christ.

CHAP. IV.

CONFESSION PROVED FROM THE TESTIMONY OF THE FATHERS WHO LIVED FROM THE YEAR 100 TO 200.

To the testimonies of the Councils, we may add the testimonies of the Fathers, as well Greek, as Latin, who flourished in each age of the church.

ST. IRENEUS.

I shall cite in the first place, St. Ireneus, who lived in the first age, almost immediately after the Apostles, who was the disciple of St. Polycarp, who had been himself, the disciple of St. John the Evangelist. In his first book, chap. 9, he thus writes of certain women, whom Marcus the heretic, had seduced: *These,* says he, *often converted to the church of God, confessed, that having their bodies exterminated as it were, by him, and inflamed by lust, they loved him to excess.*

And, speaking a little below of another who had been seduced; *When with great labour the brethren had converted her, penetrated with grief, she spent her whole time in confessing and bewailing her sins (in Exomologesi) and lamenting the crime she had been led, by this Magician, to commit.* And in the third book, chap. 4. *Cerdon,* says he, *after coming into the church, and making his confession, thus, spent his time, at one time privately teaching, at another making his confession.*

TERTULLIAN.

The second testimony I shall adduce in favour of confession, is the great Turtullian, who flourished towards the end of this same century, under the reign of Severus, as he himself informs us in his apology, chap. 4. It is thus, he writes in his book on penance, (ed. Froben) p. 484. *I presume,* says he, *that many avoid declaring their sins, or delay it from day to day, because they have more regard for their honour, than they have for their salvation; they resemble in this respect those who having contracted a disease in the hidden parts of their body, conceal it from the eye of their physician, and suffer themselves thus to be bereft of life, through an unhappy shame.* And a little after in a strain of irony: *O the singular advantage to be gained, by concealing our sin! Do we think, that by covering it from the eyes of men,* it will escape the all-seeing eye of God? Here then is a strong testimony in favour of Confession, from one who lived shortly after the Apostles. He speaks in the most explicit terms of the necessity of confessing even our most secret sins, that it is not enough to confess them to God, but we must also declare them to men; and he considers our very salvation, as depending upon the faithful discharge of this duty.

CHAP. V.

TESTIMONIES OF THE FATHERS WHO LIVED FROM THE YEAR 200 TO 300.

ORIGEN.

Origen, who lived at the beginning of the second century, after the Apostles, under the reign of Alexander Afameas and immediately after Tertullian, compares the secret sins, which burden the conscience, to indigested meat, which overloads the stomach, and says, that we must have recourse to confession, in order to rid ourselves of our sins and be cured. His words are these: *Dum accusat semetipsum & confitetur, simul evomit & delictum, atque omnem morbi digerit causam.* Hom. 2. in Psalm 37. T. 1. He adds, moreover, that we must use great discernment in the choice of our spiritual physician, to whom we are to discover the diseases of our soul; that having made choice of one, we must obey him in all things; and if he ould judge that we ought to declare any one of our faults to the assembly of the faithful, we must submit to it. Here we see, that it was he practice of the faithful in those days, on some occasions, and when specially enjoined by the Priests, to make a public confession of some of their faults, that before they made this public confession, they previously made a secret confession to the priest, and that they did not declare before the public, all the sins they had revealed in private. This testimony is no less strong than the foregoing. But Kemnitius, has taken it into his head, to distinguish here, secret sins from public ones, and to pretend that the doctrine of Origen, is, that it is sufficient to confess the former to God alone, and that it is not necessary to reveal the others to the priest, except to know from him, which those are, which may be declared in the assembly of the faithful, with fruit and edification, without exposing them to the evil consequences of slander. He maintains that this doctrine is contained in the two homilies, upon the 37th Psalm, observing, that the first treats of sins of the first sort, and the following of those of the second. But, I here challange any one, who will take the trouble to read the above mentioned homilies, to point out to me, the least foundation for any such distinction. It is all mere assertion, and but a lame contrivance to weaken the force of the testimony. Origen gives sufficiently to understand in other passages, how much he is persuaded of the necessity of confessing his most secret sins, when for example, he says: that the only means of preventing the accusation of the devil our enemy, is to accuse ourselves; that he who has carried us to offend God, will not fail to accuse us of our most secret sins, even of those we have committed in thought; but by accusing ourselves, we shall avoid his malignity. What stronger refutation can there be to the imaginary distinction of Kemnitius? This reformer may equally read his condemnation in these other words of the same Father. *If we confess our sins, not only to God, but likewise to those who have the power to heal our wounds, our sins will be effaced by him who has said: I will blot out thy iniquities as a cloud, and thy sins as a mist.* His words are: "Si revelaverimus peccata nostra non solum Deo, sed et eis qui possunt mederi vulneribus nostris, delebuntur peccata nostra ab eo, qui ait: ecce deleo ut nubem iniquitates." Hom. 17. in Lucam. T. 1. Ed. Froben. p. 272.

ST. CYPRIAN.

This great saint was contemporary to Origen, and was crowned with martyrdom in the year 258. In his sermon *De lapsis*, he employs the whole force of his eloquence, to induce the faithful to make an exact confession of their sins. Thus he speaks: *Let each one of you*, says he, *confess his faults whilst he is yet in the world; whilst his confession can be received; and whilst the satisfaction he will offer, will be agreeable to God.* Serm. de lapsis, Ed. Froben. p. 226. And relating, in another place, the example of a girl who had been signally punished by almighty God for having neglected this important duty, prior to her receiving communion: *She had deceived man*, says he, *but she could not escape the vengeance of God.* And again, in another place; *How many do we see*, says he, *daily possessed by impure spirits, because they do not confess their secret sins.* Serm. de lapsis. ed. Rigalt. p. 202; and every where reminds his flock of the all-seeing eye of God, which penetrates all things, and which suffers nothing to escape.

CHAP. VI.

TESTIMONIES OF THE FATHERS FROM THE YEAR 300 TO 400.

LACTANTIUS.

This great man, whose testimony I am now about to cite, was so celebrated for his eloquence and erudition, that he was styled the Christian Cicero. He flourished towards the end of the third, and the beginning of the fourth century. His virtue and merit rendered him so conspicuous, that Constantine entrusted him with the education of his son Crispus. But this, far from elevating, only served to render him more modest. He lived in poverty and retirement, amidst the abundance and noise of the court; and whatever presents the Emperor made him, he never failed to distribute them to the poor. He died in the year 325.

In the fourth book of his divine Institutions, chap. 17. he warns us not to keep our hearts envelloped and hid, that is to say, as he explains himself, not to conceal in the recesses of our conscience any hidden crime, under the veil of dissimulation. He then proceeds to show, that the circumcision of the Jews, was the figure of confession, and that this was the circumcision of the heart, of which the prophets spoke. *God*, says he, *who by his infinite bounty has provided us with all the means necessary to salvation, has traced out to us in the circumcision of the flesh, the true idea of penance, in order that if we discover our hearts naked, that is to say, if we confess our sins, to please God, we may obtain of him the pardon, which he refuses those who obstinately persist in their evil ways, and who conceal the sins which they have committed.* Can there be any thing stronger, or more clear than this passage, to impress upon us, the strict obligation we are under, to confess our most hidden sins?

The same Lactantius, in a work which he wrote against the Novatians, lays down confession, as a mark of the true church: It is thus he writes. *As every sect and denomination of heretics*, says he, *deem themselves Christians, and theirs to be the Catholic church, it is proper they should know that that church is the true one, in which there is confession, and penance, which heals the sins and wounds to which the weakness of our flesh is subject.* What will those Protestants who condemn and prescribe confession, say after this?

ST. ATHANASIUS.

This great Saint, was Bishop of Alexandria. His whole life was one continual struggle against the heretics of his days, and particularly against the blasphemous errors of Arius; whose history is so well known. He had been banished four times from his see, by the Roman Emperors, at the instance of the Arians; during which time he wrote many excellent works. He died at Alexandria on the 2d of May, 373, after having been bishop 43 years.

In his sermon upon these words: *Go into the village that is over against you; and immediately at your coming in thither, you shall find a colt tied, &c.* Towards the end of the sermon he speaks thus:

Let us examine ourselves, whether our chains be loosed, that we may proceed better. If they be not loosed, deliver thyself over to the disciples of Jesus: For, there are some present who can loose thee, pursuant to that power which they have received from the Saviour. For whatsoever you shall bind, says he, on earth, shall be bound in heaven: and whatsoever you shall loose on earth, shall be loosed in heaven: and whose sins you shall forgive, they are forgiven them.

ST. BASIL, AND ST. GREGORY OF NYSSA.

St. Basil, who died in the year, 378 says in express terms: *that one must necessarily confess his sins to those who have received from God the dispensation of his mysteries.* Regula 288. Tom. 2. ed. Paris, p. 728. Now, to whom has the dispensation of the mysteries of God been entrusted, if not to the Priests? Can any thing be more formal, and more decidedly opposite to what is generally pretended by Protestants? Let them say after this: that it is good, it is profitable to confess the sins that particularly burden the conscience, in order to ask counsel of the Priest or to receive his instructions; but it is not what St. Basil requires: This Father expressly says, that it is necessary: *necessarium est,* ἀναγκαῖον. Let it not be said also, that he speaks here of confession made in general terms only, whereby one acknowledges himself guilty, and a sinner; but St. Basil exacts that the confession be made, in order that the penance may be proportioned acccording to the quality of the sin. Now, how is it possible for the priest to proportion the penance without having an exact knowledge of the sin? He says, moreover, that *as one does not show the infirmities of his body to every person indifferently, but only to those who understand how to cure them, so one should not make a confession of his sins, except to those who are able to apply a remedy to them.* ibid. But is it customary for a person to say in general terms only, that he is sick? Does he not take care to specify in the most particular manner, as well as he is able, all his complaints, in order that his physician may be able to apply the most convenient remedies? It must be therefore manifest, that the intention of St. Basil is, to exact a similar conduct from the penitent, towards the physician of his soul; and this is moreover precisely the advise, which St. Gregory, the brother of St. Basil, gives to the penitents. *Boldly discover,* says he, in his orat. in mulierem peccatricem. T. 2. *to your spiritual father all that you have most hidden, put him in possession of every thing that passes in the bottom of your heart, as you would show to a physician your hidden wounds.*

ST. AMBROSE.

St. Ambrose, in his second book on penance, chap. 3. T. 2. ed. nov. Paris, p. 420. says: *that the Lord has ordained, that the greatest sinners should be admitted to the participation of the heavenly gifts, provided they do penance for their sins with all their heart, acknowledging themselves guilty, by a sincere confession.* Here we may remark the condition, which the saint requires as necessary to be reinstated, in the favour of God and participation of his holy mysteries: the sinner must declare his sins, by an humble and sincere confession. If it be pretended that he speaks only of public sins and a public confession, it is easy to show, that St. Ambrose requires equally, that the confession be made of the most secret sins; for he says in the 16th chap. of his book on penance, that he who performs an exact penance for all his sins, does not on this account receive the advantages of a reconciliation, but he must be reinstated, through the ministry of priests. But what need I recur to the words of the saint, when we have in his conduct the most complete and satisfactory proof of the point we maintain? It is said in his life, written by Paulinus, one of his deacons, and consequently a contemporary author, that he shed many tears whilst hearing the confessions of the penitents, and thereby obliged them to weep with him. This author adds, moreover, that the saint observed a profound secresy, in all that had been committed to him, and that he spoke of it, but to God alone, in order to implore his mercies.

ST. PACIAN.

St. Pacian, Bishop of Barcelona, lived under the reign of Valens. He died in the year 390, under that of Theodosius, after having governed his flock with a most edifying holiness, and distinguished himself as well by his exemplary virtues, as by his superior talents and eloquence.

In an exhortation to penance, made by this holy bishop, we have the strongest evidence, that nothng less was required of the penitents of the fourth century, than is required, in our days. He therein conjures his flock, by him, to whom the most hidden things are known, *not to conceal any thing, nor to disguise their wounded consciences.* In Parenœsi. ad. Pœnit. Biblioth. Pot. Tom. 4. p. 316. He also complains of those who address themselves to ignorant and uninformed priests, with a view to surprise them. He tells them, that there are some who confess properly their sins, and explain them sufficiently, but who refuse to submit to the painful exercises of penance. He compares them to those who calling in a physician, discover to him their wounds, but neglect to apply the remedy or observe the prescription. *ibid.*

ST. JEROME.

This great doctor was born about the year 340, and died on the 30th of September, 420, aged 80 years. In his admirable letter to Helidorus, he writes thus: *Far be it from me to say any thing disadvantageous of those, who being the successors of the Apostles, consecrate with their sacred mouth the body of Christ, by whom we are also Christians, and who have the keys of the kingdom of heaven, and in some manner judge before the last judgment. The priests,* continues he, *have not only power to forgive sins, when they baptize, but even after.* See the same, in his comment. upon the 10th chap. of Ecclesiastes; and upon the 26th chap. of St. Matthew.

ST. AUGUSTIN.

I now come to St. Augustin, one of the brightest luminaries of the Christian church, who lived from the year 354 to 430, a period of 76 years. I should never end, were I to undertake to cite all the passages which are scattered through the voluminous works of this great man, in proof of confession. I shall therefore content myself, with simply producing one or two, which set forth in the clearest and most unequivocal terms, the whole doctrine for which we contend. In his 49th Hom. T. 10. ed. Froben. p. 549. we read these words: *Let no one say,* (mark what follows) *I do penance privately with God, who knows my sins: For then in vain was it said, Whatever you shall bind on earth shall be bound in heaven: Were then the keys given in vain to the church of God? We frustrate the gospel, we frustrate the words of Christ.* And in his following Homily he adds: *that whosoever is burdened with mortal sins, and has not recourse to the keys of the church, hopes for salvation in vain.* Hom. 50. T. 10. p. 559. Now, it is easy to perceive, that amongst the mortal sins, of which he makes the enumeration, there are many hidden, and which never come before the public eye. He therefore enjoins, that the sinner, as soon as he shall have formed the sincere resolution to amend his life,repair to the priests charged with the ministry of the keys, in order to expose to them, the state of his conscience, and to learn from them, what satisfaction he is to make for his sins, exacting moreover from him, that if he has given any scandal, to be ready to repair it b a public confession, according to the advice of him to whom he shall have declared all things. *Veniat ad Antistites, per quos illi claues in ecclesia ministrantur, &c.* ibid.

CHAP. VII.

TESTIMONIES OF THE FATHERS FROM THE YEAR 400 TO 500.

ST. JOHN CHRYSOSTOM.

This great doctor was contemporary to St Augutin. He died on the 14th September, in the year 407, after having governed his flock nine years and eight months. In his third book *de Sacerdotio*. T. 5. apud Hugonem, page 509. he points out the difference between the priests of the old law, and those of the new. He says: *that the former, had the power to declare that persons were healed of the leprosy, whereas the latter* (the priests of the new law) *had the power to cure them effectually.* How does this agree with what Protestants pretend in general, viz. that the Priest has power to declare simply the benefit of reconciliation, and that he does not in any manner act as judge, to take cognizance of the cause; it is on this ground they dispense with the obligation of private and particular confession, but this principle is declared by St. Chrysostom, in the most explicit terms, to be wholly false. His words are these: *At vero sacerdotibus nostris non corporis lepram vero animæ sordes, non dico purgatos probare, sed purgare prorsus concessum est.* He adds also in the same place, *that God has given a power to the priests, which he has given neither to the Angels nor Archangels, having never said to them: whose sins you shall forgive, they are forgiven them, &c.* and a few lines after he says: *that the eternal Father, gave the power of judging to his son, in all its extent, and that this same power was given by the son of God to them.* How then can they deny this quality to the priests, if it be true, as St. Chrysostom says, that it has been communicated to them by Jesus Christ, without any reserve? And if the priests be true judges, how will they judge, if they be not informed of what should constitute the matter of their judgment?

But what need have I to dive into the principles of the saint, to find a proof of the necessity of confessing one's sins in detail to a priest, when his very words so formally point out this obligation? Does he not exact as the first duty of penance, *to condemn one's sins, and to confess them?* Hom. 9. in Ep. ad. Heb. And to prove that it is to the priest we must confess them, does he not add a little below: that we must pay that respect to the priest, which is due them, because it belongs to them to remit sin? Does he not exhort the faithful to make a sincere confession during *holy week*, by representing to them the conveniency of the time to declare their sins to the priest, and to discover their wounds to their spiritual physician? Hom. 30. in Genes. T. 1. p. 50. 51. Does he not say, that the bishop, or he who is charged with the care of souls, ought to enter into all the secret folds of the heart, making a most diligent and exact search, in order that nothing may escape him? That he must inform himself most particularly of all the diseases, in order to be able to apply the proper remedies? Lib. 2. de Sacerdot. T. 4. apud Hug. p. 500. Does he not quote the example of the Samaritan woman, in order to exhort the faithful not to be ashamed to confess their sins? Does he not openly declare to them, that should they neglect to confess their most secret sins, they will not escape the public confusion which they will have to undergo at the day of judgment before the whole world? Hom. in John. T. 3. op. 36.—What more clear?

ST. LEO, SURNAMED THE GREAT.

This learned and holy man died about 30 years after St. Austin. He began to abolish the custom of publicly confessing in the Latin church, and allowed only of confessions made in private to a priest; which shows that public confession was a point of mere discipline and consequently subject to change, and that the necessity of obtaining the absolution of a priest, after having made a faithful confession of all mortal sins, has always been deemed invariable: These are the words of this great Pope : *I forbid*, says he, *the recitation in public of the declaration which sinners shall have made of their faults in detail, giving them in writing, because it is sufficient to discover to the priests by a private confession, the sins of which they may stand guilty, for although we should commend the great faith of those, who fear not to cover themselves with confusion before men, from a great fear of God, nevertheless, as some desiring penance, may have committed sins which they may not wish, should be made public, I deem it proper to abolish this practice, lest many should deprive themselves of the remedies of penance, and withdraw through a shame or fear which they may have to discover to their enemies, actions which deserve to be punished by the authority of the laws : for the confession which is made first to God, and afterwards* (mark well) *to a priest, ought to suffice*. Epist. 80. ad. Episcopos Campaniœ.

Also in his 91st. Epistle to Theodorus, Bishop of Forojulius, he thus writes : *The manifold mercy of God has also afforded this remedy to the frailties of our nature, that the hope of eternal life may be gained not only by baptism, but likewise by the benefit of penance, and that those who have violated the grace of their baptism, by condemning themselves, may obtain the remission of their crimes, the divine bounty having so ordained it, that the indulgence of God cannot be obtained without the supplications of the priests. For our Lord Jesus Christ, the mediator between God and man, has imparted this power to the heads of his church, to impose on those that confess, a competent penance, and admit the same after a wholesome satisfaction, to the communion of the sacraments, through the door of reconciliation.* St. Leo, in this passage most clearly shows confession to be necessary, by the divine ordinance; to have been ordained by God, insomuch, that without the ministry of the Priests, no reconciliation can be obtained; and moreover adds, that the ministry of the priest, from the divine institution, consists in enjoining a penance upon those that confess, and in admitting the same through the door of reconciliation, to the communion of the sacraments. This testimony is at once so pointed, and so strong in every point, relating to confession as taught in the Catholic church, that none of the Reformers have ever offered to give a solution.

CHAP. VIII.

TESTIMONIES OF OTHER FATHERS FROM THE YEAR 500 TO THE YEAR 1215.

ST. GREGORY, THE GREAT.

I SHALL begin with St. Gregory, surnamed the great, from the splendour of his actions, as well as the lustre of his virtues, who was born about the year 540. It is to this great saint that England owes her conversion to Christianity, from the apostolic labours of Augustin, Prior of the monastery of St. Andrew, whom he had expressly sent thither, for that purpose. In his 26th homily, explaining these words of the gospel, *Whose sins you shall forgive, they are forgiven them*, he writes thus: *It must be seen*, says he, *what the offence is, and what penance has succeeded the offence, that those whom the Almighty visits with the grace of compunction, may be absolved by the sentence of the Priest. For the absolution of the subaltern judge*, (viz. the priest) *is then true, when the sentence of the sovereign judge follows.* Now, certainly the priest cannot know, whether the penitent who desires to be absolved, has done penance according to the magnitude of his offence, unless he openly confess his fault or rather all his faults: wherefore the confession of all and every sin, is absolutely necessary.

Again, in the same homily, this holy pontiff has traced out to us in the resurrection of Lazarus, an admirable figure of the conversion of a sinner, which fully discloses the sentiments and ideas of the saint on the present subject. *Every sinner*, says he, *is buried in the depth of the tomb, as long as he retains his sins in the secret recesses of his conscience; but the dead man issues from the tomb, when the sinner confesses his iniquities, of his own accord; it is therefore, to all who are dead by sin, as well as to Lazarus, it is said: " come forth," why do you conceal your sins in the bottom of your conscience? cause them to come forth by a faithful confession; let the dead issue from the regions of the tomb and appear: that is to say, let the sinner confess his sins, by exposing to view what he has concealed in the most hidden recesses of his conscience; after which, he may be loosed by the ministry of the priests, as Lazarus was loosed by the hands of the disciples of the Saviour*. Hom. 26. in Joan. T. 1. Ed. Paris. p. 1441. Here, it is scarcely necessary to remark, that St. Gregory, speaks of all sinners who are guilty of mortal sins; his words are: *omnis peccator, cuilibet mortuo in culpa;* that he alludes particularly to those whose sins are hidden, *introrsum latet, in suis, penetralibus occultatur;* that he finally, considers confession a duty equally incumbent upon all sinners, since it is on this condition only, they can be loosed by the priests, *venientem vero foras solvant discipuli.*

ST. JOHN CLIMACUS.

In the same age flourished St. John Climacus, surnamed the scholastic; in his book entitled *Climax*, he thus speaks: *But before all things, let us confess our sins to our enlightened judge; and let us be prepared, should he command us, to confess to all.* And a little below, he says moreover, that without confession, which is made to man, no remission can be obtained.

I could produce a number of other not less respectable witnesses of the faith and practice of the Catholic Church, respecting confession, in this same age, but I fear to exhaust the patience of the reader who must be, I am satisfied, perfectly convinced by this time, that the Fathers are for us. I shall therefore content myself with the two above in this age, and with citing one or two, in each of the subsequent ages, down to the year, 1215.

After the year 600, we have the celebrated Cœsarius, bishop of Arles. In his 6th, 7th, 8th, 9th, and 10th, Hom. he reasons most admirably on penance; in his 7th, principally, he tells his flock that confession and penance, purify from sin; and in his 10th, discoursing more largely on the necessity of confession, he speaks thus: *Wherefore I have often admonished you, dearest brethren, and I do again and again admonish and beseech you, as soon you perceive yourselves to be torn by the tempest of concupiscence from the shore of continence, tossed in the ocean of luxury, and to have suffered the shipwreck of Charity, to hasten to profit by confession, as by a plank from the shattered vessel; that by it you may escape the deep abyss of luxury, and arrive at the haven of penance, where you may in the more secure ground of hope, let drop your anchor, and recover your lost salvation.* Now, that Cœsarius speaks of the confession of every sin according to its species, is manifest from his seventh homily, where he compares sin to a disease, confession to its medicine, and the priest, to the physician: nor is it sufficient, as I have more than once said above, for the curing of corporal diseases, for the patient to say to his physician, that he is sick or indisposed, but he must also point out and indicate clearly to him, his complaint or complaints, if perchance he should labour under a complication of them.

After the year 700, appears Venerable Bede, whose memory is so respected by the church, that his homilies are publicly read in her office. In his commentary upon the 5th chap. of the Epist. of St. James explaining these words: *Confess your sins one to another*, he writes thus: *In this sentence*, says he, *this discretion should be used, viz. to confess our daily and light transgressions, one to another of our equals, and trust that by their prayers, we shall be saved; but to discover the foulness of our more nauseous leprosy to the priest, according to the law, and take special care to purify ourselves agreeably to his decision, in the manner and according to the measure of time he shall command.*

About the middle of the same century, Theodorus Studites in the life of St. Plato, commends the said Plato, because from his youth he had been accustomed to confess to the pastor of his soul, not less frequently than diligently, all his sins even to his most inmost thoughts.

Towards the close of this century, we find Theodolphus, who governed the church of Orleans, and who by his rare merit acquired the highest reputation with Charlemagne. He made in the year 797 many excellent regulations which are mentioned in the 7th vol. of the council of F. Labbeus. The 31st contains, that we must make a clear confession of all the sins we have committed, whether by action or in thought, to a Priest; it moreover enjoins, that the confessor interrogate the penitent, in order to find out the manner and occasion of his sin.—Why so much exactness in informing one's self of the occasions and circumstances, if at that time they did not at all admit of the obligation of confessing one's sins in detail to a priest?

After the year 800, appears the learned Raban-maur, Archbishop of Mentz, and one of the greatest ornaments of the church of Germany. In his seventh book on Ecclesiasticus, chap. 7. he thus speaks concerning the necessity of confession: *He who trangresses in the concupiscences of the flesh, and offends in any notable degree, is necessarily bound to cast off and purify himself of his ordure, by a clear confession of his sins, and thus by fasting and bodily chastisements re-*

turn to his wonted health. See the same, in his second book, de Institut. Clericorum, chap. 30.

In the same century, we have also Jonas, Bishop of Orleans, and one of the great luminaries of the church of France. In his third book de Institut. Laicali, he expresses himself, on the obligation of confession in a manner equally clear and distinct. *Should the sick,* says he, *be guilty of any sins, they will be remitted them, provided they confess them to the priests of the church, and take special care to renounce them and amend, for sins cannot be forgiven without confession; which corrects them.*

It would be easy to add to the authority of these great men, the authority of several councils, I shall however, only make mention of one, namely, that of Pavia, held in the year 850, and whose testimony is equally decisive in proving that they were not less convinced in those days, than we are at present, of the necessity of confessing in detail to a priest. After having laid down some regulations for the public penance of public sinners, the council goes on to declare: *that all who have sinned in secret, shall confess to those whom the Bishops and Archbishops have appointed to be physicians proper to heal secret wounds. And if the confessors have any doubt in the exercise of their ministry, they must consult thereupon their Bishop, without however naming the person who shall have confessed.* Council Ticinense. can. 6. T. 8. Labb. p. 63.

After the year 900, Reginon, the Abbot of the monastery of Prum, in the Diocese of Treves, celebrated for his great exactness, in the history he has left us in his Chronicles, and for his erudition in his two books, on Ecclesiastical discipline, furnishes us with a beautiful testimony in favour of confession. It is thus he writes in the 286th chap. of his first book, p. 134, ed. Paris: *Whosoever, is guilty of having sullied the spotless robe of Jesus Christ, which he had received at his baptism, must repair to his pastor, and humbly confess to him all the transgessions and all the sins by which he remembers, to have offended God, and acquit himself with the nicest exactness of whatever shall be enjoined him.*

Also, in the same century, Radulphus Flaviacensis, in his 3d book on Leviticus, chap. 7. writes thus: *It is necessary that those who confess their sins, should declare all that occurs to their memory, developing themselves to the Lord, and not reveal one thing, and conceal another.*

After the year 1000 flourished the great Peter Damien, less illustrious by the nobility of his birth and his high dignity as cardinal, than for his eminent piety and profound learning. This holy and learned divine has left us a sermon, wherein he treats of the rules of a good confession, and of the obstacles that prevent the making it well. Amongst other things, he there tells us, that nothing combats and surmounts the grace of God more effectually, than human fear; that when we blush at confessing our sins, we are less afraid of the judgments of God, than those of men: that reason, in short, urges us to confess, and God who sees all things obliges us to it. Serm. 58. 2d. of St. Andrew. p. 139. Ed. Paris. Again, in another place of the same sermon: *the fourth degree*, says he, *is the confession of the mouth: this is fully to be made; and not a part only to be declared, and the other part withheld; or that light sins are to be confessed, and the more grievous concealed, &c.* And a little farther down, speaking of the priest, the confessor: *he must take special care,* says he, *not to make any mention of those things, he has received under the seal of Confession.*

Before I proceed to the next century, I cannot forbear citing a singular example of the integrity of confession, as related by this same very grave and learned author, in his epistle to Desiderius, concerning the miracles of his time.—When Hugue, the Abbot of Clunium, says he, conducted me to his monastery, a certain aged brother lay in the Infirmary, labouring under a very severe and painful distemper. As soon as he discovered the Abbot to be present, filled with joy, he began to implore the divine clemency. O Lord, I beseech thee, said he, to whom nothing is hidden, if there be any thing within me whereof I am guilty, and which I have not as yet confessed, do thou, in thy mercy bring it to my mind, that I may clearly confess it to my Abbot whilst he is here present, and being judged by him, who above all others, has this power over me, I may be absolved. Having said this, he immediately heard a voice which distinctly said to him: Yes, yes, there is certainly something, which you have not yet confessed. Whereupon, as he heard only the voice, but did not see whence it came; continuing his prayer, he thus proceeded: Express clearly to me, O Lord, what this is, that having confessed, I may correct my fault. When, the same voice immediately indicated to him what he had so fervently demanded to know, which he immediately acknowledged to have committed; and then calling the Abbot to him, he confessed it: and a few days after terminated his life by a most edifying death.

Whether this fact, as related above, be true or false, matters very little; although there can be no just reason, considering the historian that relates it, to discredit it. It is sufficient however, for me, that it prove, as it most unquestionably does, that confession was practised in those days, and that it was then deemed, as essentially necessary to salvation, as it is considered to be now.

This age also gives us, St. Anselmus, Archbishop of Canterbury, who was born in August, 1033. In his Hom. upon the ten lepers, he explains these words of Jesus Christ: "Go, show yourselves to the priests," &c. of the obligation which is incumbent upon all sinners, to address themselves to the priests of the church, in order to be purified by confession. "Go, show yourselves to the priests, that is to say, (observes this holy doctor,) discover faithfully to the priests by an humble confession, all the stains of your interior leprosy, in order that you may be cleansed. As they went, they were cleansed, because as soon as sinners abandon their crimes, and condemn them, having the intention to confess, and a firm resolution to do penance for them, they are freed from them, in the eyes of him who sees their interior....they must notwithstanding, after this, repair to the priests, and ask absolution of them."

After the year 1100, we have the great St. Bernard, so celebrated both for the extraordinary sanctity of his life, and the lustre of his miracles, and the one of all the Fathers of the church, for whom Luther expressed the greatest consideration. Writing on the seven degrees of penance, he thus expresses himself: What does it avail, to tell one part of your sins, and to suppress the other? to purify yourselves by halves, and to leave the other half sullied? Is not every thing open to the eyes of God? What! will you dare to conceal any thing from him, who holds the place of God, in so great a sacrament? And speaking of the Knights Templars, he uses these words, of the book of Deuteronomy,* "the word is very nigh unto thee, in thy mouth "and in thy heart," in order to give them to understand, that it is not enough for the word to be in the heart, that it must likewise be in the mouth: that being in the heart, it produces therein a salutary contrition, and being in the mouth, it removes the evil shame that prevents confession, *confession*, says the saint, *which is absolutely necessary;* and a little after he exhorts the priests, not to absolve those who feign

* Deut. 30. 14.

repentance for their sins, unless they confess them at the same time. Ed. Mabillon T. 1. p. 1168. St Bernard died in 1153.

In the same age flourished Hugues de St. Victor, so renowned for his eminent learning that he was styled a second St. Austin. He asks how these words of the fifth chapter of St. James, are to be understood, viz. " Confess your sins one to another, and pray for one ano-" ther, that you may be saved :" and immediately answers, that " these words mean that you must confess not to God only, but also " to man, who holds the place of God; confess one to another, that is " to say, the sheep to the shepherds, inferiors to superiors; they who " have sins, to those who have the power to remit them. But why " confess? Why! for what reason? In order that you may be sa-" ved; that is to say, you will not be saved, unless you confess." Lib. 2. de sacramentis fidei, Edit. Mogunt. p. 495. This author died in 1139.

In the same age, also, lived Yves of Chartres, who was reckoned the oracle of his time. In a sermon which he preached at the commencement of Lent, he thus addresses his audience: " All, whatsoe-" ver you have committed, whether by the secret suggestion of the " devil, or the advice of another, must be declared in confession in " such a manner as to eradicate them from the heart, because all sins " are washed away by such a confession." Serm. 13. in capite jejun. apud Laurentium Cottereau, part 2, p. 291.

We may add likewise Richard de Saint Victor, one of the greatest theologians of his age, who died in 1173. In a treatise on the power of binding and loosing, page 330, edit. Rothomagi apud Joannem Bertelin chap. 5, he no less points out the necessity of confession in these words: True penance, says he, is a detestation of sin, with a firm resolution to avoid and confess it, and to make satisfaction for it; and adds in the eighth chap. that if the penitent neglect to look for a priest to receive his confession and absolve him, he will not escape everlasting punishment.

After the year 1200, we have the celebrated Council of Lateran, held under Innocent III. in the year 1215, and at which both the Greek and Latin Church assisted. It consisted of 412 bishops, amongst whom were the Patriarchs of Constantinople and Jerusalem; the Legates of the Patriarchs of Antioch and Alexandria; 71 Primates, Metropolitans, Abbots, and superiors of religious orders, to the number of above 800, and a vast number of delegates of Archbishops, Bishops, Abbots, Priors, and Canonical Chapters. There were likewise present at it, the Ambassadors of the Roman Emperor; of the Emperor of Constantinople; of the King of France; the King of England; the King of Hungary; the King of Jerusalem, the King of Cyprus; the King of Aragon; besides a great number of envoys sent by other sovereigns, princes, cities, &c. &c.

The 21st canon of this council (being the 4th general council of Lateran) enjoins "That all the faithful of both sexes shall confess "their sins, at least once a year, and fulfil to the utmost extent of "their ability the penance that shall be appointed them, and shall "devoutly receive the sacrament of the eucharist, at least at Easter: "unless the priest for a reasonable cause shall deem it proper to "withhold them from it for a time; under the penalty, should they "not comply, of exclusion, whilst living, from the pale of the church, "and of privation, when dead, of christian burial. Wherefore it is "the wish of the council, that this salutary canon be frequently pub- "lished in the churches, that no one may exempt himself, under the "pretext of ignorance: but if any, for just reasons, should wish to "confess their sins to another priest, they must first ask and obtain "leave of their own pastor, as otherwise he shall not have power "either to loose or to bind him."

"Every priest must, like skilful physicians, be wise and discreet in "administering oil and wine to the wounds of the patient, diligently "enquiring into the circumstances as well of the sin as of the sinner, "by which he may prudently know how to advise him, and what re- "remedy to apply, making use of every experiment to effect his cure.

"But above all, he must take the utmost care not to betray the "sinner either by word, by sign, or in any other way; but if, in any "case, he stand in need of prudent counsel, he must ask it in such a "manner as not to give the slightest and most distant intimation of "the person. And if any one shall be so presumptive as to reveal "what has been committed to him at the tribunal of penance, he shall "not only be deprived of his sacerdotal function, but shall also be "confined within the walls of a monastery, there to do penance all the "days of his life." Thus the council.

Many of the reformers, and amongst others principally Kemnitius, a disciple of Melancthon, in his Exam. Concil. Trid. have pretended, that the doctrine of sacramental confession was unknown in the church prior to the above council of Lateran. How far this assertion is correct, the reader is enabled at once to judge from the foregoing testimonies, to the number of not less than thirty, and of the most learned, respectable, and holy men in every age, from the apostles down to the year 1200. What must we think after this, of the so much boasted of *reformation*, when one of its avowed and most prominent doctrines, viz. "that the confession of sins made to men, is not necessary to salvation," rests upon the bare assertion of a few individuals born in the sixteenth century, without the least shadow of foundation, and in direct contradiction to the faith of the whole christian world in every age! The Council, far from establishing the necessity of Confession, supposes it already established. It has done no more than regulate and appoint the time when each of the faithful is to comply with this duty. The obligation of confession is as ancient as christianity itself, and was perfectly known before the Council, as the above testimonies sufficiently shew; but many lukewarm and indolent christians neglecting to acquit themselves of it, the Church judged it proper to urge them to it, by a salutary law, which should awake their attention. Thus they might with the same propriety have said, that the Council of Lateran established also the precept of communion, because it enjoined that all the faithful should communicate at Easter, as to say that this Council established the precept of confession, because it commanded that each of the faithful should make his confession, at least once a year.

Certainly, if the most distinguished authors who wrote during the eleven centuries preceding the Council of Lateran, have unanimously admitted the necessity of confession, in the manner specified; if at that time the practice of confessing was no less established in the armies and courts of princes, than in cloisters and monasteries; if in all cases where a person was in danger of death, confession has been thought necessary, to dispose him to appear before the tribunal of God; if before approaching the holy table, they always made it an indispensable duty to present themselves to a priest in order to declare the sins they had committed, and receive his absolution; if, in all ages, they have considered those as heretics who have dared to combat the necessity of confession, it cannot be denied that Kemnitius and his associate reformers have erred most egregiously, in fixing the origin of the precept of confession, at the commencement of the thirteenth century, and in giving Pope Innocent III. as the man who caused it to be received and adopted by the Council of Lateran. Now, nothing is more easy than to furnish the most satisfactory proofs of each of the above points.

With regard to the first, viz.: that the most distinguished authors who wrote during the eleven centuries preceding the Council of Lateran, have unanimously admitted the necessity of confession, I believe no one will question, who will take the trouble to read the five preceding chapters. I shall therefore, attend solely to the points that follow.

EMPERORS AND KINGS CONFESSED.

In the first place, I will shew that emperors and kings had their confessors, as all Catholic Princes have at this day; I shall content myself with simply naming some, and pointing out the authors, who inform us of it King Thiery I. (*a*) had in the 7th century, for his confessor St. Ausberg, Archbishop of Rouen; St. Viron Bishop of Ruremond, (*b*) was in the same century, the confessor to Pepin, the father of Charles Martel. St. Eiden, Bishop of Wexford in Ireland, heard the confession of Brandubh, king of that Island, after having raised him to life, as it is expressly mentioned, (*c*) in his life. St. Martin, a monk of Corbia, (*d*) was the confessor of Charles Martel, in the eighth century. St. Corbinien Bishop of Frisingua, (*e*) heard the confession of Grimoald, duke of Bavaria. Offa, a king in England, according to the relation of a Protestant, (*f*) had for his confessor a priest named Humbert. We find in the ninth century, that St. Aldric Bishop of Man, was according to Mr. Baluze, (*g*) the confessor of Louis, the meek; that Donatus Scot, Bishop of Peluze, was, according to Ughel, (*h*) the confessor of Lothaire, the son and successor of Louis; in the tenth century, St. Udaldric, bishop of Augsburg, (*i*) was confessor to the emperor Otho. William, Archbishop of Mentz, (*k*) heard the confession of St. Matilda, wife of Henry surnamed the bird-catcher, in his last sickness. Didacus Fernandus, (*l*) was confessor to Ordonnius II. king of Spain. In the eleventh century, I shall cite only Queen

---

(*a*) 2. Sœcul. Benedict. p. 1055. (*b*) Bolland. 7. Maii. T. 2. p. 313. (*c*) Bolland. 31. Jan. T. 2. p. 1118. (*d*) 1. part. 3. Sœcul. Bened. p. 462. (*e*) 1. part. 3. sœcul. Bened. p. 511. (*f*) Spelman. T. 1. Conc. (*g*) Miscell. T. 3. p. 5. (*h*) Italia. sacra. T. 3. p. 173. (*i*) Dietmar lib. 2. Chron. Auth. Brunsw. p. 333. (*k*) Bolland. 14. Martii. T. 2. 369. (*l*) Yepez. in Chron. Ord. s. Bened, T. 4. p. 450.

Constantia, wife of the pious Robert, (*a*) who had for her confessor a priest of the Diocess of Orleans, named Stephen; and in the twelfth, Henry I. king of England, who had for his confessor Atheldulf, Prior of St. Oswald, (*b*) and afterwards Bishop of Carlisle, the king having founded this new Bishoprick to gratify his confessor.

THE ARMIES HAD THEIR CONFESSORS.

It must not be thought, that during the ages of which I have just spoken, the armies were without their confessors; these were supplied no less than the courts of princes. The first Council of Germany, celebrated under the auspices of St. Boniface, in the year 742, informs us of this. It is there said in the second Canon, (*c*) that each Colonel shall be provided with a priest, who shall hear the confessions of the soldiers, and impose on them an appropriate penance. Charlemagne made nearly a similar regulation, which may be found in the fourth article of his Ecclesiastical chapters. (*d*) William of Sommerset, a Religious of Malmsbury commends the Normans, (*e*) for employing the whole night in confessing their sins, before they engaged in battle.

THE MULTITUDE OF PENITENTS WHO PRESENTED THEMSELVES FOR CONFESSION.

What I have already stated would be sufficient to convince any unprejudiced mind, that anterior to the council of Lateran, the practice of confession was very general amongst the faithful; but the multitude and crowd of penitents who presented themselves at the tribunal of penance, furnishes me with a new proof which ought not to be suppressed.

Nicephorus, the keeper of the Archives, a Greek author, of the seventh century, according to Labignus, and of the ninth, according

---

(*a*) Tom. 2. Spicil. Acheri. p. 676. (*b*) History of England by Andrew Duchere. edition by Duverdier, T. 1. L. XI. p. 449. (*c*) Quisque Prœfectus unum Presbyterum secum habeat, qui hominibus peccato confitentibus judicare, & indicare pœnitentiam possit. Tom. 6. Labb. p. 1534. (*d*) Tom. 7. Labb. p. 1165. (*e*) Tota nocte confessioni peccatorum vacantes. Lib. 3. de Gestis Anglorum Cap 15.

to Coccius, informs us, (a) that the Bishops were at first the only persons who attended to the ministry of reconciliation, but not being in sufficient number to hear the multitude of penitents, they were obliged to commit the care of them to those monks who joined to the priesthood an approved and exemplary virtue.

THE PRIESTS DURING MASS PRAYED FOR THOSE WHO CONFESSED TO THEM.

THIS was the constant practice of the Greek church; as to the Latin church, it does not appear, that there existed any distinction relatively to this article, between secular and regular priests, both having been indifferently employed in hearing confessions; it appears even, that all those who were honoured with the priesthood, were at the same time charged with the care of directing consciences, as may be seen from the Gallican Mass, which Illiricus has presented to the public, and which on this account ought to be less suspected. It is as ancient at least as the eighth century. The priest there prays, in more than ten places, (b) for all those who were in the habit of confessing to him; whence it may be easily inferred, that every priest who celebrated mass, was also ordinarily the confessor of many penitents.

But why should I recur to authorities to prove the generality of the practice of confessing, prior to the council of Lateran, in order to conclude that there must have existed a law at that time, obliging the faithful to confess their sins, when we have monuments of the tenth, and even of the eighth century, wherein the time of satisfying this law, is positively and expressly laid down.

A TIME EXPRESSLY APPOINTED FOR CONFESSION.

REGINON, whom I have already cited, makes mention, at the beginning of his second book on Ecclesiastical discipline, of a regulation of the Council of Rouen, touching the questions a bishop ought to put in

---

(a) Negotii tœdio frequentiâque multitudinis & turbulentia fatigati id operœ ad Monachos transmisêre. De potestate ligandi et absolvendi. Bibl. Patrum, Edit. Colon. Tom. 12. p. 547. (b) Pro omnibus quorum confessiones suscepi. Le Cointe ad annum 60. 1. T. 2. p. 499. p. 406, p. 514.

the visit of his diocess; and it is there said, (*a*) that a bishop should not fail to inform himself of all those persons who shall have passed, in his parish, a whole year without confession, and who shall not have made it, particularly at the beginning of Lent. Where we may see that this was the time specially marked out for complying with the obligation imposed by the law of confession.

Chrodegandus, bishop of Metz, who died in 767, exacted still more. In his rule it was required, (*b*) that every religious should confess every Saturday, and that the other faithful of his diocess should do it at least thrice during the year, namely, before the festival of Easter, Christmas and St. John, during the three Lents which were at that time observed, exhorting one another to arm themselves with courage to declare their sins with great sincerity, and adding that it is from an humble and sincere confession that pardon is to be obtained, and without this, no pardon is to be expected.

To assert after this, that before the thirteen century, the precept of Confession was unheard of, that the obligation of confession originated at the Council of Lateran, and that it was Innocent III. who first imposed it, is to betray in the face of the world, the grossest ignorance and temerity, to speak of things one knows nothing about, and upon which he has not even been willing to inform himself; but I have other still stronger proofs yet to produce.

THE SICK, IN DANGER OF DEATH, ALWAYS CONFESSED.

Venerable Bede relates in his history that a certain Courtier of the King of the Mercians, (*c*) having fallen dangerously ill, the King, who had a high esteem for him in consequence of the eminent servi-

---

(*a*) Si aliquis ad confessionen veniat vel unâ vice in anno, id est in capite Quadragesimæ. Lib. 2. Interog. 65. p. 228.

(*b*) In tribus Quadragesimis populus fidelis suam confessionem sacerdoti faciat, et qui plus fecerit melius facit. Monachi in uno quoque Sabbato confessionem faciant. Quando volueris confessionem facere, viriliter age, & noli erubescere, quia inde veniet indulgentia & sine confessione non est indulgentia. Cap. 32. T. 1. Spicil. Acheri. p. 228.

(*c*) Lib. 5. Cap. 14. tom. 2, edit. Colon. p. 130.

ces he had rendered him, went to see him and exhorted him to set his conscience in order by a good confession. The sick man replied, that although he was fully resolved to confess, yet he preferred not to do it whilst he was sick, but to wait until he should recover his health, lest he might be reproached with having confessed through fear of death. The King, zealous for the salvation of his courtier, and apprehensive for him from the debauched life which he had till then led, continuing to press him by new instances, this unfortunate man declared to him that it was now too late, and that he had already received his judgment. From this passage of the ancient history of England, it will be seen what the persuasion of the eighth century was touching this point, and how fully impressed they were, at that time, of the indispensable necessity of a good confession, to dispose one to appear before God.

But this is not the only example I have to produce; it is said in the life of St. Philbert, founder of the Abbey of Jumiege, who lived in the seventh century, (a) that one of his Monks being speechless and in the agonies of death, the holy Abbot accosted him with great mildness and tenderness, and requested him, if he had yet any sin left upon his conscience, to signify it by squeezing his hand; the sick man having accordingly given him this sign, St. Philbert repaired to the church to beseech of God to restore him the use of his speech, lest, by not confessing his sin, the devil should have power to seize upon his soul at her exit from the body. (b) God heard the prayer of the saint; the sick man recovered his speech, confessed his sin, and died shortly after in the peace of the Lord.

Peter the Venerable, a man of the first quality, who had cultivated with great care the talents which nature had given him and the advantages of his birth, writes (having learnt it from a religious of St. Angeli, an occular witness of the fact he relates) that a certain religious of this Monastery, (c) after having been for some time in his

---

(a) Sæcul. 2. Bened. p. 821.

(b) Ne adversarius animam pro abscondito crimine, valeret sub verrere in barathrum inferni. 2 Sœc. Bened. p. 821.

(c) Unde scias nullatenus te posse salvari, nisi quod perniciosè cælaveras, salubriter studeas confitendo manifestare. Lib. 1. miracul. cap. 4. T. 22. Bibl. pag. 1089.

agony, suddenly recovered from it, and declared that he had seen a venerable personage who warned him to confess a certain particular sin which he had concealed until that time, declaring to him very distinctly, that he had no salvation to expect if he did not confess it before he died.

I am well aware of the manner in which our adversaries, who are not much inclined to give credit to these sorts of histories, will treat these facts; but though they should claim the right to regard what is related even by the gravest and most creditable authors, as fabulous, yet they cannot but admit at least this fact, that there was a general persuasion at that time of the necessity of confession. This is sufficient at present for my purpose. But let us produce other proofs founded on the great precautions that have always been taken to prevent the sick from dying without confession.

PRECAUTIONS TAKEN TO PREVENT THE SICK FROM DYING WITHOUT CONFESSION.

The monks of Fulda presented a request to Charlemagne, wherein they besought him, to prevent their taking the infirm and decrepid from the monasteries, and removing them to some of their dependencies, "lest they should die without confession."(a)

The sixth council of Paris held in 829, forbids bishops to give such commissions to curates as will oblige them to absent themselves from their parish, because, adds the council, (b) "It may often happen, "that the sick may die without confession, and children without bap- "tism."

The sick who are in danger of death, says the first council of Mentz, held in the year 846, (c) must be excited to make a faithful and sincere confession of all their sins, and the penance must be pointed out to them which they would have to do, were they in health, without exacting, however, of them to do it as long as they are sick. A council in England, held in the kingdom of Kent, in the year 787, went so far as to forbid (d) any one to pray for those who should, through their own fault, die without confession.

(a Antiquitates Fuldenses. Christof. Broveri ex Offic. Plant. lib. 3 Cap. 12. Art. 5. Libelli supplicis p. 223. (b) Can. 29. T. 7. Labb. p. 1619. (c) Can. 26. Tom. 8. Labb. p. 49. (d) Concil. Calchutense T.6 . Labb. p. 1872.

From these specimens the reader will be able to judge how far Kemnitius and his brethren have been justifiable in advancing, that before the council of Lateran, the obligation of confessing one's sins to a priest was not known, or rather, whether it be not a concerted design in these gentlemen, to decry the practice of confession, by making it pass for a novelty, and at the same time the desire of acquiring the reputation of learned and penetrating men, by determining with nicety and precision, the time and place of its origin, that carried them to invent this fiction.

THE FAITHFUL CONFESSED THEIR SINS BEFORE THEY APPROACHED THE HOLY TABLE.

But this will appear still clearer by the care which the Faithful always took to purify their conscience, by confession, before they approached the holy table. Can any thing be stronger on this subject, than the exhortations of a holy Religious of the sixth century? You would not dare, says Anastasius of Sina, to touch the garments of a king with filthy hands, and how will you dare to receive the King of kings, in a heart sullied by mortal sin? "Confess therefore your sins "to Jesus Christ through the ministry of the priests, (*a*) condemn your "actions and be not ashamed to do it; for there is a shame which be- "gets sin, and another which is converted into glory and procures the "favour of God."

What is left us on the same subject by St. Paulinus, Patriarch of Aquila, who lived in the eighth century, is not less precise and energetic. "Let every one prove himself," says this celebrated author with the Apostle, (*b*) "before he receives the body and blood "of our Lord Jesus Christ. In order to prepare ourselves worthily "for it, let us have recourse to confession and penance; let us care-

---

(*a*) Confitere Christo per sacerdotes peccata tua, condemna actiones tuas, & ne erubescas, est enim confessio adducens peccatum, & est confessio adducens gloriam & gratiam. Hom. de synaxi in Auctuario Combesis T. 1. p. 890. (*b*) Antea ad confessionem & pœnitentiam recurrere debemus, & omnes actus nostros curiosius discutere, & peccata obnoxia; si in nobis comperimus, cito festinemus per confessionem & veram pœnitentiam abluere ne cum Juda proditore diabolum intra nos cœlantes pereamus. T. 6. August. p. 199.

"fully examine all our actions, and if we discover in ourselves any "grievous sins, let us hasten to obliterate them by confession and true "repentance, lest keeping the devil, after the example of Judas, hidden "within us, we also perish like him."

After this, we need not be surprised to find in the formularies of confession which the ancients have left us, and which differ but little from the examens found in the prayer-books now in use amongst us, we need not be surprised I say, to see therein amongst the more grievous sins, which formed the subject of accusation, that of having approached holy communion with a sullied conscience, and without having taken the precaution to purify it by a good confession. This is expressly mentioned in the formulary of St. Fulgentius, (*a*) who died at the beginning of the sixth century, and in that of Egbert, Archbishop of York (*b*) who died in the eighth. Both express this sin in the same terms: "I accuse myself," say they, (*c*) "of having received the body and "blood of the Lord, knowing myself to be unworthy, and to be in the "state of sin; and without having prepared myself by a good confes- "sion, and a sincere repentance." Whence it may be easily seen, that all the faithful who were sensible of having their conscience stained with any grievous sin, considered it as an indispensable duty to confess before they partook of the holy mysteries. It has even often happened, that God has made it appear, in a manner equally sensible and miraculous, to those who had neglected to take this precaution, how unworthy they were to approach the holy table.

Fortunatus, Bishop of Poitiers and an author of the sixth century, relates of St. Marcellus, Bishop of Paris, whose life he wrote, (and we find the same thing in the ancient Breviary of Paris,) (*d*) that a certain man, wishing to receive holy communion, found himself as it were invisibly bound, and remained immoveable, without power to approach the altar, whilst the others passed in order to the holy table. St. Marcellus, surprised at so extraordinary an event, asked this man the reason of it, who frankly acknowledged to him his temerity in having presented himself, without having previously accused himself

---

(*a*) In sacrament. S. Gregor. p. 226. (*b*) Apud Morin de Administrat. pœnit. in appendice p. 13. (*c*) Ego corpus & sanguinem Domini polluto corpore sine confessione & pœnitentiâ indignus accepi. (*d*) The 3d of November in the Lessons of St. Marcellus apud Seb. Cramoisy, an. 1650.

in confession of a certain grievous sin. But having repaired his fault by a good confession, he was permitted to communicate with the others.

Peter the Venerable, relates an event very similar to this, of a young man, who having engaged in a criminal commerce, with a married woman, fell dangerously sick; a priest was called in, says this author, (a) "according to the custom of the church," to hear his confession, and to administer to him the holy *Viaticum*; this young man, not only did not confess his crime, but being even interrogated by the priest, went so far as to deny it. After which wishing to receive the sacred Host, he could not swallow it, although he was able to take every other thing; which having greatly terrified him, he entered into himself and made a sincere confession of all his sins. The author who relates this fact, names the very persons who were present when it took place, and mentions, that he had it from their own mouth.

THOSE HAVE ALWAYS BEEN CONSIDERED HERETICS WHO REFUSED TO ADMIT THE OBLIGATION OF CONFESSION.

Can one desire more evident traces of the constant use of confession, and of the invariable idea of the faithful, touching its necessity? Yet, this is not all I have to say on this subject; I have still other witnesses to produce, and who say far more than all I have yet cited; they inform us, that those have always been considered heretics, who have dared to combat the necessity of confession.

As early as the third century, we find the use of the keys in absolving a penitent after an humble Confession, regarded as a distinctive mark of the true church. "You must know," (b) says Lactantius, the most eloquent man of his time, and who was still more recommendable for his zeal in defence of religion, "you must know that that is the true "church in which there is confession and penance.

Alcuin, the master of all the men of letters who flourished in his time, and so consummate in every kind of literature, that he was

---

(a) Invitatus est ad eum more Ecclesiastico Presbyter, ut ejus confessionem susciperet. Lib. 1. miracul. cap. 3.p. 22. Bibblioth. Pat. p. 1089. (b) Sciendum est illam esse veram ecclesiam, in quâ est confessio & pœnitentia. T. 3. Bib. Pat. p. 588.

commonly styled the universal man, and the secretary of the fine arts, informs us, that there arose in his time, that is to say, towards the end of the eighth century, certain heretics who refused to confess. It was against them that he wrote his 71st epistle, according to the edition of M. du Chene; and the 26th, according to that of Canisius. He therein exhorts (*a*) the authors and followers of that error to walk in the footsteps of the Fathers, and not to introduce new sects contrary to religion and the catholic faith. "Beware," says he, "of the poisonous leaven which has been lately introduced; and eat of the wholesome and pure bread of the true faith, in sincerity and truth."

Geoffroy, abbot of Vendome, who died in 1130, observing that a man named William, who had been his regent, favoured a sentiment prejudicial to the integrity of confession, and that to support it, he had strained a passage of Venerable Bede, wrote a very strong and pressing letter to him, to induce him to relinquish his error; amongst other things he particularly observed to him, (*b*) that faith cannot subsist, nor be kept entire without giving to the words of Bede a very different sense from that which he had given them (*c*): he concluded his letter by assuring him, that the obligation of confessing all mortal sins, is most certain, and that nothing is more constant than this precept.

Could Kemnitius and his reforming brethren, be ignorant of all these testimonies, touching the use of confession prior to the Council of Lateran? It is impossible.

(*a*) Sequimini vestigia SS. Patrum, & nolite in Catholicæ fidei in religionem novas inducere sectas, cavete vobis venenosum erraticæ inventionis fermentum, sed in sinceritate & veritate mundissimos sacræ fidei comedite panes. Ep. 71. T. 2. p. 417.

(*b*) Hos juxta fidem catholicam intelligere non possumus. Aliter determinanda est ista sententia—ut fidei nostræ integritas conservetur. T. 21. Bibl. Pat. ed. Col. p. 55.

(*c*) Certum est, nihil hoc certius, omnia peccata vel crimina confessione indigere & pœnitentiâ. Ibidem.

PROOFS DRAWN FROM THE PRACTICE OF THE GREEKS, IN FAVOUR OF CONFESSION.

WHAT renders them still more inexcusable is, that they could not be ignorant of the practice of the Greek * schismatics, who confess even to this very day, in the same manner as Roman Catholics do. This alone ought to have furnished them with a reflection perfectly natural

---

* The Greeks were perfectly united to, and in communion with the Mother Church until the year 864, when Photius, a wicked, ambitious, and intriguing man, intruded himself into the patriarchal see of Constantinople, expelled Ignatius through the favour of the emperor Michael, and cut himself off from her communion. Being afterwards deposed and excommunicated by the eighth general council held at Constantinople in 869, most of the Greek Bishops who had taken part with him returned to the Church, made their submission, and the two churches were again united. Things continued in this state until Michael Cerularius, patriarch of Constantinople, thought proper in 1053, to renew the same fatal division which Photius had begun. After every effort was made by Pope Leo IX. to reclaim him and his rebellious adherents without effect, he was also formally condemned and excommunicated. The Greeks persevered in this schism until the year 1274, when they were once more united in the second council of Lyons, (fourteenth general) after having abjured their schism, received the profession of faith of the Latin and Roman church, and acknowledged the supremacy of the Holy See. This union lasted but until the death of the then emperor, when a new breach was made by the disaffected Bishops, which lasted until the year 1439, at which time a new attempt was made to effect a union in the celebrated council of Florence. At this council the emperor and the patriarch of Constantinople assisted in person, with twenty archbishops of the East, and a vast number of other Greek ecclesiastics of distinguished merit and capacity. The patriarchs of Alexandria, Antioch, and Jerusalem, sent their deputies. After all the difficulties had been cleared up, the emperor, the patriarch, and the Greek bishops, gave a profession of faith, conformable to that of the Roman Catholic church, in which they acknowledged in particular the procession of the Holy Ghost from the

and every way calculated to precaution them against the error into which they have given, and which they have disseminated with so much assurance. For I would fain ask of these able chronologists whether it was before or after the Council of Lateran, that the Greek

---

Father and the Son, the Pope to be the visible Head of the Universal church. The words of the Council are these: "We define the "holy apostolical see and the Roman pontiff to be invested with the "supremacy in the whole world, and that the same Roman pontiff is "the successor of St. Peter, the prince of the apostles, and the vicar "of Jesus Christ, and head of the whole church, and the father and "teacher of all christians, and that full power is given to him by "Jesus Christ our Lord, in St. Peter, to feed, guide, and govern the "universal church." After this, a union was agreed upon by both churches, and a decree drawn up containing all those points which the Greeks had before contested, which was signed by the Pope, by the patriarchs, and the other Greek prelates, excepting Mark, bishop of Ephesus, who constantly refused to subscribe it. Thus were the Greeks after so many unhappy relapses, for the last time united in communion with the Mother Church, which union diffused an universal joy throughout the Catholic world. But this joy was of short duration. When the emperor and Greek prelates returned to Constantinople, they found the clergy and people of that schismatical city strangely prepossessed against the union. These abused in the most wanton manner, those who had signed it, and eulogised the bishop of Ephesus for having alone had the courage to refuse his consent. Those who had assisted at the council of Florence, intimidated by this tumult, renounced what they had done, and thus was the schism finally consummated. Some years after, Pope Nicholas V. a pontiff of distinguished piety, reflecting upon the many useless efforts which had been made to effect the conversion of the Greeks, wrote them a letter, in which, after having dwelt upon the preparations which the Turks were making against them, he exhorted them to open at length their eyes upon their past obstinacy and to return. "It is now a considerable time," said he, "that the Greeks have "abused of the patience of God, by persevering in their schism. "God, according to the parable of the Gospel, waits to see whether "the fig-tree, after so much care and cultivation, will at last yield

schismatics submitted to the practice of auricular confession? If the precept of confession was acknowledged and practised among them before the Council of Lateran, that Council consequently could not be the author of it; and if it be only since the Council, that the Greek schismatics confess, how came they to have so much complaisance as to imitate us in a new and troublesome practice, who, as every history informs us, have always been in the habit of reproaching and exclaiming against the Latins, for the most trifling changes, even in things of mere discipline?

Can it be for a moment supposed, that they would have chicaned so much about the tonsure and beard of our priests, the fast of Saturday, and the chant of the *Alleluia*, and when required to subject their consciences to a new and difficult law, when it was proposed to erect the necessity of confession into a *dogma*, they would not only remain silent upon so considerable a change in doctrine, but even act in concert with the Latins, in tamely submitting to a yoke, against which the pride of man is naturally so inclined to rebel and reclaim?

Who will believe such paradoxes? It is a fact well known that more than eight centuries have elapsed since the Greek schismatics first separated from the catholic church; since then, * auricular confession

---

"fruit; but if, within the space of three years, which God of his in-"dulgent mercy still grants them, it yieldeth none, the tree shall be "cut down to the very root; and the Greeks shall be visited by those "ministers of divine justice whom God shall send to carry that sen-"tence into execution which he has already pronounced in heaven." For the literal accomplishment of this prediction, we refer our readers to every ecclesiastical history.

* The Greeks agree with Roman Catholics not only in the practice of auricular confession, but also in almost all those points in which our adversaries dissent from us; as the following testimonies, drawn solely from protestant writers, sufficiently prove.

1. "With Rome," says Sir Edwin Sandys, "the Greek church concurs in the opinion of transubstantiation, and generally in the sacrifice and whole body of the mass." Relat. of Western Relig. p. 233. See also Dr. Potter, in his answer to Charity Mistaken, p. 225, and Bp. Forbes de Euch. L. 1. c. 3. p. 412.

2. "The sacrifice of the Mass is used by the Greeks, for the quick

is as much in use among them as it is among us, and they are no less persuaded than we are of the necessity of it, this practice and the general persuasion of all christians touching the necessity of this prac-

---

and the dead," says Alex. Ross in his View of the Religions of Europe, p. 479.

3. "The Greeks of Venice and all other Greeks," says Bishop Forbes, Consid. Modest. de Sacr. Euch. p. 422, "adore Christ in the eucharist, and who dare either impeach or condemn all these christians of idolatry." "When the sacrament is carried through the temple," says Alexander Ross, p. 479, "the people, by bowing themselves, adore it, and falling on their knees kiss the earth."

4. "The Greeks reckon seven sacraments," says the Atlas Geographicus out of Sir Paul Ricaut, vol. 2, p. 1724, "the same with the church of Rome."

5. "They are no less for church authority and tradition than Roman Catholics are," says Alexander Ross, p. 479.

6. "They agree (with Rome) in praying to saints; in auricular confession; in offering of sacrifice and prayers for the dead," says Sir Edwin Sandys. "They place much of their devotion," says Alexander Ross, "in the worship (he should say veneration) of the blessed Virgin Mary, and of painted, but not carved images; in the intercession, prayers, help, and merits of the saints, whom they invocate in their temples," p. 479.

As for auricular confession, the Atlas Geographicus also takes notice out of Sir Paul Rycaut, p. 1722. 1. "That the Greeks of note are obliged to confess four times a year; their clergy once a month, and the labouring people once a year: the priests oblige them to confess every thing, saying, they cannot otherwise release them."

And as for prayers for the dead, "they believe," says Alex. Ross, p. 479, "that the souls of the dead are bettered by the prayers of the living."

7. "They do not hold," says Alex. Ross, p. 479, "a purgatory fire, (that is to say, they are not willing to acknowledge a fire in purgatory; nor are Catholics obliged to hold there is) yet they believe," says he "a third place between that of the blessed and the damned, where they remain who have deferred repentance until the end of their life. But if this place be not purgatory, I know not what it is, nor what the souls do there."

tice, must necessarily be anterior to the separation of the Greeks from us. Here is a reflection which even good sense ough naturally to have suggested to Kemnitius and his reforming brethren, and hich

---

8. "The Greeks place justification," says the same author, "not in *faith* alone, but in works."

9. "They celebrate their liturgy in the old Greek tongue, which they scarce understand," says the same writer, p. 481, and Mr. Breerwood, in his Enquiries, chap. 2, p. 12, tells us "that the difference is become so great between the present and the ancient Greek, that their liturgy yet read in the ancient Greek tongue, is not understood, or but little of it, by the vulgar people."

10 "Their Monks," says Alex. Ross, "are all of St. Basil's order; the patriarchs, metropolites and bishops, are of this order, and abstain from flesh: but in Lent and other fasting times, they forbear also fish, milk, and eggs," p. 481.

11. "The same author, p. 496, in remarking the differences between the Greeks and protestants, gives us to understand that "they permit not marriage to their priests after their ordination."

Thus far Protestant witnesses, respecting the consent of the Greeks, with the church of Rome, in the greatest part of our modern controversies with Protestants. To which Archbishop Whitgift, in his defence against Cartwright, Tract. 8. p. 473, adds the doctrines of free-will, merits, &c. And indeed so many other articles might be added, that we may advance with truth, that setting aside the dispute about "the procession of the Holy Ghost," (which together with the ambition of Photius, gave the first origin of the schism) and the controversy, about consecrating in unleavened bread, (from which Michael Cerularius, took occasion to renew the breach) the faith of both churches would to this day have been the same. For as to the article of the Pope's supremacy, it neither was any occasion of the breach at first, nor ever obstructed any of the negotiations, that have so often since been made for the re-union of the churches, since we do not find in history, that the schismatics, ever objected much to this, so that their disowning the Pope's supremacy, may be considered, but as the natural consequence of their schism: for what rebel, whether in church or in state, would ever yet acknowledge that authority by which he was condemned.

What has been here said of the tenets of the Greeks, is to be ex-

independently of the knowledge of books and those authors who have written on confession, should have prevented them from taking a ground which they must have known to be untenable, and for which

---

tended also to the Melchites in Syria, the Georgian and all those people that are of the Greek faith and communion in Asia; as also to the Russians, or muscovites in Europe, who are of the same religion: for whose doctrine and ceremonies, see Alexander Ross. p. 486, 487, 488. in short to the Armenians, who are very much spread through Persia, Mesopotamia, both the Armenians, &c. &c.

As a further confirmation of the above, I must not omit to set down the answer of Jeremias, Patriarch of Constantinople in 1574, to some Protestant Divines of Wittemberg, who had presented him the confession of Ausbourg, translated into Greek, for his approbation. This confession was accompanied with a letter in which, as they knew that the Greeks highly approved of the seven first councils, in order to flatter them, they hadinserted the following deceptive clause: " We hope, (said they) that although there may exist between us a difference in some ceremonies, by reason of the distance of places, you will nevertheless perceive that we have introduced no innovation in the principal things necessary to salvation; and that we embrace and hold, as far as we are able to understand, the faith which has been taught us by the Apostles, Prophets, and holy Fathers inspired by the Holy Ghost, and by the seven councils established and founded on the holy Scriptures." It was impossible for these Wittemberg divines not to see that these words written to Greeks, would naturally give them to understand and believe, that the Reformers did actually receive the seven first councils; which, however, they knew was not true, principally with regard to the seventh council. It is therefore very visible that they would not be sorry to see the Greeks led into this mistake to their advantage, and esteem them more devoted and attached to the Fathers and councils, than they were in reality, provided this deception, should render them more favourable to their doctrine.

But the Greeks were not to be so easily ensnared. Jeremias, the then Patriarch of Constantinople, saw through their design, and in his reply to their articles, expatiated at some length and with great freedom upon the novelty of their opinions, and condemned all

we reproach them with so much justice. This is one of those ignorances that may be styled voluntary and affected, fostered and maintained by passion, the spirit of party, a vicious obstinacy and a mali-

---

their errors. This he did in three separate letters, which were afterwards published with the whole correspondence, in 1581, and in which he, at the same time, pointed out the great disagreement in their belief. In his last letter to them, he thus expresses himself, speaking of the sacraments.

"Since you admit, says he, some of them only, and even these "with errors, and reject the others as mere traditions which are not "only, not contained in the scripture, but even are contrary to it, "by corrupting the texts, as well of the old as of the new testament, "in order to accommodate them to your own sense: since you pre-"tend that the divine John Chrysostom, who approves of Chrism, "suffered himself to be carried away by the torrent; and that by thus "rejecting the Fathers, you arrogate to yourselves the title of Theo-"logians: since you believe the invocation of saints to be a vain and "idle notion; you despise their images, their holy relics and the "honour which is paid them, in imitation of the Jews; since you "abolish the confession of sins, which we make one to another, and "the monastic life so much resembling that of Angels; we declare "to you, that the words of the scripture which contain these truths, "have not been interpreted by such like Theologians as you, nor "was St. Chrysostom, nor any of those genuine Theologians ever "carried away by the torrent. This saint, and those resembling "him, were men full of the Holy Ghost. They have wrought "miracles and wonders, both during their life-time and after their "death; and these are the men who have explained the scripture to "us, and who having received these traditions as being necessary and "pious, have transmitted them to us, as it were, from hand to hand, "through an uninterrupted tradition: Ancient Rome observes and "embraces many of them. How, therefore, could you be so bold "as to believe that you have considered all these things better, than "both ancient and new Rome? And how have you dared to aban-"don the sentiments of those genuine Theologians, in order to pre-"fer yours to theirs?" And in order to rid himself entirely of all future importunities, he concludes his third answer, in the following

cious envy to render the most holy practices of the catholic religion contemptible; an ignorance for which there is no excuse either before God or before men.

---

manner: "We pray you to give us no farther trouble, and to write "to us no more, nor to send us any more of your writings upon these "matters. You treat those great luminaries of the church, those "great Theologians too much as your equals. You pretend "to honour them with your lips, but you discard them in effect; and "you wish to destroy the efficacy of our arms, which are their di- "vine discourses, by which we are able to combat your opinions. "Thus you will rid us of trouble. Go then your own way, and write "to us no more on the subject of dogmas, but, if you are willing, "only upon topics of mere civility and friendship." This was the last letter of the Patriarch Jeremias to the Protestants, who expected, or rather hoped, to find him a warm admirer of the doctrines of the Reformation; and in order to succeed the better, had taken care to prepare the way, (after the example of Melancthon, who had already sent an insidious letter to Joseph, his immediate predecessor in the Patriarchate of Constantinople, to which he received no answer) towards conciliating his esteem, by declaring that they received and acknowledged the seven first general councils, which they knew to be irreconcileable with their principles, and which they had already more than once publicly disclaimed and rejected. I regret that my limits will not permit me to insert the whole of this curious correspondence, which displays at once, in a manner equally clear and authentic, the great disagreement existing between the Greeks and Protestants, in almost every point in which Protestants dissent from us, and at the same time how perfectly (two points alone, as mentioned above, excepted, and one of which protestants hold as well as we) they agree and have always agreed with us: But I trust that what I have given of it, will suffice for my present purpose.

CHAP. IX.

THE DIVINE INSTITUTION OF CONFESSION PROVED BY OTHER ARGUMENTS.

HAVING given the authority of the scripture, the tradition of the councils, the testimonies of the Fathers, and the practice of the church in every century and in every country, where the religion of Jesus Christ has been known or established, I shall now proceed to offer in proof of the divine institution of confession, several arguments drawn from reason which will place this truth above all doubt, and beyond the possibility of contradiction.

1. I prove it, in the first place, from its antiquity. For, all human institutions in the church are found to derive their origin either from some general council, or from the decrees of some Pope: but, that confession existed in the church before the decree of any council or of any Pope, may be seen from the testimonies cited above; since St. Ireneus, Tertulian, St. Cyprian, and Origen, lived not only before the convocation of the first general council, namely the Nicene, but before every other council, provincial not excepted, and every Pope who has issued any Bull, touching sacramental confession, as has been sufficiently proved above by the testimonies, both of the councils and Fathers and their respective dates.

Again: That confession is of divine institution, I prove from this well known axiom of law, viz: *In dubio, melior est conditio possidentis:* that is to say: If a man has enjoyed the quiet, and undisturbed possession of a certain property for a length of time, and it cannot be shewn, that he acquired or holds the same unjustly, the law will always support and maintain him in his possession, because it presumes always in favour of him who is in possession; and this very possession is considered by law a sufficient title: the justness of which decision, is founded upon this other maxim: *Nemo presumitur malus donec robetur; i. e.* no one is presumed guilty until he be proved. Now let this be applied to confession. The Catholic church has been in possession of confession, these eighteen hundred years: If not; let the contrary be proved. Let it be shewn, 1st. Who the artful impostor was, that first intruded it into the Christian world; 2dly in what century, or age of the church this innovation took place; 3dly in what country it was first introduced; 4thly who were the chief abettors of this strange dogma; and 5thly, who were they that opposed it. He who denies the divine institution of this sacrament, must be able to point out each of these five points: for, it is a fact well known to all who have the slightest knowledge in church history, that at the most trifling and insignificant innovations or changes that have taken place in the Christian world, every one of the above points can always be ascertained. Now as this is impossible in regard to confession; we must conclude that the author of confession, is our divine saviour Jesus Christ himself, according to the celebrated rule laid down by St. Austin, lib. 4. de Bapt. c. 6. where he says, (*a*) that when any doctrine is found generally received in the church, in any age whatsoever, whereof there is no certain author, or beginning to be found, then it is sure, that such a doctrine comes down from Christ and his apostles.

2. I prove it, in the second place, from the difficulty of establishing such a law: for if there be any thing in the Catholic church, which may be considered hard and difficult, it is most assuredly confession. What is there, in effect, more irksome and disagreeable than for an emperor, a king, or persons of the highest distinction, to be compelled to reveal to the priests, who are but sinful men like themselves, all their most hidden and shameful abominations of whatever nature or species, or however painful the discovery may be to the feelings of the penitent, to submit to the judgment of these same priests, and to undergo the penalty enjoined by them? So great is the difficulty attending such a matter, that it may be safely pronounced incredible, that any prelate would ever dare to make, or introduce such a law; or that he would ever be able to persuade the people to receive and submit to it for so many ages; unless it were indeed established, supported and encouraged by a divine command, a divine institution, and a divine promise. Divine, therefore, must be the authority which has brought the minds of men to submit to confession, and divine the promise, that has brought them to submit to it willingly.

(*a*) Quod universa tenet ecclesia, nec a conciliis institutum, sed semper retentum est, auctoritate apostolicâ traditum rectissime creditur. S. Aug. lib. 4. de Bapt. c. 6.

3. The third argument is drawn from its great utility: for, an humble confession, brings always with it so many real benefits and advantages, that if there were no other proof of its divine institution, these alone would suffice. For, whether we consider God, or whether the priests who govern his church by his authority; whether we take the whole church in general, or only each of the faithful individually, the signal utility of confession every where appears.—First, we discover in this scheme the wonderful mercy of God, who does not here extort the confession of the guilty, after the manner of terrestrial judges, in order to condemn them after having confessed; but like a charitable physician, in order to heal their wounds, as soon as they shall discover them: also his justice, which checks the pride of the sinner, by the humility of confession, and which exacts that those who did not blush to do what was shameful, should undergo the confusion of confession.—2dly, Great advantage is derived therefrom to the pastors of souls, who by the confession of the sheep, become acquainted with their diseases, and thus are better enabled to apply to each one the most convenient remedies, as well in private by their counsels, as in public by their discourses. 3dly, The utility of confession both to church and state, is no less apparent: for many evils which can never be remedied by public courts of justice, are without difficulty corrected by the tribunal of penance. Witness the number of restitutions daily made, which would never be made without it:—Witness the many families divided by mortal dissentions, from time immemorial, that are reconciled and meet together again in the kiss of peace and friendship:—Witness the many baneful effects of slander and detraction, which are arrested and destroyed by the retractions and reparations of penitents, who are obliged to discharge this duty at the risk of their very characters, under the penalty (in case of refusal) of being deprived of absolution, and consequently of the benefit of the sacrament:—Witness the many unjust contracts that are dissolved by it, the many thousands of vices and disorders most injurious to the community, which are eradicated, and which the civil authority would in vain attempt to suppress:—Witness, in short, the many dangerous conspiracies, and other foul compacts, which have been from time to time, and are still detected and eluded by the confessor's wise and prudent counsel to the penitent, and caution to the state.—*Lastly*, the principal utility that accrues from confession, is received by those who discharge as they ought, this duty with integrity and fidelity.

For, to say nothing of the inestimable benefit of having their sins remitted them, and of being reinstated into favour with God, which Jesus Christ has solemnly promised, Mat. 18. 18. and John 20. 22, 23, they will receive also many other advantages; such as a present comfort and ease of conscience, a remedy against future sins, directions and prescriptions from the minister of God, for curing the spiritual maladies of the soul, &c. 2dly, that by this short passing confusion, which will last but a moment, they will escape the dreadful shame of having their sins written on their foreheads at the last day, to their eternal confusion, *when the Lord*, according to the apostle St. Paul, 1 Cor. 4. *will bring to light the hidden things of darkness, and will make manifest the counsels of the hearts.* These and many other advantages, of which frequent mention is made in the works of the holy fathers, are obtained by every sincere penitent upon making a faithful and exact confession of his sins.

4. The fourth and last argument, I shall offer in favour of the divine institution of confession, is drawn from the infalibility of the church, which has repeatedly and solemnly declared this truth in her general councils, and emphatically taught the same in every age. This declaration alone of the Catholic church, the oldest and only church that has descended in a direct line from the Apostles down to us, and which St. Paul styles *the pillar and ground of the truth*, ought indeed to suffice to resolve every difficulty on this subject, and banish for ever all doubt. But as our adversaries, for reasons best known to themselves, are not willing to concede this privilege to the church, of never erring in matters of faith, I shall proceed to establish it, by such arguments, as I trust, will leave no doubt upon any unprejudiced mind. This truth, in fact, is the more important, as it not only offers an invincible argument in favour of confession, but puts an end at once to every dispute on matters of religion.

THE CHURCH CANNOT ERR IN MATTERS OF FAITH.

In order that the question may be fairly stated, and leave no room for equivocation, I first define and understand the word, *Church*, to be that society of faithful, founded by Jesus Christ, propagated by the Apostles, continued by the posterity of the first Christians, perpetuated to us by the faithful, always governed by pastors, inheritors both of the faith and of the sees of their predecessors, spread over the earth, and visible in all ages, in the exercise of the functions of the sacred ministry.

Now it is to this church, that Jesus Christ has made his promises: It is this church, which has subsisted from her first establishment without any interruption, and which will subsist to the end of time: It is in short, this church which cannot teach errors contrary to faith. Three propositions which I shall establish by the most convincing and undeniable proofs.

First Proposition. I say then first, that it is to the church, such as I have represented her to be, namely, to a church visible by the continuity of the faithful, the uninterrupted succession of her pastors, and the exterior functions of the sacred ministry, that Jesus Christ has made his promises. To be convinced of this, it is enough to read what precedes and what follows the promises, which Jesus Christ has made to his church: it will be immediately seen, that to attach any other idea to the church of which Jesus Christ speaks, is to sport with the scripture, and to abandon one's-self without reserve to the most absurd and ridiculous imaginations.

Let the reader then examine the promise which was made in the 16th chap. of St. Matt. v. 18. where it is said: *Thou art Peter;* (a) *and upon this rock* (b) *I will build my church; and the gates of hell*

(a) *Thou art Peter, &c.* As St. Peter, by divine Revelation, here made a solemn profession of his faith of the divinity of Christ; so, in recompense of this faith and profession, our Lord here declares to him the dignity to which he is pleased to raise him, viz. That he, to whom he had already given the name of Peter, signifying a rock, St. John 1. 42. should be a *rock* indeed, of invincible strength, for the support of the building of the church; in which building he should be, next to Christ himself, the chief foundation stone, in quality of chief Pastor, ruler, and governor; and should have accordingly, all fullness of ecclesiastical power, signified by the keys of the kingdom of heaven.

(b) *Upon this rock, &c.* The words of Christ to Peter, spoken in the vulgar language of the Jews, which our Lord made use of, were the same as if he had said in English, " Thou art a rock, and

(a) *shall not prevail against it.* Let him observe also, that immediately after these words, our divine Saviour adds, addressing himself to Peter, v. 19. *And I will give to thee the keys of the kingdom of heaven: and whatsoever thou shalt bind upon earth, it shall be bound also in heaven: and whatsoever thou shalt loose upon earth, it shall be loosed also in heaven:* Can any thing be more plain? Can words be clearer? Is there not here a church pointed out, in which there are both pastors and sheep, in which they absolve and in which they condemn, in which they bind obstinate sinners, and in which they loose such as are contrite, and consequently, in which the ministerial function is visibly exercised? But was the visible exercise of the ministry to be confined to the time of St. Peter? Was it not to extend to future ages, and to be continued by the successors of this apostle? It is then manifest that he had here a visible and a successively continued society in view, and that it is to such a church he has promised, that "the gates of hell shall never prevail against it."

Let us again examine this other promise of the Saviour in the 28th chap. of St. Matt. v. 20. *Behold, I am with you all days, even to the consummation of the world,* and let it be observed that these words were not addressed to the apostles until after they had received the

---

"upon this rock I will build my church." So that by the plain course of the words, Peter is here declared to be the rock, upon which the church was to be built; Christ himself being both the principal foundation and founder of the same. Where also note, that Christ, by building his house, that is, his church, upon a rock, has thereby secured it against all storms and floods, like the wise builder, Matt. 7. 24. 25.

(a) "*The gates of hell,*" &c. That is the powers of darkness, and whatever satan can do, either by himself, or his agents. For as the church is here likened to a house or fortress, built on a rock; so the adverse powers are likened to a contrary house or fortress, the gates of which, i. e. the whole strength, and all the efforts it can make, will never be able, to prevail over the city or church of Christ. By this promise we are fully assured, that neither Idolatry, heresy, nor any pernicious error whatsoever, shall at any time prevail over the church of Christ.

order to go and to preach throughout the whole earth, and to baptize all nations. *Go ye, therefore,* said our divine Saviour to them, *and teach all nations; baptizing them in the name of the Father, and of the Son, and of the Holy Ghost;.....and, behold, I am with you all days, even to the consummation of the world.* Is not this the same as if he had said: Go and preach, I shall be with you when you preach. Go and baptize, I shall be with you when you baptize. Who is there that does not see here a church visible both in the preaching of the gospel, and in the administration of the sacraments? A church which is to extend herself throughout the whole earth, since she is charged with teaching and baptizing all nations? And when our Lord adds, *all days,* who is there that does not see, that the promise is not confined solely to the apostles, who were to die as all other men, but likewise extended to their successors, whose succession was to last to the end of the world, and whom Jesus Christ solemnly promises never to abandon.

What can be stronger than the words of St. Paul, to confirm the idea which every Catholic forms of the church, in combining her perpetuity with her visibility? Does not this apostle style her in the 3d chap of his 1st epist. to Timothy v. 15, *the pillar and ground of the truth?* But of what church does he speak in this place? Is it of a society of persons apart, unknown to one another, united by no other tie than that of an interior faith of which they give no exterior proof? Does he not speak of the house of God perfectly disposed in all its parts? Of a visible society, governed by bishops and priests, whose most minute duties he has taken care to mark out? And does not the same apostle assure us in the 4th chap. of his epistle to the Ephesians v. 11. that there will always be *pastors and teachers for the perfection of the saints, for the work of the ministry, unto the edification of the body of Christ:* (namely his church) *till we all meet in the unity of faith and of the knowledge of the Son of God,* which will be manifested to us in all the splendor of his glory on the day of his second coming.

Let but a moment's reflection be indulged upon those many passages of holy writ where mention is made of the duration of the church, and it will be every where seen that this duration is always linked to a state of visibility, as if the Holy Ghost had taken the precaution to baffle all chicane, and every artifice which a mind averse to a state of dependance, might be inclined to use as a pretext to shake off the yoke of authority.

If, notwithstanding all that I have said, the reader should have still some prepossession left for this visionary phantom of an invisible church, so artfully devised to elude the promises of Jesus Christ, I would fain ask him how we should manage in these cloudy days of an eclipsed church, to satisfy the precept of Jesus Christ, who directs us, Matt. xviii. 17, to repair to the church with our complaint, to hear her sentence, and peaceably to submit to her decisions: I would ask him, to whom ought the idolaters, Jews, and Mahometans, to address themselves, in order to embrace a pure and orthodox faith, and to enter into the true way of salvation: I would ask him who has dispensed those privileged souls composing the said invisible church, with openly professing their faith, notwithstanding the express command which the Saviour of the world has given to all christians, Matt. x. 32, to confess him before men, if they did not wish to be disowned by his heavenly father, and the declaration of the apostle, couched in terms no less formal, Rom. x. 10, that it is absolutely necessary *to confess the faith with the mouth*, to be saved. I should be glad to know also, whether these interior faithful, exempt from the common contagion, have communicated in the use of holy things with the crowd under the dominion of error and idolatry: if they have, how comes it that they have not rendered themselves guilty of the same prevarication? And if they have avoided participating in the mysteries of the profane and straying multitude, how is it that they have not been remarked? and how happens it, that no historian has ever recorded it? I would also request him to inform me, of what use or of what benefit have the general councils been in repressing the heresies which have arisen in the church since the birth of christianity, if the promises of Jesus Christ have not been made to a visible church. Behold then the decisions of all the general councils subject at once to a revision, as flowing from a tribunal which has nothing in it to render us secure or confident. Behold all the heretics of past ages, such as Arians, Macedonians, Nestorians, Eutichians, Pelagians, &c. again let loose upon the world, a wide door is opened to them, they have but to thrust themselves into an invisible church, which they can with all ease and propriety form, to shelter themselves from the anathemas of the church visibly assembled in her councils. It cannot be denied that these and such like questions are not a little embarrassing, and that it would be vain to attempt giving them a satisfactory answer; it cannot either be denied, that of all the protestant writers, none have ever explained themselves more rationally on the present matter, than the celebrated Melancthon, author of the Ausbourg Confession, and who next to Luther was the most active in bringing about the pretended reformation. Here are his own words, which will be found in the preface to his works.* "We must necessarily admit," says he, "a visible church; for it is evidently of her "that the Son of God speaks when he says, *tell the church:* and St. "Paul when he says: *that we are made a spectacle to the world, and* "*to angels, and to men.* But how a spectacle," he demands, "if it "be imperceptible? What will be the effect of these inconsiderate "speeches which deny the existence of any visible church? Is it "not sufficiently apparent, that they go to destroy at once the testimony of all antiquity, to annul every decision the church has ever "made, and to introduce the most licentious of all anarchies?" Thus Melancthon.

I cannot believe, after such solid reasons, that any doubt will remain upon the mind of any unprejudiced reader, respecting the truth of the first proposition which I have advanced above: I shall therefore proceed to the second.

Second Proposition. I say that this visible church, and which is so easily known by the continuity of the faithful, the succession of her pastors, and the exterior functions of the sacred ministry, has not ceased since her first establishment to be the true church of Jesus Christ, and that she will never cease to be that true church to the end of time. This proposition will be seen, at first sight, to be but a natural consequence of the preceding one; for if it be to the church such as I have represented her, that Jesus Christ has made his promises, it will doubtless be this same church which will have experienced and which will always experience the effects of these promises, and consequently when we meet with persons who are so bold as to assert that the faith began to be altered in the fourth century, that

---

* Necesse est fateri esse visibilem Ecclesiam, de qua filius Dei inquit, dic Ecclesiæ, & de qua Paulus ait, sumus spectaculum toti mundo, Angelis & hominibus. Quale spectaculum est quod non cernitur? Quò spectat autem hæc portentosa oratiò quæ negat esse visibilem ullam Ecclesiam? delet enim omnia testimonia antiquitatis, abolet judicia, & facit anarchiam infinitam.

error has been always encreasing, and that for upwards of a thousand years before the reformation undertaken by Luther, the church governed by bishops, instead of remaining the faithful spouse of Jesus Christ, had become a miserable prostitute, what can we think of those who discourse in this manner, but that an excess of inconceivable prejudice has so bewildered their minds as to deprive them of the good sense and reason which they should naturally have to reflect, that by their fine system of religion they make of Jesus Christ a false prophet, and worse, than this, an impostor as unfaithful in fulfilling his promises as he was lavish in making them.

Is it not somewhat surprising that persons who are for ever boasting of their care and attention in adhering closely to the text of the scripture, and who make of this pretended attention the fundamental maxim of their reformation, when the question relates to the article of the church, which is the most important of all others; of that article which the apostles have thought proper to place in their creed immediately after what is necessary to be believed of the three divine persons, is it not, I say, somewhat surprising that these very men will then hold a language directly contradictory to that of the scripture? Jesus Christ says that the gates of hell shall not prevail against his church, and they dare to say that error has prevailed against her; Jesus Christ promises to be with the successive body of pastors, all days, even to the consummation of the world, and they dare to say that Jesus Christ has abandoned this body of pastors during many ages; Jesus Christ commands us, Matt. xviii. 17, to hear the church, under the penalty of being regarded as heathens and publicans, and this without fixing any bounds to the submission he exacts from us to her, and they pretend that there may be cases in which not only one may dispense with receiving the decisions of the church, but wherein he is even obliged to combat them. St. Paul styles the church *the pillar and ground of the truth;* and these make her a feeble ozier bending under the weight of error; the same apostle declares to us that there will always be true pastors and true doctors, it being absolutely necessary for the support and preservation of the church; and they pretend that for a very considerable time there were only false pastors, false doctors, who merited rather the title of seducers and teachers of falsehood. Is not this a good set-out to dispose us to credit them on their word, when they assure us with so much confidence that in what respects belief, their first care, or rather their only object, is to follow the letter of the sacred text, which they hold up as the only and invariable rule of their faith? Who is there that does not remark here the most palpable contradictions, and will not deem that cause at least suspicious, which is thus defended?

THIRD PROPOSITION. I now pass to the third proposition, and say that the church, of which I continue to speak always in the same sense, and under the same idea, which I at first traced of her, has not at any time and never will be able to teach errors contrary to faith. The proof I shall give is plain and explicit. It is this. If the church should at any time teach errors contrary to faith, she would cease from that instant to be the true church; for nothing can be imagined more incompatible with, or more proper to deprive her of this, her quality of the true church of Jesus Christ, than errors contrary to faith. Now it has been demonstratively proved that the visible church spread over the whole world, discoverable by the continuity of the faithful, the succession of pastors cannot conformably to the promises of Jesus Christ, which have been made to her, ever cease to be the true church, therefore, we must conclude at the same time, that this church, taken always in the same sense, cannot teach errors contrary to faith. Here is a very short and a very simple reasoning, but which terminates at once all controversies on matters of religion; and until it be answered (which will never be done with any success) we have a right always to refuse, if we please, to enter upon the discussion of any particular article. It is a sure ground. The authority of the church, supported by the promises of Jesus Christ, is a firm rampart against every attack that can be made upon us. The church of Christ, cannot err in matters of faith, therefore, all her decisions are true, all her doctrine the true faith of Christ. Therefore the confession of sins, taught by the same church, to have been instituted by Christ and to be necessary to salvation, was indeed instituted by Christ and is indeed necessary to salvation.

In vain will it be pretended, by way of palliation, and in order to reconcile the principles of the reformation, with the above strong texts of scripture, in favour of the church's infallibility, that the church of Christ was never utterly destroyed, but only in a state of decay; that faith was not entirely extinct, but only obscured; that the truths of the gospel were altered, but not annihilated; all this fine modification will not save the promises of Christ, nor justify those, who by pretending to respect them, only give them a more vital stab. To shew at once the absurdity of it, I will only observe that: Either the church, has taught errors, or she has not; either the errors which she has taught were prejudicial to salvation, or they were not; if the church has not taught errors prejudicial to salvation, it was wrong to separate from her, for a separation from the church, could not in its origin and cannot in its continuance be but unjust, unwarrantable, criminal and damnable; if the church has ever taught errors prejudicial to salvation, she is then completely overturned and destroyed: for what is it that can effect her destruction, if it be not errors prejudicial to salvation? Or to express the same in other terms which will more clearly elucidate this thought, if the church has never taught errors prejudicial to salvation, how and in what sense can she be styled *the pillar and ground of the truth?* Of what avail has the ever present assistance of Jesus Christ been to her? Who will ever be able after this to reconcile to his mind the idea of a church built upon a rock, and having nothing to fear from the united efforts of the powers of hell, if it be true to say, that the wild imaginations of a few headstrong men, have sufficed to triumph over her?

CHAP X.

PROTESTANTS IN FAVOUR OF CONFESSION.

LET us now hear our adversaries themselves, on this important subject. And to begin with the chief of the Reformers: Luther in the seventh tome of his works in his example, whether the Pope has power to command confession; thus writes: "I look upon private "confession, says he, to be a very precious and salutary thing. O "how much ought all Christians to rejoice that it exists, and to thank "God that he has permitted and given it to us. Two reasons, continues "he, ought powerfully to excite us to confess willingly and cheerful- "ly. The first is, the holy Cross, that is, the shame and confusion "for a person to accuse himself of his own accord, before other men, "and to be tried by them. O if we but knew what pain, this voluntary "confusion prevents, and how propitious it renders God, when a man "thus humbles and annihilates himself, we would dig up confession "from the very earth. No fasting, no prayers, no indulgence, no "suffering, can contribute so much as this voluntary shame to render

"a man humble, that is to say, susceptible of grace. And would
"to God, it were a custom to confess publicly before the whole world,
"our secret sins, as St. Austin did. O God! how soon should we
"become men rich in grace! And why are we so much ashamed before
"one man, when we shall have to endure so much on our death-bed;
"which is not far distant, before God, all his angels, and the devils,
"which will go infinitely harder with us; all which we may now
"easily prevent, by this momentary shame before one man. Besides,
"I do not know, whether a person can have a true and lively faith
"who is not willing to suffer so much, and to take up so small a piece
"of the cross. The second reason which ought to incite us to make
"a voluntary confession, is the precious and noble promise of God,
"Matt. 16." *And whatsoever thou shalt loose upon earth, it shall be loosed also in heaven;* and John 20. 23. *whose sins you shall forgive, they are forgiven them.*—Thus Luther.

Again, in his second tome, fol. 84. edit. Lat. Wittemberg, 1546, he says: "There is no doubt but that the confession of sins is neces-
"sary and commanded by God. But private confession which is
"now in use, pleases me in every regard, and is not only useful, but
"even necessary. I would not that it were not; nay I rejoice that it
"is in the church of Christ, because it is the only remedy to an afflict-
"ed conscience."

Again, in his book against the Anabaptists, and *alibi*, he declares, speaking of the church of Rome, that "she is the true church, the
"pillar and ground of truth, and the most holy place. In this church
"God miraculously conserves baptism, vocation and ordination of Pas-
"tors, the image of the crucifix, *the remission of sins, and absolution*
"*in confession*," &c. And again,—"We confess that under the Pa-
"pacy are many good Christian things, yea, all that is good in Chris-
"tianity, and that we had it from thence: For we acknowledge that
"under the Papacy, is the true scripture, true baptism, the true sa-
"crament of the altar, *true keys for the forgiveness of sins*, true office
"of preaching, true catechism, as the Lord's prayer, the ten com-
"mandments, and the articles of the faith. I say, moreover, that un-
"der the Papacy is true Christianity, even the very kernal of Chris-
"tianity."

In the Ausburg confession or apology, art. 11. 12. 22. Apol. de pœnit. p. 167, 200, 201, it is expressly laid down, that "Absolution
"ought to be retained in confession; that to reject it, is an error of

" the Novatians, and a condemned error; that this absolution is " a true sacrament and properly so called; that the power of the keys " remits sins, not only in the sight of the church, but also in the sight " of God." And in Luther's little catechism, which is unanimously received throughout the whole party, we find these words: " In the " sight of God we must hold ourselves guilty of our hidden sins: but " with respect to the minister, we must confess those only, which are " known to us, and which we feel within our hearts." And the better to discover the Lutherans conformity with us, in the administration of this sacrament, the reader need only refer to the absolution, which, as the same Luther in the same place sets it down, the confessor gives the penitent, after confession, in these terms: " Do you not believe " that my forgiveness is that of God?" "Yes," answers the penitent. " And I," replies the confessor, " by the orders of our Lord Jesus " Christ, forgive you your sins, in the name of the Father and of the " Son, and of the Holy Ghost." Do Protestants know their own doctrine, and that of the Father and Patriarch of their reformation, when they inveigh so loudly against us for believing in the utility and necessity of confession, and when they charge it with being a licentious practice? If they do not hold with the belief and practice now, it certainly is not because their founder did not strenuously recommend it.

The church of England also, is so well convinced of the divine institution of confession, that she enjoins a special charge to be given to those of her communion, to confess their sins upon two occasions. The one, when about to receive communion they shall find their conscience charged with any grievous sin, which we call mortal; the other when they are sick. It is thus, the minister addresses them in the conclusion of his exhortation before communion, as laid down in the book of common prayer, (latest edition printed in England)..........." And " because it is requisite, that no man should come to the holy communion, but with a full trust in God's mercy, and with a quiet conscience; therefore if there be any of you, who by this means cannot " quiet his own conscience herein, but requireth further comfort or " counsel; let him come to me, or to some other discreet and learned " minister of God's word, and *open his grief;* that by the ministry of " God's holy word, he may receive the benefit of *absolution*, together " with ghostly counsel and advice, to the quieting of his conscience, " and avoiding of all scruple and doubtfulness."

With regard to the second occasion, wherein the church of England enjoins a special confession to be made to the minister; we find it expressly noted in the same book, in the order for the visitation of the sick. It is thus we there read: "Here shall the sick person be moved "to make a special confession of his sins, if he feel his conscience "troubled with any weighty matter. After which confession, the priest "shall absolve him, (if he humbly and heartily desire it) after this "sort: Our Lord Jesus Christ who hath left power to his church, to "absolve all sinners who truly repent, and believe in him, of his great "mercy, forgive thee thine offences: And by his authority committed "to me, I absolve thee from all thy sins, in the name of the Father, "and of the Son, and of the Holy Ghost. Amen." The reader will perhaps be a little surprised to hear, that this is the identical form of absolution used in the Catholic church.

But it will not be improper here, to take notice, that the book of common Prayer, published by and with the approbation of the bishops, clergy and laity of the Prostestant Episcopal church, in the United States of America in convention, and which has been generally adopted by said church, since the first day of October, in the year of our Lord 1790, does not contain in the exhortation before communion, as taken down above, the words, *the benefit of absolution*, nor in the order for the visitation of the sick, any part of the above preamble and formula of absolution, which have been entirely expunged. What reason could have induced the bishops, clergy, &c. of the United States, to make the above extraordinary alteration and omission, whether it was their disbelief in the efficacy of the Absolution of the minister, which however, was thought and believed during the long interval between the days of Edward the sixth, when the liturgy was first compiled to the epoch of the American Revolution, to be a real *benefit*, and so great a *benefit*, that it was considered some *could not quiet their conscience without it*, as may be seen in the warning, for the celebration for the communion, and still more clearly inculcated in the order for the visitation of the sick, in the English book of common Prayer, or whether they deemed the above to be incompatible with the constitution, and laws of our constitution, and *that blessed liberty wherewith Christ*, as they say in the preface, *hath made us free*, and which they declare also, to be one of the many reasons which influenced them in the charges which have been made, or whether they considered the absolution of the minister to be an unessential point of doctrine, or a point of mere discipline, subject to *such changes and alterations as local circumstances might require*, I will not pretend to say. But certain it is, that to me as a Roman Catholic, and consequently not much accustomed to changes, this omission has appeared not a little surprising; especially as the words of the Episcopal formula of absolution, viz. *Our Lord Jesus Christ, who hath left power to his church, to absolve all sinnsrs who truly repent, &c*............And these others.—*And by his authority committed to me, I absolve thee from all thy sins, &c.*—have always led me to believe that they considered themselves as ministers empowered by Christ to absolve (not to declare them to be absolved, as their present revised book of common Prayer says) truly repentant sinners, and consequently, *absolution*, to have been divinely instituted, and as I do not find any mention made in any part of said revised book, of their having, since the American Revolution and independence, received from heaven any other equivalent means whereby they can, (as a *dernier resort*) *quiet the conscience of the guilty, and remove* from the poor unhappy, though repentant sinner, *all scruple and doubtfulness*.—Be this however as it may, I do not think, they, *at least* no more than the Lutherans, can with any propriety, charge that with being a *licentious practice*, namely, *confession with the use of absolution*, which they themselves once followed as well as we, which they have so very recently left off, and which their own acknowledged mother church, the church in England holds with, to this present day; or find any fault with us for preferring, having availed ourselves also, of that same *blessed liberty, wherewith Christ hath made us free*, and which our constitution has left us the free enjoyment of, to adhere to what was practised by us, long before Edward the sixth, and what we mean, old fashioned as we are, to carry with us, in spite of every new fashion, to the grave, and our successors and immediate posterity, to their graves, and so on to the end of the world.

But to resume.—I say that the above warning, before the communion of the English Episocpal church and her formula of absolution as set down in her Book of Common Prayer, in the order for the Visitation of the sick, shew evidently that this said church holds, that Jesus Christ is the author of the confession which is made to the ministers of his church, that it is founded upon the divine word of Scripture, and that they do indeed possess the power to absolve all sinners truly repentant, and consequently that all sinners are obliged to make a special declaration or confession of those sins with which their conscience reproaches them. It is true that the Puritans, the Presbyterians, the Anabaptists, and some other religious sects made a formal petition to king James, in the year of our Lord one thousand six hundred and four, at the conference held at Hampton court, to have confession abolished; but the king, far from granting their petition, confirmed the said practice, as may be seen in the 113th Canon of this same Conference, page 8, and 46, where, in conjunction with all the bishops of the realm, he declares, in quality of head of the English church, confession to be apostolical, that is to say, of divine institution. He speaks the same language, and with equal force in his Meditations upon the Lord's Prayer, where he says: "As to myself, "I do heartily approve of confession, even when made in private to "a minister, and I could moreover wish that it were more practised "amongst us; for I consider it to be a most excellent thing, and every "way calculated to prepare men for worthily receiving the holy sa-"crament."

And to shew that the real belief of the Episcopalians, is as I have stated it above, and to put this matter beyond all dispute, I shall cite two Episcopalian doctors of the English church. Mr. Bayle, the first I shall name, declares himself so decidedly in favour of confession, in his book against the Presbyterians, entitled, *The Practice of Piety*, that, I believe, no catholic will be found more favourable to confession than he is in the 51st article, page 627, (edit. 13.) These are the very words he makes use of in his exhortation to a sick man, to make a sincere confession of his sins to a minister; "Send," says he, "and "enquire after some holy and religious minister; not only that he may "pray for thee, but that he may impart to thee, after a confession and "an unfeigned sorrow and repentance, the absolution of thy sins: for, "as God hath called him to baptize thee in the repentance and remis-"sion of thy sins, so also he hath given him a vocation, a power and "authority, provided thou doth repent, to absolve thee from thy sins: "for, the Lord hath said to him: *And I will give unto thee the keys* "*of the kingdom of heaven: And whatsoever thou shalt bind on earth* "*shall be bound in heaven; and whatsoever thou shalt loose on earth* "*shall be loosed in heaven.* And again: *Verily I say unto you,* "*Whatsoever ye shall bind on earth, shall be bound in heaven, and* "*whosesoever sins ye remit they are remitted unto them.* Now, it is "not said, Whose soever sins ye declare to be remitted; but whose "soever sins ye remit: they therefore remit sins, because Jesus Christ "remitteth the sins through their ministry, as it was Jesus Christ who "loosened Lazarus, by the hands of his disciples."

The same minister, in the conclusion of his discourse, after naming many other ministers who had the highest esteem for confession, goes on, and says: "Another faithful pastor highly commends "and advocates this practice, and Luther himself declares, that he "would rather forfeit a thousand worlds, than consent that private "confession should be abolished and put out of the church. The "church of England," it is thus he concludes, "has therefore wisely "and justly maintained at all times, the truth of this doctrine."

The second doctor of the Episcopal church I shall cite is Bishop Andrew in his court sermon on John 20. 23. *Whose sins you shall forgive, they are forgiven them.* "We are not," says he, "the ordi-"nance of God thus standing, to rend off one part of the sentence: "Three are here expressed; three persons: 1st. The person of the "sinner *(whose sins)*; 2dly, Of God *(they are forgiven)*; 3dly, Of "the priest, *(you forgive)*. Three are expressed; and where three "are expressed, three are required; and where three are required, "two are not enough. It is *St. Augustin*, that thus speaketh of this "ecclesiastical act in his time; (An. 400.) Let nobody say within "himself, I repent in private, I repent before God: God who pardons "me, knows I repent from my heart. Then to no purpose was it said, "*Whatsoever you shall loose on earth, shall be loosed in heaven*: Then "to no purpose were the keys given to the church of God; we make "void the gospel, we make void the words of Christ." Thus these two Episcopalian doctors.

I could cite many other divines of the church of England to corroborate the same, but, I think, what I have already given, will suffice. If, however, more will be required, more shall be given later.

The Presbyterian church also, if we may be allowed to judge from a work printed under the inspection of a committee appointed by the General Assembly of the Presbyterian church of the United States, equally advocates, though in a manner somewhat different, the utility and importance of confession. In a catechism containing, as it is said in the title-page, a brief but comprehensive summary of the doctrines and duties of christianity, translated chiefly from a work of professor Osterwald, by Samuel Bayard, (printed New-York, page 99.) I read the following questions and answers:

Q. " Is confession of sin necessary?

A. " Yes; without confession we cannot obtain pardon. 1 John 1. 9. " *If we confess our sins, he is faithful aud just to forgive us our sins,* " *and to cleanse us from all iniquity.*

Q. " In what manner are we to make confession?

A. " It is not sufficient to acknowledge in general that we are sin- " ners; we ought to confess in the presence of God the particular sin " of which we are guilty.

Q. " Are we to confess our sins to any but God?

A. " It is our duty to confess them to our neighbour, when they " have been committed against him, to the church when they come " under its cognizance; and to our pastor when we may have need of " his counsel."

What was the impression also of the celebrated Grotius, another Protestant, touching confession? " I am persuaded," says he, in annot. ad Consult. Cassandri, art. 40. tom. 4. fol. 621. " that the confession, " not only of public, but also of secret sins, has its advantages, which " is also confessed by the greatest part of protestants."

But what shall I say of the Protestant ministers of Strasbourg? These were so fully convinced of the advantages, importance and necessity of private confession, that they did every thing in their power to re-establish it in their churches. The history of this transaction I shall set down in a few words; it is one of the most singular and extraordinary that has perhaps ever occurred since the era of the reformation. It is to M. Scheffmacker I am indebted for it.

These protestant ministers, having it in contemplation to give a new edition of their ritual, about the year 1670, examined with the nicest care and attention what alteration it would be proper to make touching the articles contained therein, and after having made their remarks thereon, presented a written paper to the magistrate containing thirty-one articles by way of doubts and questions, respecting the changes which they judged convenient or necessary, submitting the whole, however, with great deference, as they express themselves, to the ultimate and sovereign decision of the magistrate. The sixth article of this paper spoke of communion, and they expressed a desire therein that the people should henceforth receive communion kneeling, as well to conform to the custom of the church of Saxony, whence they said they had derived the pure word of God, as to shew their belief in the real presence of Jesus Christ in the eucharist; they moreover added, that as St. Paul enjoined that every knee should bow in the name of Jesus, it was far more just every knee should bow before his person. The magistrate gave his answer to this article in these few words: *Let there be no innovation.*

The last article of the paper treated of confession, which was far more lengthy than all the others put together. An evident demonstration that they had it most at heart, and therefore wished to defend it in the best possible manner. In fact, they alledged proofs of every description to prevail upon the magistrate to consent to the re-establishment of private confession. The same custom existed then which exists now among the protestants of Strasbourg; they confessed by bands and companies, twenty or thirty persons presenting themselves at a time, to receive the same absolution. The ministers wished to change this custom, and to exact that each one in particular should make known the state of his conscience, and be absolved separately and alone; it was with a view to induce the magistrate to sanction this alteration, that they quoted in their memorial the eighth article of the Ausbourg confession, the apology, the eighth article of Smalcad, the book of concord under the article of predestination, the agreement made with the church of Wittemberg, more than twelve Lutheran authors, the very words of the Strasbourg ritual, p. 32 and 295, the opinion of John Marbach, and John Schmidt, two ministers highly esteemed in that city, and especially the text from the 20th chap. of St. John: *Whose sins you shall forgive, they are forgiven them*, &c. after which they concluded their request by observing that from a regard they had to the oath they had taken at their ordination, not to approve of any thing which might have a tendency to taint the doctrine contained in the confessien of Ausbourg, and in the apology, they thought themselves obliged to make this remonstrance touching confession; and that they might not be suspected to be influenced in this by any temporal interest or gain, they therein declared that they would cheerfully renounce all the emoluments which might arise from it, promising to forbear receiving *the piece of money* which the penitents were accustomed to present in the other Lutheran churches. The magistrate, to all this mass of reasoning, proofs, citations, &c. contented himself with simply writing in the margin of the memorial these few words by way of answer: *This is a novelty which must not be introduced.*

It must be acknowledged that these ministers took great care to say that they were far from having any intention to re-establish the confes sion of *papists*, the fact is, they had already rendered it too odious to venture to recommend such a measure as this; besides, according to them, it was an insupportable burden, a cruel torture to the conscience; it is thus they represent it in their memorial. Yet it is very certain that they were far from being satisfied with the manner of confessing, as then in use among them, and which is practised still to this day; they wished for something more, and desired that each one should acquaint his confessor in private with his interior dispositions, and if he should discover himself to be guilty of any grievous sin which gave him uneasiness, he should repose so much confidence in his confessor as to open it to him; but I would fain ask of these gentlemen, whether their object was to impose on penitents an obligation to declare their secret sins, or whether, to leave them at full liberty to confess them only to God. If they pretended that there was no obligation on penitents, and that they were not in any manner obliged to declare their sins, how could they flatter themselves with the idea that these would come of their own accord and without being led to it from a principle of duty, and what effect would this new ordinance have produced upon rational minds? And if they considered it to be indeed a duty incumbent on them, was not this to re-establish the confession of *papists* under another name. What more do catholics contend for, than that confession is a duty imposed by God himself, and divinely instituted? However it may be, they have sufficiently manifested by this proceeding, how greatly they esteemed the confession of secret sins, and if they have not been so bold as to exact it, they have at least strongly recommended it, and still more strongly desired to see the practice of it revived.

And as to the unfavourable opinion they had formed of our confession, and which they took so much care to foster and encourage in the mind of the magistrate, and which we see equally prevalent amongst the reformed churches in this country, this must be solely attributed to the ancient calumnies of the leaders of the reformation, (which I am sorry to be obliged so repeatedly to say, but which I shall fully make appear) and especially upon those disseminated by Kemnitius, or as he is otherwise called *Chemnitz*, the disciple of Melancthon, who alone upon the single article of confession, in his work published against the council of Trent, has slandered us in more than six or seven notable places.

In the first place, he charges us, tom. 1. p. 354, n. 40, with exacting a thing impossible, pretending that we require of penitents, to remember all the sins which they have committed: now, we have never said that they were obliged to remember all their sins, but only to declare those which they should remember after a diligent and reasonable examen. He lays an obligation on us, in the second place, p. 353, n. 50, to confess all sins without distinction. Now, we distinguish between mortal and venial sins, and in no manner pretend that these last named form any part of the necessary matter of confession. He accuses us, in the third place, p. 359, n. 1, with exacting a detail of all the circumstances; and we require nothing more than that the penitent should declare those which alter or change the species of the sin, or which aggravate it in a notable degree. There is certainly a wide difference between stealing one dollar, and stealing an hundred, between sinning with a single person, and sinning with one married. These are the circumstances with which it is necessary to acquaint the confessor; with regard to such as are indifferent, we not only willingly dispense penitents with declaring them, but even request and entreat them not to cumber their confession with them. In the fourth place, if Kemnitius be believed, p. 359, n. 1, we make the remission of our sins depend upon the recital we make of them, that if we should happen to omit one, all the rest would be considered as nothing worth: and we say continually that an involuntary omission which proceeds from pure forgetfulness, does not in the least prejudice or prevent the confession from being good. He charges us, in the fifth place, p. 354, n. 20, with expecting to merit the remission of our sins by the exactness and fidelity of our confession, and reproaches us for striking thereby at the root of gratuitous justification, which proceeds solely from the merits of Jesus Christ. Now, we declare with the council of Trent, sess. 6, c. 8, that nothing of what precedes justification, merits the grace of justification, and that we do not deem the confession of the sinner, to speak strictly, as a meritorious work, but as a condition which God requires, and without which he will not receive us into favour, nor apply to us the merits of his dear Son. Can we say after this that much credit is due to Kemnitius for his great fidelity and correctness in stating the doctrine of his adversaries? Or rather does it not manifestly amount to being convicted of imposture and bad faith? And does it become an honest and upright dealer to employ means so unjust and unwarrantable, to render the doctrine of his adversaries odious? Yet this has been done, this is done, and this will always be done in a bad cause. It has been so foretold, and we must expect it.

But to return to the ministers of Strasbourg. What shall we think of their extraordinary conduct? The whole body of ministers in that extensive city, from the highest to the lowest, are convinced in their mind that important changes ought to be made in certain usages in the church of Strasbourg, and especially respecting the administration of the sacraments. They make the strongest representations on this head to the magistrate, signed by the whole body of ministers; but why does not this body take upon itself and in its own name, to make the regulations it deems necessary? Is it not the depository of ecclesiastical authority? Why have recourse to an authority purely secular, which has been created and established by God only to decide law-suits, and to make regulations of civil policy, and which is invested with no power to judge or decide in matters which concern religion? But this is not all; they address themselves to the magistrate, not to act in concert with him, and avail themselves of his protection, which in some respect would be tolerable, but to submit the result of their ecclesiastical deliberations with a full and entire deference to his ultimate and sovereign decision. Who are they that thus submit all their ideas and lights? And to whom do they submit them? masters and doctors in the church, who are willing and ready to listen to those as oracles who were once their scholars, and who know no more about religion, than what they had learnt in the days of their youth from these very masters who now consult them; pastors who submit to the judgment of their flock; persons whom professional duties attach to the constant study of religion, and who promise an unrestrained deference to all that shall be decided by those, whom domestic cares, the management of public concerns, commerce, or profane studies, devote to things altogether of a different nature.

Yet these are the persons who declare to these ministers, that they must not shew any external marks of respect by their geneflections, at the time of receiving the holy communion: that they must not confess singly and in a manner calculated to discover the true state of their conscience. It is true, that the whole body of the Strasbourg ministers, was of a different opinion, and after having maturely considered and weighed the matter too; but nevertheless, the heads of civil and political departments must be believed possessed of superior lights in matters of religion. This, no doubt, was the principle which directed and influenced these ministers, and which rendered them so docile to the laconic refusal noted in the margin, and which was to serve as the answer to all their demands.

How much are they to be pitied, who stray from the paths marked out by providence. These same ministers and their reforming ancestors, were for ever raising their voice, and exclaiming against the tyrannical and imperious authority of the councils; they were unwilling to submit to the judgment of the bishops, who are the true and proper judges in religion, since they have been indeed constituted, Acts 20. 28. by the Holy Ghost himself, *to rule the church of God;* and they servilely crouch to a secular magistrate, they offer to receive instruction from those whom they ought to instruct, in short they submit to a sentiment in direct contradiction to the one they had themselves proposed without offering the least reply. How can they after this, boast of the conformity of their doctrine and rites with the holy scripture. They declare it to be their belief, that Jesus Christ ought to be adored in the Eucharist, and that penitents ought to confess their sins, one by one and in private; they cite scripture to prove and support their sentiment; the magistrate is of a different opinion, or does not find such an alteration convenient; they acquiesce in the sentiment of the magistrate, and yet equally proclaim to the people, that they always follow the scripture and conform to it throughout; what can we think after this? Can illusion go farther, can it manifest itself more sensibly?

The reader will pardon this digression, which is somewhat long, but which I have deemed very proper, to shew the great regard and esteem which our adversaries themselves have for auricular confession.

In the above transaction at Strasbourg, we have seen the Protestant clergy of that city, presenting a remonstrance to the magistrate, to have confession restored, but now I shall shew the reverse of the case, viz. the Protestant magistrates themselves, of the illustrious city of Nuremberg, strenuously urging the same. So general was the decay of piety which ensued, (as Erasmus, though by the bye, no zealous advocate for the Catholic church, and even Luther himself testify) and so great the degeneracy of morals which was brought on by the change of religion, and by enfranchising men from the powerful curbs and penitential exercises of fasting, abstinence, confession, and other religious duties, and which the magistrates of the above named city were so sensible of, that they solemnly petitioned the emperor Charles V. to re-establish auricular confession among them by an imperial law, as a check upon the prevailing libertinism, alledging, that they had learned by experience, that since it had been laid aside by them, their commonwealth was over-run with sins, against justice and other virtues, heretofore unknown in their country, and that restitution for injustices committed, was scarce any longer to be heard of. The petition (as the historians of those days inform us) only moved the court to laughter, as if a human law could compel men to the confession of the secrets of their consciences, and as if it was to be expected that any attention would be paid to the ordinance of man by a people who disregarded the institution of God, as the emperor replied. See Gahan's hist. of the church.

So much for Protestant testimonies in favour of the utility and importance of sacramental confession. Let us now see what the opinion of philosophers and free-thinkers is, on this subject. In order not to swell the Appendix too much, I shall confine myself to a few only. " There is not perhaps a wiser institution," says Voltaire, in Rem. on the Trag. of Olympia. " Most men when they have fallen into " great crimes, naturally feel remorse. The law-makers, who estab- " lished mysteries and expiations, were equally studious to prevent " the guilty from yielding to despair and relapsing into their crimes,"

" Confession," says the Philosophical Dictionary, art. *The Parson's Catechism*, " is an excellent thing, a curb to inveterate wicked- " ness. In the remotest antiquity, confession was practised in the " celebration of all the ancient mysteries. We have imitated * and

* It is altogether unnecessary to examine this imitation particularly, as the author seems himself to reject it in the following passage, where on the contrary, *it is human wisdom*, that has *perceived the utility and embraced the shadow of so useful an institution.* It is well known, the philosophers would fain derive from the ancient nations all the Christian customs and practises. And their efforts have been seconded by a performance of Dr. Conyers Middleton, entitled, *A letter from Rome:* but this work has been so completely refuted by the Rt. Rev. Dr. Challenor, that I shall take no farther notice of it. My sole object at present is to shew the homage these very men pay to the importance and utility of confession.

"sanctified this wise practice; it is excellent to induce ulcerated "hearts to forgive; and to make thieves restore what they have un- "justly taken from their neighbour."

"The enemies of the church of Rome," say the annals of the Emp. tom. 2. p. 41. "who have declared against this wholesome institution, "seemed to have deprived the world of the best check that could be "given to vice. The sages of antiquity were themselves sensible of "its importance. If they could not impose it on man as an obligation, "they established the practice for those who aspired to a life of greater "purity. It was the first expiation of the initiated among the Egyp- "tians, and in the mysteries of Elusinian Ceres. Thus has the Chris- "tian religion sanctified a practice of which God permitted, that hu- "man wisdom should discover the utility and embrace the shadow."

The author of the Philosophical and Political history of the commerce of the Indies could not refuse, in vol. 3. p. 250. his encomiums to confession. "The Jesuits have established, says he, a theocratical "government in Paraguay, but with a peculiar advantage to the reli- "gion on which it is built. This is the practice of confession, a prac- "tice of immense benefit as long as its ministers will not make a bad "use of it. * This alone stands in lieu of penal laws, and watches

---

* No Catholic will deny that in confession, as in every thing else, there have been some abuses, from which the church has laboured and still labours to reclaim, by her authority, those who have deviated from the established rules. There have been severities, and there have been laxities: some appeared to have considered confession as a bare recital of sins, without attending to the penitential feelings from which it must flow, like the stream from its fountain head. Others have made it a benefit of such difficult access, that there is scarce any aspiring to it. What does this prove, but that people may reason very ill upon things that are very good in themselves and very true? The evils occasioned by the indiscreet zeal of some confessors, have been few and transitory, but the good effects of confession, are daily and permanent. Would the philosophers have people renounce eating and drinking, because some gluttons have killed themselves by eating too much? Do the abuses hinder confession from being a curb to licentiousness, an abundant source of wholesome advice, an heartfelt consolation to souls afflicted for their sins? Does

"over the purity of morals. In Paraguay, religion more power-
"ful than the force of arms, leads the culprit to the feet of the magis-
"trate. There it is that, far from palliating his crimes, religion
"prompts him to aggravate them; instead of eluding the punishment,
"he comes to beg it on his knees: the more severe and public it is, the
"more it pacifies and composes the conscience of the criminal. Thus
"the punishment, which every where else frightens the guilty, is here
"a comfort to them, as it smothers remorse by expiation. The people
"of Paraguay have no civil laws, being unacquainted with property,
"nor have they any criminal laws, because each individual accuses
"himself, and inflicts on himself voluntary punishment. All their laws
"are precepts of religion. The best of all governments, would be a
"theocracy, in which the tribunal of confession were established, if
"always directed by virtuous men, and upon rational principles."

The celebrated Addison, being in Italy, could not behold the inscriptions from Holy Writ on the confessionals, without feeling himself struck, and relating them with a pious complacency.—These in-

---

confession cease to be an excellent means of improving the seeds of virtue in well disposed minds, of preventing the growing passions, from smothering them in others, from affording a support to innocence, from repairing the depredations of theft, from drawing closer the bonds of charity, from keeping up the love of peace, of subordination, of justice, of every virtue, from eradicating the habits of waywardness, dissention, rebellion, and all kinds of vice?

A thing well worth observing, and really supernatural and miraculous, is the seal of confession, entrusted every day to thousands of priests, often, alas! ill qualified for the profession, and capable of any other prevarication, and yet so faithfully kept. Scarce can all church history, furnish one example of infidelity in this point. If in making this observation, one should reflect on the inconsistence of mankind, on the curiosity of some, and the loquacity of others, on the nature and importance of the affairs entrusted to the ministers of this sacrament, whereof the revelation would often have astonishing effects, on the means which various interests, avarice, jealousy, and other passions, fail not to try, in order to compass their ends, &c. there will remain no doubt but that God watches over the preservation of his own work. *De Feller's Phil. Cat.*

scriptions were the following: *Let tears run down like a torrent day and night, give thyself no rest, and let not the apple of thy eye cease.—I will arise, and will go to my father, and say to him: Father, I have sinned against heaven and before thee.—Whatsoever you shall loose upon earth, shall be loosed also in heaven.—Turn, O my soul, into thy rest.—Go, and now sin no more.—He that hears you, hears me.—Come to me all you that labour, and are heavy laden, and I will refresh you.—The just man shall correct me in mercy, and shall reprove me.—See if there be in me the way of iniquity: and lead me in the eternal way.—From heaven the Lord hath looked, upon the earth; that he might hear the groans of them that are in fetters: that he might release the children of the slain.* And indeed these inscriptions are very expressive of the spirit and effects of the sacrament of penance.

CONCLUSION.

The doctrine of the Catholic church touching penance and sacramental confession, is then as ancient as Christianity itself. It is in fact the only sound and natural construction which can be put upon the tenth article of that admirable *symbol* which was framed by the Apostles under the direction of the Holy Ghost, and which is universally received throughout the Christian world. There must, unquestionably, have been a particular reason, and a reason worthy of the Holy Ghost, who inspired the Apostles, which prompted them to insert in their *Creed*, their belief in the *forgiveness of sins*, immediately after the article relating to *the Catholic church*. The same eternal wisdom which regulated the beautiful order that reigns in the material world, has in like manner regulated that which reigns in the creed.

For what else could they have intended by this admirable order of the articles of our faith, if it be not, that they wished to let us know thereby, that the forgiveness of sins is one of the greatest advantages of the church; that it is a prerogative granted to and held by her; that it is in her bosom, and in her bosom only, man can enjoy this precious advantage; that she is the true *Jerusalem*, (*a*) in which the true *Temple* exists, and the true *Probatic Pond*, (*b*) which heals all sorts of diseases; that in her only are found the true waters of the Jordan, which cleansed Naaman,(*c*) of his leprosy,; that she is that mysterious *Inn*, in which the true Samaritan effects the cure of the traveller (*d*) whom he finds wounded on the road to Jericho?

It is indeed true and unquestionably true, that to pardon sin in itself, to wash away its stain, to efface its character, to restore to the soul her lost charms, her original beauty, is a right which belongs in so peculiar a manner to God, that no creature however powerful, or however perfect he may be supposed, can ever dare pretend to it. This divine right, is a title which he attributes to himself in the scripture,

---

(*a*) Gall. 4. v. 16. (*b*) John 5. 9. (*c*) 4 Kings, 5. 14.
(*d*) Luke 10. v. 33.

to the exclusion of all others. *I am,* does he say by the mouth of his Prophet, *I am he, that blot out thy iniquities for thy own sake.*(*a*)

He alone is the creditor who can forgive this debt, which is due to him only; he alone the physician capable of healing this wound; it is incurable to every one else. It is God who is offended by sin, and infinitely offended; he alone can forgive man this infinite injury.

He alone who has created man, has the power to renew him, to purify him, to sanctify him, to *create* in him *a clean heart, and renew a right spirit within his bowels* (*b*). If the Jews blasphemed against Jesus Christ, because he had said to the man sick of the Palsy: *Son, be of good heart; thy sins are forgiven thee,* (*c*) if they were mistaken, it was not because they said, that it belonged but to God, to *forgive sin;* but because they refused to acknowledge him to be God who had wrought so divine a work, and which demonstrated to them the truth of this invisible miracle, which he had just operated in the soul of the man sick of the palsy, by the visible miracle which they themrelves had witnessed, and which he had wrought upon the body of this sick man.

But this power of remitting sin, which God alone has by nature, Jesus Christ has as God, because he is the same God with his Father, and all that belong to the Father, belong to him.(*d*) He has it likewise as man, in consequence of the *hypostatical* union of his sacred humanity, with the divine person of the word. And this he gives us evidently to understand by these words, which he addresses to the Jews, when healing the man sick of the palsy: *But, that you may know that the son of man hath power on earth to forgive sins, then, saith he to the man sick of the palsy: Rise up, take thy bed, and go into thy house.*(*e*) He possesses this power as Saviour, because he has purchased it at the price of his blood. It was to exercise it, that he came down from heaven. The prophets had foretold, that he would come *to blot out our iniquity.* The adorable name of *Jesus,* which heaven had given him before his birth, and which he received eight days after, (*f*) was a pledge of the salvation and remission which he brought us. He is called Saviour, but because he came to save his people and to save them *from their sins.*(*g*) If St. John the baptist announces him, it is(*h*)

(*a*) Isaiah, 43. 25. (*b*) Ps. 50. v. 12. (*c*) Mat. 9. 2. (*d*) John, 17. 10.
(*e*) Math. 9. 6. (*f*) Math. 2. 21. (*g*) Luke 2. 21. (*h*) John, 1. 29.

as *the lamb of God who taketh away the sins of the world.* If he dies on a cross, it is *to blot out the hand-writing of the decree which was against us.*(a) If he sends his Apostles throughout the world, it is to preach every where the remission of sins.(b)

But this is not yet all, this power so divine, so peculiar to God, so consoling to the sinner he imparts to man, to sinful man, in order to facilitate to him, that precious grace which had cost him his life and blood. He imparts it to his Apostles. He imparts it through his Apostles to their successors. He imparts it in their person to his church, to be exercised by his ministers, through all succeeding ages.

Go, said he to his Apostles, (c) *As the Father hath sent me, I also send you.* He has sent me *to save the world,* (d) you also shall become in some sort its saviours. He has sent me to destroy sin, to sanctify sinners, to reconcile man with him. Go and complete the great work. Preach every where the remission of sin. It is the fruit of my death; it shall be the end and effect of your ministry.

But in order that it should not be understood, that they had to announce or proclaim it only, or to promise it on his part, he associates them with him in this divine power. He wishes that they themselves should remit sin; that they should remit it in his name and on his part. In quality of sovereign judge, both of the living and of the dead, he constitutes them his subalterns; he imparts his authority to them, to raise even the dead to life, and to save sinners. He engages himself, to ratify in heaven, the sentence they shall have pronounced on earth.

This is in effect what he promised to St. Peter and to all his apostles, and what he imparted to them all after his resurrection *Thou art Peter,* said he to the prince of the apostles, (e) *and upon this rock I will build my church,.....And I will give to thee the keys of the kingdom of heaven : and whatsoever thou shalt bind upon earth it shall be bound also in heaven : and whatsoever thou shalt loose upon earth, it shall be loosed also in heaven.* He made afterwards the same promise, and in the same terms to his other apostles.(f) *Amen I say to you, whatsoever you shall bind upon earth, it shall be bound also in*

(a) Coloss. 2. 14. (b) Luke, 24. 47. (c) John, 20. 21.
(d) John, 3. 17. (e) Matt. 16. 18, 19. (f) 18. 18.

heaven; and whatsoever you shall loose upon earth, shall be loosed also in heaven. And in order that no doubt might be ever entertained either of the sense of his promises, or of the nature of the power promised; he himself explained it when he gave it to them. *Receive ye the Holy Ghost,* said he to them breathing on them after his resurrection, *Receive ye the Holy Ghost, (a) whose sins you shall forgive they are forgiven them; and whose you shall retain, they are retained.*

It can therefore be no longer said, *If one man shall sin against another, God may be appeased in his behalf: but if a man shall sin against the Lord who shall pray for him? (b)* This is no longer impossible from the time that the Son of God became man, and imparted his power to man. But is it to the person of the apostles he has limited and confined this power? No; he imparted it equally to the church in the person of the apostles. It passes from the apostles to their successors, they impart it to those whom they appoint to succeed or assist them in the functions of the priesthood, and whom they associate with them in the divine work with which they are charged. As the fruit of the death of Jesus Christ was to subsist always, so it was to be always applied and communicated. As the sacred ministry of the sanctification of man was to pass from the apostles to their successors, so this power of remitting sin was in like manner to be transmitted to them. They have sent others as they themselves were sent.

The power of remitting sin is like that of baptising, teaching and imparting the Holy Ghost, which the apostles have transmitted to their successors together with the episcopacy or priesthood. Jesus Christ, according to his promise, *is with them,* teaching, baptising, and remitting sin, *to the consummation of the world (c).* And consequently, to the consummation of the world, they teach, baptize, and remit sin, in the name and by the authority of Jesus Christ, or rather it is Jesus Christ who remits it through their ministry. " The priests, says St. Chrysostom, " lend their tongues and hands to Jesus Christ; " but it is God himself who does all in them and through them."

It is then to the church and for her benefit, that this power is given, and it is to last as long as she herself lasts. It is an irrevocable gift which Jesus Christ has conferred upon her, and *his gifts are without*

(a) John 20, 22, & 23. (b) 1 Kings, 2. 25. (c) Matt. 28, 19.

repentance. (*a*) It is to the apostles, as heads of the church, and her representatives, this power is given. The church, at the death of the apostles, who are her fathers, has had and will always have children, heirs of their power, and whom God himself raised up in their room, to be the *princes of the earth*, of that true promised land which he has given to his people, in which he has established his worship, and in which he distributes his favours. "It was the whole body of the church," says St. Austin, (*b*) "that Peter represented, when Jesus "Christ promised him, that whatever he should loose on earth, should "be loosed in heaven." Which made this Doctor also say: "That "it is the peace and unity of the church which remits sin; that who-"soever is not in the unity of his body, can have no part in this re-"mission. That it is the rock that binds, and the rock that looses; "that it is the dove that retains sins, and the dove that remits them; "that it is the unity of the church which remits them and which re-"tains them." Thus St. Austin.

It is by her ministers she exercises this power. They alone have the power to bind or to loose sinners, and to do towards those who are dead, as to the soul, what the apostles did in regard to Lazarus whom Jesus Christ raised to life. To them alone, as spiritual physicians, it belongs to discern between leper and leper. To them alone it belongs to pronounce on earth sentences which are ratified in heaven.

It is in administering the sacraments they exercise this power. For it is to these sacred signs that Jesus Christ has been pleased to attach his grace. It is in baptism they efface original sin, since it is in this sacrament that we are washed, cleansed, justified, regenerated in Jesus Christ, and from *children of wrath* by our birth, (*c*) we become *children of God* by his grace. (*d*) It is by the sacrament of penance, that the sins committed after baptism are remitted to true penitents. It is in this sacrament that we find a second plank in our ship-wreck. It is this second penance, as Tertullian styles it, which God has established in his church to open it to those who knock at the door, and in order that after the first door of innocence, namely, baptism, is shut, as it can be received but once, the condition of sinners might not be without resource.

(*a*) Rom. 11, 29. (*b*) S. Aug. lib. 3 de Bapt. cont. Donat. c. 17. (*c*) Eph. 2 v. 3. (*d*) Rom. 8. 16.

Such has been the faith of the catholic church in every age. If the power which she possesses of remitting sin be founded upon the most divine titles, she has preserved the most authentic possession of it. All the fathers of the church bear testimony to it. All the councils, in regulating the discipline of penance, have furnished additional proofs of the power of the church to remit sin. What the apostle did in regard to the incestuous Corinthian; (*a*) what the apostle St. John did in regard to the captain of the robbers, whom he brought over to repentance, and afterwards reconciled to the church, the same have the pastors of the church done and will continue to do in all succeeding ages. The church, in condemning the Montanists and Novatians, who wished to contest or limit her power, did but arm herself against them to preserve this precious *deposit;* and when in these latter days the protestants arose to dispute this power, they had already received their judgment and condemnation from the tradition of all ages. By their separation they have deprived themselves of the consolation and resource enjoyed by the children of the church. Their opposition and sophistry will never take from the church what she has divinely received, and what she has always preserved. They themselves are the only sufferers by their secession.

(*a*) 2 Cor. 2. 10.

NOTES REFERRED TO IN THE TRIAL.

THE POPE'S SUPREMACY.

CATHOLICS believe that the bishop of Rome, the successor of St. Peter, Prince of the Apostles, to whom Christ gave the keys of the heavenly kingdom, *Math.* 10. 2. *&c. &c.* and whom he entrusted with the special care of his flock, *John* 21. 17. *Math.* 16. 18. 19. is the visible head upon earth, of the whole Catholic church. It is no article of Catholic faith that the Pope is in himself infallible, separated from the church, even in expounding the faith. Nor do Catholics, as *Catholics*, believe that the Pope has any direct or indirect authority over the *temporal power* and jurisdiction of foreign princes, or States. Hence if the Pope should pretend to absolve or dispense with the subjects or citizens of any country from their allegiance, on account of heresy or schism, such dispensation would be null and void; and Catholic subjects or citizens, notwithstanding such dispensation or absolution, would be still bound in conscience to defend their prince and country, at the hazard of their lives and fortunes, (as far as Protestants would be bound) even against the Pope himself, should it be possible for him to attempt an invasion.

The subjoined queries which were sent, at the request of Mr. Pitt, to six of the Catholic universities, with the answers to the same, will clearly evince this point, and at once do away every unfavourable impression on this head.

Extracts from the Declarations and Testimonies of six of the principal Universities in Europe, on the three following Propositions, submitted to them at the request of Mr. Pitt, by the Catholics of London, in 1789.

THE PROPOSITIONS.

Has the pope, or cardinals, or any body of men, or any individual of the church of Rome, any civil authority, power, jurisdiction, or pre-eminence whatsoever, within the realm of England?

P

2. Can the pope or cardinals, or any body of men, or any individual of the Church of Rome, absolve or dispense with his majesty's subjects from their oath of allegiance, upon any pretext whatsoever?

3. Is there any principle in the tenets of the Catholic faith, by which Catholics are justified in not keeping faith with Heretics, or other persons differing from them in religious opinions, in any transaction, either of a public or a private nature?

Abstract from this answer of the Sacred Faculty of Divinity of Paris to the above queries.

After an introduction according to the usual forms of the university, they answer the first query by declaring:

Neither the pope, nor the cardinals, nor any body of men, nor any other person of the church of Rome, hath any civil authority, civil power, civil jurisdiction, or civil pre-eminence whatsoever in *any* kingdom; and, consequently, none in the kingdom of England, by reason or virtue of any authority, power, jurisdiction, or pre-eminence by divine institution inherent in, or granted, or by any other means belonging to the pope, or the church of Rome. This doctrine the sacred faculty of divinity of Paris has always held, and upon every occasion maintained, and upon every occasion has rigidly proscribed the contrary doctrines from her schools.

Answer to the second query.—Neither the pope, nor the cardinals, nor any body of men, nor any person of the church of Rome, can, by virtue of the keys, absolve or release the subjects of the king of England from their oath of allegiance.

This and the first query are so intimately connected, that the answer of the first immediately and naturally applies to the second, &c.

Answer to the third query.—There is no tenet in the Catholic church, by which Catholics are justified in not keeping faith with Heretics, or those who differ from them in matters of religion. The tenet, that it is lawful to break faith with Heretics, is so repugnant to common honesty and the opinions of Catholics, that there is nothing of which those who have defended the Catholic faith against Protestants, have complained more heavily, than the malice and calumny of their adversaries in imputing this tenet to them, &c. &c. &c.

Given at Paris in the general assembly of the Sorbonne, held on Thursday the 11th day before the calends of March, 1789.

Signed in due form.

UNIVERSITY OF DOUAY.

January 5, 1789.

At a meeting of the Faculty of Divinity of the University of Douay, &c. &c.

To the first and second queries the sacred faculty answers—That no power whatsoever, in civil or temporal concerns, was given by the

Almighty, either to the pope, the cardinals, or the church herself, and, consequently, that kings and sovereigns are not in temporal concerns, subject, by the ordination of God, to any ecclesiastical power whatsoever; neither can their subjects, by any authority granted, to the pope or the church, from above, be freed from their obedience, or absolved from their oath of allegiance.

This is the doctrine which the doctors and professors of divinity hold and teach in our schools, and this all the candidates for degrees in divinity maintain in their public theses, &c. &c. &c.

To the third question the sacred faculty answers—That there is no principle of the Catholic faith, by which Catholics are justified in not keeping faith with Heretics, who differ from them in religious opinion. On the contrary, it is *the unanimous doctrine* of Catholics, that the respect due to the name of God so called to witness, requires that the oath be inviolably kept, to whomsoever it is pledged, whether Catholic, Heretic, or Infidel, &c. &c. &c.

Signed and sealed in due form.

UNIVERSITY OF LOUVAIN.

The faculty of divinity at Louvain, having been requested to give her opinion upon the questions above stated, does it with readiness—but struck with astonishment that such questions should, at the end of this eighteenth century, be proposed to any learned body, by inhabitants of a kingdom that glories in the talents and discernment of its natives. The faculty being assembled for the above purpose, it is agreed with the unanimous assent of all voices to answer the first and second queries absolutely in the negative.

The faculty does not think it incumbent upon her in this place to enter upon the proofs of her opinion, or to shew how it is supported by passages in the Holy Scriptures, or the writings of antiquity. That has already been done by Bossuet, De Marca, the two Barclays, Goldastus, the Pithæuses, Argentre Widrington, and his majesty king James the First, in his dissertation against Bellarmine and Du Perron, and by many others, &c. &c. &c.

The faculty then proceeds to declare that the sovereign power of the state is in no wise (not even indirectly as it is termed) subject to, or dependant upon any other power, though it be a spiritual power, or even though it be instituted for eternal salvation, &c. &c.

That no man nor any assembly of men however eminent in dignity and power, not even the whole body of the Catholic church, though assembled in general council, can, upon any ground or pretence whatsoever, weaken the bond of union between the sovereign and the people; still less can they absolve or free the subjects from their oath of allegiance.

Proceeding to the third question, the said faculty of divinity (in perfect wonder that such a question should be proposed to her) most positively and unequivocally answers—That there is not, and there never has been, among the Catholics, or in the doctrines of the church of Rome, any law or principle which makes it lawful for Catholics to break their faith with Heretics, or others of a different persuasion from themselves in matters of religion, either in public or private concerns.

The faculty declares the doctrine of the Catholics to be, that the divine and natural law, which makes it a duty to keep faith and promises, is the same: and is neither shaken nor diminished, if those with whom the engagement is made, hold erroneous opinions in matters of religion, &c. &c.

Signed in due form on the 18th of November, 1788.

UNIVERSITY OF ALCALA.

To the first question it is answered—That none of the persons mentioned in the proposed question, either individually, or collectively in counsel assembled, have any right in civil matters: but that all civil power, jurisdiction and pre-eminence are derived from inheritance, election, the consent of the people, and other such titles of that nature.

To the second it is answered, in like manner—That none of the persons above-mentioned have a power to absolve the subjects of his Britannic majesty from their oaths of allegiance.

To the third question it is answered—That the doctrine which would exempt Catholics from the obligation of keeping faith with Heretics, or with any other persons who dissent from them in matters of religion, instead of being an article of Catholic faith, is entirely repugnant to its tenets.

Signed in the usual form, March 17th, 1789.

UNIVERSITY OF SALAMANCA.

To the first question it is answered—That neither pope, nor cardinals, nor any assembly or individual of the Catholic church, have, as such, any civil authority, power, jurisdiction or pre-eminence in the kingdom of England.

To the second it is answered—That neither pope nor cardinals, nor any assembly or individual of the Catholic church, can, as such, absolve the subjects of Great Britain from their oaths of allegiance, or dispense with its obligations.

To the third it is answered—That it is no article of Catholic faith, with Heretics, or with persons of any other description, who dissent from them in matters of religion.

Signed in the usual form, March 7th, 1789.

UNIVERSITY OF VALLADOLID.

To the first question it is answered—That neither pope, cardinals, or even a general council, have any civil authority, power, jurisdiction or pre-eminence, directly or indirectly, in the kingdom of Great Britain: or over any other kingdom or province in which they possess no temporal dominion.

To the second it is answered—That neither pope nor cardinals, nor even a general council, can absolve the subjects of Great Britain from their oaths of allegiance, or dispense with their obligation.

To the third it is answered—That the obligation of keeping faith is grounded on the law of nature, which binds all men equally, without respect to their religious opinions; and with regard to Catholics, it is still more cogent, as it is confirmed by the principles of their religion.

Signed in the usual form, February 17th, 1789.

[To the declaration of the universities, it will not be amiss to add also, the declaration of Pius VI. of venerable memory, in a letter to the Roman Catholic Bishops of Ireland.]

"The Roman Catholic Archbishops of Ireland, at their meeting in Dublin, in 1791, addressed a letter to the Pope, wherein they described the misrepresentations that had been recently published of their consecration oath, and the great injury to the Catholic body, arising from them..........

"After due deliberation at Rome, the Congregation of Cardinals appointed to superintend the ecclesiastial affairs of these kingdoms, returned an answer (of which the following is an extract) by the authority and command of of his holiness:

"*Most Illustrious and most Reverend Lords, and Brothers,**

"We perceive from your late letter; the great uneasiness you labour under since the publication of a pamphlet entitled, *The present state of the Church of Ireland,*—from which our detractors have taken occasion to renew the old calumny against the Catholic religion with increased acrimony; namely, *that this religion is by no means compa-*

---

* The original Latin will be found in opposite columns in Dr. Troy's Pastoral Instruction, 1793—(Coghlan, Duke-street.)

tible with the safety of kings and republics; because, as they say, the Roman Pontiff being the father and master of all Catholics, and invested with such great authority, that he can free the subjects of other kingdoms from their fidelity and oaths of allegiance to kings and princes; he has it in his power, they contend, to cause disturbances and injure the public tranquillity of kingdoms, with ease. We wonder that you could be uneasy at these complaints, especially after your most excellent brother and apostolical fellow-labourer, the Archbishop of Cashel,* and other strenuous defenders of the rights of the Holy See, had evidently refuted, and explained away these slanderous reproaches, in their celebrated writings."—In this controversy a most accurate discrimination should be made between the genuine rights of the Apostolical See, and those that are imputed to it by innovators of this age for the purpose of caluminating. *The See of Rome never taught, that faith is not to be kept with the heterodox:—that an oath to kings separated from the Catholic Communion, can be violated:—that it is lawful for the Bishop of Rome to invade their temporal rights and dominions.* We *too* consider *an attempt or design against the life of Kings and Princes even under the pretext of religion, as an* HORRID *and* DETESTABLE CRIME."..........

.........." At the very commencement of the yet infant church, blessed Peter, Prince of the Apostles, instructing the faithful, exhorted them in these words:—*Be ye subject to every human creature for God's sake, whether it be to the king as excelling, or to governors as sent by him, for the punishment of evil doers, and for the praise of the good; for so is the will of God, that by doing well you may silence the ignorance of foolish men.* The Catholic church being directed by these precepts, the most renowned champions of the Christian name replied to the gentiles when raging against them, as enemies of the empire, with furious hatred; *we are constantly praying*, (Tertullian in Apologet. chap. xxx.) *that all the emperors may enjoy long life, quiet government, a loyal household, a brave army, a faithful senate, an honest people and general tranquillity.* The Bishops of Rome, successors of Peter, have not ceased to inculcate this doctrine, especially to missionaries, lest any ill-will should be excited against the professors of the Catholic faith, in the minds of those who are enemies of the Christian name. We pass over the illustrious proofs of this fact preserved in the records of ancient Roman Pontiffs; of which yourselves are not ignorant. We think proper, notwithstanding, to remind you of a late admonition of the most wise Pope Benedict XIV. who in his regulations for the English missions, which are likewise applicable to you, speaks thus:—*The vicars Apostolic are to take diligent care that the missionaries behave on all occasions with integrity and decorum, and thus be-*

---

* Dr. James Butler.

come good modes to others; and particularly that they be always ready to celebrate the sacred offices, to communicate proper instructions to the people, and to comfort the sick with their assistance; that they by all means avoid public assemblies of idle men, and taverns.................. The Vicars themselves are particularly charged to punish in such manner as they can, but severely, all those who do not speak of the public government with respect."

"England herself can witness the deep-rooted impressions such admonitions have made on the minds of Catholics. It is well known that in the late war, which had extended to the greater part of America, when most flourishing provinces, inhabited, almost by persons separated from the Catholic church, had renounced the government of the King of Great-Britain; the province of Canada alone, filled as it is almost with innumerable Catholics, although artfully tempted, and not yet forgetful of the old French government, remained most faithful in its allegiance to England. Do you, most excellent Prelates, converse frequently on these principles; often remind your suffragan Prelates of them: when preaching to your people, exhort them again and again *to honour all men, to love the brotherhood, to fear God, to honour the king.*

"Those duties of a Christian are to be cherished in every kingdom and state, but particularly in your own of Great-Britain and Ireland, where, from the benevolence of a most wise king, and other most excellent rulers of those kingdoms towards Catholics, no cruel and grievous burden is imposed; and Catholics themselves experience a mild and gentle government. If you pursue this line of conduct unanimously; if you act in the spirit of charity; if, while you direct the people of the Lord you have nothing in view but the salvation of souls, adversaries will be ashamed (we repeat it) to calumniate, and will freely acknowledge that the Catholic faith is of heavenly descent, and calculated not only to procure a blessed life, but likewise, as St. Augustin observes in his 138th letter, addressed to Marcellinus, to promote the most lasting peace of this earthly city, inasmuch as it is the safest prop and shield of kingdoms. *Let those who say* (the words are those of the holy Doctor) *that the doctrine of Christ is hostile to the Republic, produce an army of such soldiers as the doctrine of Christ has required; let them furnish such inhabitants of provinces, such husbands, such wives, such parents, such children, such masters, such servants, such kings, such judges, finally such payers of debts and collectors of the revenue, as the doctrine of Christ enjoins; and then they may dare to assert that it is inimical to the republic: rather let them not hesitate to acknowledge that it is, when practised, of great advantage to the republic.* The same holy Doctor, and all the other fathers of the church, with one voice, most clearly demonstrate by invincible arguments, that the whole of this salutary doctrine cannot exist with permanent consistency and stability; or flourish except in the catholic society; which is spread and preserved all over the world by communion with the See of Rome as a sacred bond of union, divinely connecting both. From our very high esteem and affection for you, we earnestly wish that the great God may very long preserve you safe. Farewell.

Rome, 23 *June*, 1791.

As your Lordship's most affectionate brother,

L. Cardinal Antonelli, Prefect.

A. Archbishop of Aden, Secretary."